Ace That Interview

Solving the Puzzle of Getting the Offer You Want

Yin-So Chen

Bonzai Press

Published by

Bonzai Press.

All rights reserved. No part of this book maybe reproduced or transmitted in any form without written permission except in the case of brief quotation/citation. For more information please contact the publisher.

Ace That Interview

Copyright © 2015 Yin-So Chen

ISBN: 978-1-943599-00-4

Library of Congress Control Number: 2015910438

Disclaimer

The information in this book is compiled based on the experiences of the author, which may or may not be suitable for your particular situation. Therefore, the author and the publisher make no representation or warranties with respect to the accuracy or completeness of the contents of this book and specifically disclaim any implied warranty or merchantability or fitness for a specific purpose. You should consult with a professional where appropriate before utilizing the advice, strategies, or steps contained herein. Neither the publisher nor the author shall be liable for any loss of profit or any other commercial damages, including but not limited to special, incidental, consequential, or other damages. Proceed at your own risk.

To My Mother.

Contents

Chapter 1   Introduction 1

Part I   Knowledge is Power 7

Chapter 2   What an Interview is Really All About 9

Chapter 3   Types of Interviews 15

Chapter 4   Interview Misconceptions 21

Chapter 5   Having the Right Mentality 29

Chapter 6   The Interview Process 37

Part II   Mastering Interview Flow 43

Chapter 7   First Impression Counts 45

Chapter 8   Meet and Greet - the Secret to Small Talks 55

Chapter 9   Interview Opening 65

Chapter 10   Manage the Interview Body Flow .... 7⸱

Chapter 11   Building Rapport The Easy Way 81

Chapter 12   Interview Closing 91

Part III   Ace The Interview Questions 95

Chapter 13   Traditional Interview Questions 97

Chapter 14   Behavioral Interview Questions 107

Chapter 15   Skill Interview Questions 115

Chapter 16	Brainteaser Interview Questions	129
Chapter 17	Ace in the Hole – Presenting Your Big Idea	139
Part IV	Practice Makes Perfect	147
Chapter 18	Craft Your Winning Plan	149
Chapter 19	Know Thy Enemy - Research, Research, Research	157
Chapter 20	Know Thyself - Refresh and Synthesize	165
Chapter 21	Practice! Time for Mock Interviews!	175
Chapter 22	The Night Before	185
Part V	Alternative Interview Types and After Interview	193
Chapter 23	Remote Interviews	195
Chapter 24	Panel Interviews	203
Chapter 25	After Interview - Follow-Up	209
Chapter 26	Getting the Deal You Want	225
Chapter 27	It is Just the Beginning	255
Appendix 1	Bibliography	265

Acknowledgements

Writing a book is a monumental undertaking. There is no way this book could have been completed without the diligent help and feedback of others. Any flaw in this book is simply my own failing in incorporating all the excellent ideas and suggestions in a timely manner.

In last name alphabetical order:

- April Anderson
- Dmitri Bouianov
- Yin-Ting Chen
- Michele DeFilippo
- Bernard Farber
- Doran Hunter
- Jasper Kuria
- Wenshen Lee
- Khanh Nguyen
- Oksana Odnovol
- Dr. R. S. Parks
- Sunil Puri
- Ronda Rawlins
- Mandy Tsui
- Cherie Tsui

Thank you for help making this book possible, everyone!

Chapter 1

Introduction

Have an interview coming up, and want to prepare for it?

Congratulations on your upcoming interview!

You have worked hard in your career, built up an impressive resume and developed deep skills in your area of expertise. You further have shined and polished your resume, inquired for the right jobs with the right companies, and now you are getting the call you've been waiting for.

Excited? Great.

Nervous? Good.

You are not alone. While you are excited about the positive prospects, you are also understandably concerned that you might end up tanking the interview and face rejections.

The interview scene is, in many ways, very similar to the dating scene. For most of us, dating is a challenge; we feel awkward on dates, especially if we have been "out of practice" for a while. All we want is to skip the initial awkward phase to go directly into a steady relationship so that we do not have to keep dating. And if we ever have to get back out to the dating market again, we find ourselves rusty from being out of it for so long, and we will have to work hard to regain the "dating skills" we had before. Few of us ever gain enough practice to consider ourselves "dating experts."

Similarly, few of us have enough interview experiences to consider ourselves expert in interviews, since we usually just want to get jobs and stay on them, not to become experts in undergoing interviews. And even if we did well the last time around, it has been a while, and our interview skills can be quite rusty.

The biggest concern of any candidate is that when we find the job that we are qualified for, we end up failing the interview because we could not demonstrate our skills to the demand of the interviewers.

No wonder you are concerned. But fear not – interviewing is a learnable skill, and you can become an expert (again) by putting some effort into it.

The goal of this book is simple and straightforward – to provide you with the knowledge and the tools needed for you to learn and master interview skills, no matter what your skill level is right now. To that end, we will cover interviewing from 10,000 feet high to gain an overall understanding of the moving pieces of interviews, and then all the way down to the ground to tackle how to answer particular types of interview questions.

Who Can Use This Book

This book is written for anyone who wants to know more about how to ace job interviews, specifically the beginners.

Like many other skills, interviewing is all about the **fundamentals**. Fundamentals are what everything else is built on, and if you have a strong grasp of the fundamentals, the sky is the limit. Even when you become advanced, focusing on the fundamentals always pays dividends.

Furthermore, interview skills can be **subtle**. The same sentence, said by two different persons, can have completely different effects on the same interviewer. Thus, it is especially important to understand the reasons behind why something works in the first place, and to do that, one has to go back to understand the fundamentals.

This book is designed to cover not just **what to do**, but also **why you would do them** in an interview. If you are a person who likes to understand the why, this is the book for you.

Conventions of This Book

Below are the conventions used in this book.

We use **bold** for emphasis in the book.

This is what a quote looks like:

> *To be or not to be, that is the question.*
> *-- Hamlet, Shakespeare.*

This is what a note looks like:

> This is a note. It's meant to discuss a related point to the surrounding text.

This is what an important text looks like:

> **This is an "important" block for highlighting important text, like a principle or rule to remember.**

This is what a conversation dialog looks like, for one or more people:

Author This is a conversation block. It's used to denote words spoken by one or more people.

You	I see. Can we keep talking?
Author	We will. Stay tuned.

> Political correctness is nice, but makes reading slower if we keep on using "he and/or she." We will default to "he," unless otherwise noted in the rest of the book.

Organization of This Book

The book is divided into separate parts to first give you the high level overview, and then gradually dive into each of the main topics.

The high-level overview applies to everyone, so it makes sense for you to start from Part I. We will then proceed into the specifics of the interview, and then cover the methods to prepare for your interview, and finally end on what happens after the interview, including negotiations.

As this is a book written for general job seekers, you will likely find that some chapters speak to you more than others. For example, if you are great at making first impressions and build rapports than answering specific questions, feel free to focus on the question chapters more than the impression and the rapport chapters. Use the book according to your needs.

Part I - High-Level Interview Knowledge

In Part I (page 7), the goal is to cover the basic foundational knowledge about job interviews.

- What exactly is an interview about (page 9) – perspectives matter. Make sure you have the appropriate perspective for job interviews.
- Types of interviews (page 15) – the different types of interviews you can expect to encounter.
- Misconceptions about interviews (page 21) – thoughts you might have about interviews that just ain't so.
- Having the right mentalities (page 29) – prepare yourself efficiently and correctly by having the right mentalities.
- The process of an interview (page 37) - a quick high-level glance at the interview process.

Part II - Interview Structural Analysis

In Part II (page 43), we will take a look at the structure of an interview for an in-depth study in order to successfully handle interviews.

- How to make the best first impression (page 45).
- How to meet and greet smoothly and properly (page 55).
- How to handle the interview opening (page 65).
- How to build rapport with your interviewer (page 81).
- How to properly close your interview (page 91).

Part III – Interview Questions

In Part III (page 95), we will look in-depth at the types of questions that are asked in interviews, and discuss the best way to handle these questions.

- How to handle traditional interview questions (page 97).
- How to handle behavioral interview questions (page 107).
- How to handle skill interview questions (page 115).
- How to handle brainteaser interview questions (page 129).

Part IV - Prepare for Interviews

In Part IV (page 147), we will learn how to prepare for interviews.

- Planning for your preparation (page 149) – failure to plan is planning to fail. Put yourself in a good position to win by proper planning.
- How to gather intelligence (page 157) – the more you know about the other party, the more you will be prepared.
- Refresh yourself (page 165) – you will also need to know about yourself to complete the puzzle of preparation.
- How to conduct mock interviews (page 175) – make the most of your stage preparation.
- Getting into the optimal state of mind (page 185) – techniques for relaxing yourself and taking your nerves away.

Part V – Alternatives and After Interviews

Finally, in Part V (page 193), we talk about how to handle alternative interview types and what comes after the interviews.

- Remote interviews (page 195) - how are remote interviews differ and how to handle them.
- Panel interviews (page 203) - how are panel interviews differ and how to handle them.
- After interview (page 209) - how to properly follow up after the interview.
- Negotiations (page 225) - how to get the deal you are looking for.
- Where to go from here (page 255) - how to analyze your results and continuously improve yourself going forward.

Conclusion

Interviewing is a skill, and skills can be acquired. This book provides you with the knowledge that you need to master the skill.

One can never have too much knowledge if the goal is mastery. Read on if you accept the challenge to improve your interview skills.

Without further ado, let's get your journey to great interviews started!

Part I
Knowledge is Power

Is there such a thing as knowing too much? Perhaps, but not when it comes to acing your interviews!

As stated earlier, fundamental pieces of knowledge are the building blocks for applications and true mastery. Although you might have read about some of them before, going through them will only make your foundation sounder.

In this section, we will take a look at the following base concepts:

- What exactly is an interview about? (page 9)
- Types of interviews (page 15).
- Misconceptions about interviews (page 21).
- Having the right mentalities (page 29).
- The process of interviewing (page 37).

Chapter 2

What an Interview is Really All About

> What if you need to hire someone? Hiring someone can give you insight into what people look for when hiring, and that knowledge will aid you in your interviews.

Many people think of interviews as the way/process for them to get jobs. This answer is correct, but it is incomplete, and unfortunately misleading for when they need to find jobs.

If you want to succeed at interviews, you need to understand the bigger picture, and that means not just to see things from your side, but **also from the interviewer's side.**

Interviewing is not only a method for you to get the job; it is the opportunity employers have to find the best person among a group of candidates.

The following two diagrams show a more complete view, both from yours and the employers' perspective.

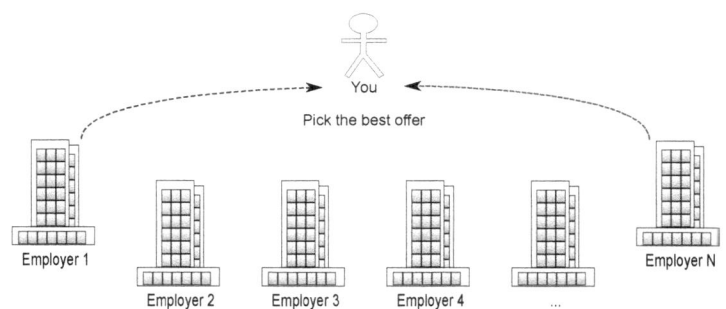

Figure 2.1 - Your Perspective - Pick the Best Offer

From your perspective, your objective is to get more than one offer, so you can select the best one.

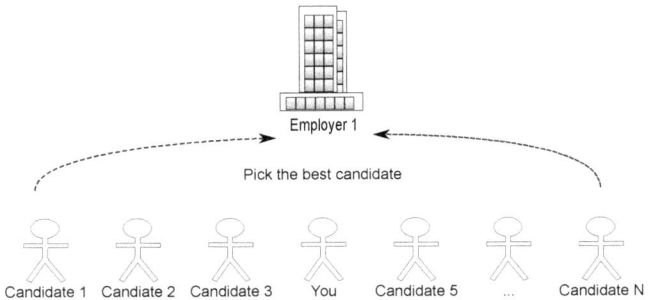

Figure 2.2 - Employer's Perspective - Pick the Best Candidate

The employer, on the other hand, wants to select the best worker from the candidates, and will only give the offer to the best candidate. In other words, only a single person will win each job. The second best candidate, no matter how great, only gets selected if the first candidate turns it down.

So for each offer you wish to receive, you need to emerge from employer's selection process as the **winner of the competition**. The second best receives no offers.

Even just for one offer, you need to compete with other candidates. You need to come out as the best person for the job.

> **An interview is a competition. Get used to it, and get ready to compete.**

Rules of the Competition

To compete well, you should also know the actual rules of the competition; otherwise you will be disadvantaged against those in the know.

You seldom compete directly with other candidates, of course. Interviewing is a much more like an individual sport – more similar to gymnastics or figuring skating, where one person goes at a time, than to tennis, swimming, and obviously not basketball.

The similarity to gymnastics or figure skating doesn't just end there. They are also similar in that you have judges to score your performance. The interviewers are equivalent to the judges of those games, who bring their own interpretations and subjectivity to bear on the actual outcomes. Just like these sports, interviews are about as subjective as they come. Where it's worse than gymnastics or figure skating is that the evaluation criteria are not only fuzzy to you, they are fuzzy to even many of the interviewers, as they are seldom verbalized and quantified. When the rules are hazy, it makes preparations more difficult.

Luckily, while the rules aren't verbalized, they can readily be inferred since most employers have common wants and needs.

> **All you have to do is to put yourself in their shoes and think like an employer.**

What Would You Do If You Were to Hire Someone?

Let's say you need to hire a plumber. What would you be looking for?

Obviously, you have some plumbing problems that need to be solved, be it a plugged drain or a leaking faucet. So immediately you are not going to just hire anyone. You tried that by asking your friends to help out for free, and it didn't work so you are back to paying someone. **You now need to hire someone who can actually solve your problems.**

But would any plumber do? Imagine that the first plumber showing up to your house is someone who looks and smells like he just finished rolling around in a dirt track, would you want to spend much time "interviewing" him instead of quickly showing him the door? If the next person who shows up were dressed in neat clothing with good hygiene, wouldn't you feel much better interviewing him?

That's only the well-known first impression problem (page 45) – a bad first impression really turns most people off and dooms the chance to be hired. But even if you do not care about people's appearances too much, you still need to know confidently that he can solve your problem. So let's say that when you show one of the plumbers the problem, he seems at a loss for words on why the problem happens and how to fix it, does he give you the confidence that he can actually do the job? If another plumber was able to quickly pinpoint the root cause and actually show you how it can be fixed, wouldn't you more likely believe him than the plumber who fails to explain to you the problem?

Let's quickly recap. When you are hiring a plumber, you are looking for the following

- Someone who is presentable enough so you can start interacting with him
- Someone who can talk to you, so you can understand what is actually going on so they can earn your trust

- By proxy, the successful communication gives you a comfort level that he can actually do the work

Basically, every hiring decision is made with these basic criteria in mind. Of course, the actual details differ for every job and there might be more complex requirements, but every hiring decision will involve the above.

The Meaning of an Imperfect Process

You might have realized what we've described above is an imperfect process. Just because someone can articulate how certain things are done doesn't mean that he will do the job well, let alone being the best at doing the job.

You are of course right. But think of it this way – short of actually having the person do the work, how else would you know for sure?

Even when you create a smaller "test scenario," it will not fully duplicate what the person will encounter in the work, but just a portion of it. And it's a much more costly way of interviewing – a cost you might not want to incur for the particular job.

Hence, for most jobs, the interview process as we have come to know it is the standard verification approach, and communication skills serve as the proxy to actual skills.

The implication of this imperfect process, however, is important for you as a candidate to understand the following

- Even if you can do the work well, unless you can articulate to people about your skills, people won't know
- And if you are not presentable, people will not be able to focus on your communication!

It also means that if your communication skill is great, you are actually likely to beat out someone who is better at the job than you are, but couldn't get his points across!

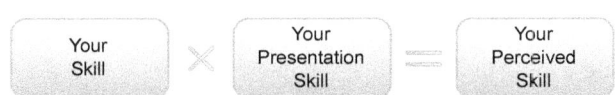

Figure 2.3 - Your Skill X Your Presentation Skill = Your Perceived Skill

For many technical folks, the above is a challenging lesson to absorb, partly due to their focus on the actual work rather than on the "packaging," and partly because they believe "people should not judge a book by its cover."

Hopefully the exercise above will show to you that even with the best intentions, the general tendency to pick up a book by its cover is alive and well, and you ignore the tendency at the risk of your own peril.

Luckily for the more technical jobs, people frequently do grant more leeway when it comes to presentations, and even on communications, especially on the soft-touch side. But they will not allow much leeway on technical communication, because the jobs will heavily depend on it.

You might be Einstein. Just remember that he couldn't get the job he wanted for a long time.

You don't want to be like Einstein when it comes to finding a job.

Conclusion

Use the following as a short rule to remember about the priority of your focus, in this order:

- Be Presentable so people can focus on what you have to say.
- Be Articulate so people can understand what you say.
- Be Knowledgeable so what you say actually makes sense.

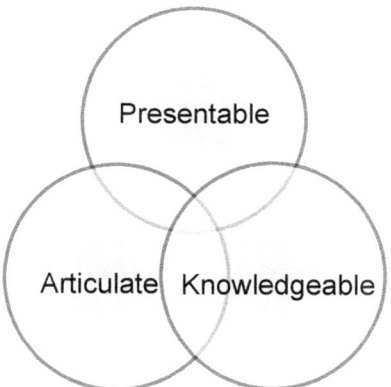

Figure 2.4 - The Triumvirate of Interview Foundations

We will go through the each of the above criteria in later chapters.

Chapter 3

Types of Interviews

> Do you know what types of interviews you are likely to get into? Looking at the types of interviews will help you prepare.

We have looked at interviews from the interviewer's perspective. Now let's look at how interviews actually work.

Let's first see the different types of interviews from both interviewer's and interviewee's perspectives.

We can roughly categorize interviews either by the communication mechanism or by the interview format.

By Communication Mechanism

One way to categorize interviews is via the communication mechanism. If the candidate and interviewers are in the same location and thus communicating in-person, it's an in-person interview; otherwise it's a remote interview.

In-Person

An in-person interview (also known as a face-to-face interview) is where you meet with the interviewer for the interview. You are likely to meet at the employer's premise or a public place.

The advantage of in-person interviews is straightforward from an interviewer's perspective – this is the **best way for the interviewer to get the most information about a candidate.** From an interviewee's perspective it's the same - it's the best way for you to present yourself.

The disadvantage is the **cost** involved, as it takes more time and money to set up in-person interviews (especially if traveling is required) for both the interviewers and interviewees.

If you are scheduled for a remote interview, you should expect a follow-up interview in person if you do well, since usually companies do not make offers solely based on the outcome of remote interviews.

Given their importance, the majority of this book focuses on in-person interviews.

Remote

The opposite of in-person interviews are remote interviews. In the past, this pretty much meant phone interviews, where you will be conversing with one or more interviewers over the phone. Videoconferencing is becoming a workable alternative these days.

The advantage of remote interviews is that they enable interviewers to consider candidates who are too far away to come in for a in-person interview, since often the company has to bear expenses for flying in candidates.

The disadvantage, from an interviewer's perspective, is the lack of having face-to-face interactions. Face to face interaction is still irreplaceable today even with the advancement in technology.

Hence, remote interviews are often used as filters before an in-person interview.

From your perspective, you might or might not be more comfortable having a remote interview, since for some questions it can be harder to answer remotely than in person (luckily, those questions are seldom asked in remote interviews, since it's also harder for interviewer to get the answer), and you also lack the nonverbal feedback you have in an in-person interview.

If you are applying to a job out of town, you should plan for remote interviews.

Much of the in-person interview techniques apply equally well to remote interviews, and we will talk about the differences in the Remote Interviews chapter (page 195) after we study the general techniques.

By Formats

Besides categorizing by location, we can also categorize interviews by their formats. There is a variety of different ways you can be interviewed. Below we will take a look the most common formats that you are likely to encounter.

One-On-One

This is most common form of interview formats. Depending on the position you apply for, you can have one-on-one interviews with one or more persons (separately) from the company.

The advantage of the one-on-one interview format is that **it gives the interviewer the best sense of you as a person,** since your attention is solely on the interviewer, and vice versa.

The disadvantage of one-on-one is that the interviewer does not observe how you behave with a group of people, and how you interact with others in a team setting, but as long as there are multiple interview sessions, this disadvantage is somewhat mitigated.

As this is the most common format, the topics in this book assume this format unless explicitly mentioned otherwise.

Panel

The main difference between panel interviews vs. one-on-one interviews is that in panel interviews, multiple interviewers will interview you at once, although sometimes a panel interview can arguably be classified as a one-on-one interview if only one of the interviewers ask the majority of questions.

The advantage of the panel interview format is that it **generally reduces the overall timeframe for conducting the interview,** since most if not all interviewers are involved on the panel in a single session. Interviewers can also take turns to observe you while you are responding to another interviewer's questions. Furthermore, panel interviews usually generate higher pressure for the candidates since candidates must pay attention to multiple interviewers at once.

The disadvantage from interviewers' perspective is that often a panel interview requires more time commitment from each one of them comparing to the one-on-one format, and at the same time they each get less personal time with you.

Besides the above differences, panel interviews will basically be the same as one-on-one interviews.

Panel interviews will be addressed in the Panel Interviews chapter (page 203) in more detail.

Group

Although interviews are usually an "individual sport," some companies like to **put all candidates together and have them interview at the same time.** This is known as a group interview. It looks similar to a panel interview, but it differs from a panel interview in that panel interviews consist of multiple interviewers instead of multiple interviewees. However it's possible that the group interview is also a panel interview, since it's often easier to conduct a group interview with multiple interviewers.

Picture the boardroom in the TV Show The Apprentice®, and you can get a feel of what a group interview is like.

Group interviews can be in the form of a written exam, and it's possible to be an oral exam as well, but it can be hard to evaluate individuals separately in a group interview.

Group interviews are generally employed with the primary goal of pitting candidates against each other, such as in The Apprentice® or sports try-outs. One of potential benefits of group interviews is that employers get to see candidates in a group setting, but since the amount of attention interviewers can devote to each candidate is limited, what can be seen is also limited. In jobs where it's important to evaluate each candidate as thoroughly as possible, there are better ways to evaluate candidate interactions.

This format is probably most often seen in jobs like sales (think The Boiler Room) and still relatively rare otherwise. We will not cover group interviews in this book.

Simulation

These are the biggest and baddest interviews one can get into. Basically, the goal of this interview format is to simulate what would happen on your job and see how you would handle it.

An example where you might come across simulation interviews is a senior management job, as it usually takes a senior position to justify the cost of the simulation. For the interview, you will be interacting with people acting as your peers, direct reports, customers, or superior(s), and you are expected to solve many problems during the course of the interview, with your performance heavily monitored, analyzed, and graded.

Another example is the process to become a U.S. Navy Seal. In order to become a Seal, an applicant will undergo six months of an intensive training course known as BUD/S (Basic Underwater Demolition/SEAL) where they are being evaluated. Anyone who cannot stand the long grueling training that simulates the difficulty of the job conditions is eliminated.

Simulation interviews are as close to the actual jobs as you can get, short of seeing the person actually performing on the job. Instead of interviewers asking you questions, you are going to dive in directly to work on tasks and solve problems that simulate the actual job environment. Such simulation gives the best predictor for your on-the-job performance.

Besides getting as close as possible to the real thing, the biggest advantage is that it generates an enormous amount of pressure for you to perform under the spotlight, so for those high pressure jobs that demand your ability to stay cool and perform under pressure, this type of interview will draw out whether you have that in you.

If you are a candidate who strongly believes that actions speak louder than words, you might actually prefer such a format, since it does give you the actions, rather than endless interview questions.

The biggest disadvantage of such an interview is that it is, compared to other formats, very costly to conduct; thus it is not economically feasible to utilize this approach for all job positions.

Unless you are applying for some senior executive positions or high-pressure positions such as astronauts or international men of mystery such as James Bond, chances are you will not be subjected to such an interview format.

As simulation interviews are highly job-specific and thus difficult to generalize them except at the very high level, they will not be covered in this book.

Conclusion

Now you know the different types of interviews you can potentially encounter in your career. Knowing what they are will help you prepare your interviews accordingly, which we will cover in the remainder of the book.

We will next take a look at the common interview misconceptions.

Chapter 4

Interview Misconceptions

> Misconceptions can reduce your chances for success by giving you the wrong lessons. Let's take a look at the common ones.

Interviews can seem like an opaque process for most of us, because we do not get to see things from the interviewer's perspective. This, unfortunately, generates prevalent misconceptions about interviews in general, and quite a few targeted toward the interviewers.

"It's All About Me."

We have previously covered this misconception in What an Interview is Really All About (page 9), but it is worth repeating, as thinking this way does have interview performance implications.

Interviewing is about the potential employer having a need to be satisfied, and your ability to target and demonstrate meeting the particular need will be the difference between being hired and not hired.

What this means is that your answers should be as little about yourself as possible. This is not a typo – your answer should be **as little about yourself as possible.** They aren't interested in you. They are interested in **what you can do for them.**

Even when they are asking about your background, they aren't really interested in your background, unless it has some relevance to them.

Hence, do not talk about yourself. **Talk about what and how you can help them.**

An example of when you should guide yourself toward how you can help them:

Interviewer   Tell me about yourself.

You   (Don't do this)

I was born in a small town in Alabama, and growing up loving all things about Karate. My personal hobby is to music, and I play Guitar Hero in my spare time.

(Do this if martial arts are relevant)

I have trained in martial arts extensively for the past ten years, and my skills will be useful as your personal security guard.

Examples where you should help steer the conversation if your interviewer is off-topic:

Interviewer So you are a martial artist?

You (Don't do this)

Yes, I love all things about Bruce Lee and I have all of his films...

(Do this if martial arts are relevant)

Yes, I have cross-trained in multiple martial art disciplines and I believe that makes me a better-rounded security guard for you.

(Do this if martial arts are irrelevant)

Yes, I have been training in martial arts since I was a teen, and my training really teaches me about the discipline of hard work, patience, and diligence, and I believe my character building will help me contribute to your cause.

"Interviewers Are Here to See Me Fail."

See how this particular myth is perpetuated from the first myth? If you think that the interview is all about you, then it's easy to think that interviewers are here to see you fail.

But if the interview were not really about you, why would the interviewer want to see you fail?

As a matter of fact, you need to understand this

All interviewers, no matter how tough, want to see you succeed.

To understand why, again you need to think from the interviewers' perspective. Think of what happens to the interviewers if you do not pass the interviews. It means they will have to continue their search!

Without having sat on the other side of the table, it can be hard to realize the following:

- Interviews take time away from productive work.
- Interviews take efforts to prepare and coordinate.
- Interviewing is draining for most people.
- The longer a job stays vacant, the more loss in productivity the company suffers.

All interviewers want is that the next person coming in for an interview is the person whom they will offer the job!

While there may be some egotistical interviewers who take a sadistic pride in torturing the candidate, most are simply creating a bar that they want you to pass, to ensure that they get the best candidate possible.

"I'm the only nervous person in the room."

This is also untrue – interviewers get nervous too. Not all interviewers are seasoned interview professionals. Many have limited interview experiences as well. You might actually come across first-time interviewers.

It is also possible for a person more junior than you to interview you, since people realize that having as many eyeballs as possible increase the chance of having a good hire. Although it's a good idea, having junior persons interviewing a senior person can contribute to their tension as well, since they will have to think about their own performance should you be hired.

So take heart, in that you just might be in a good company when it comes to being nervous, and that you might be able to use the situation to your advantage, since you know as a nervous person, you want to be soothed and calmed, and a nervous interviewer will also want the same thing.

"It's better to have the friendly interviewers and easy questions."

It can feel better to have the friendly interviewers, but having friendly interviewers doesn't mean you will get a better score. People can interview friendly but grade tough, and tough interviewers often know that they will have to give allowances to interviewee's responses since they are aware that they make people nervous.

Easy questions are the same way – just because you have easy questions doesn't mean you will do better. Many interviewers take the approach of giving a candidate easy questions once they figure out that the candidate cannot work with hard questions.

No need to spend time analyzing whether the questions are easy or hard. Until you have enough experience for an objective evaluation, the question of easy or hard is subjective to your personal experience, and not necessarily to the interviewer.

"Everybody gets the same interview questions."

Not everyone gets the same interview questions, solely due to that if they keep using the same questions, eventually people will wise up and be prepared for these particular questions. This is the reason why companies don't spend much effort worrying about the interview question sites out there.

In reality, each interviewer has a repertoire of questions to select from, and some might even create questions on the fly. Their goal isn't to get the difficulty of questions to be exactly the same, but rather to pick questions according to the interviewees' ability to answer them. Hence, it's likely that a superior candidate will get harder questions and an inferior candidate will get easier questions. The key for the interviewer is to simply track the difficulty of the questions asked, and they can use that to gauge the capability of the interviewees.

"It's better to answer I don't know than trying to figure out the answer to a question."

This actually depends on the particular question. There are questions that are designed to actually test on what you don't know (page 129), and if you answer you don't know to those questions, you will lose points.

We will address this in more detail when we get to Part III (page 0).

"The best-qualified person will get the job."

While technically speaking this is a true statement, the real answer, as we have already alluded to, is that the "best-qualified person" **from the interviewers' perspective** will get the job.

This is because interviewees often have difficulty in actually getting across their real skills, so interviewers have to make-do with what they can glean from the interviews. The person who has the best communication skills and can get the ideas across will likely win over a candidate who has stronger skills but cannot get the ideas across.

You don't want to be the person who cannot get their ideas across.

"Looks don't matter. Skill is all that matters."

This is a corollary to the above myth. Presentations are always critical. There are probably many interviewers out there who do not care about appearances and are willing to overlook that. But are you willing to bet your chance on the likelihood that none of your interviewers care?

Do not chance it to prove some principle. Play it safe with adherence to human nature when it comes to presentations and packaging. Even when your interviewers tell you to dress casual, it doesn't mean a sloppy casual. Make sure you take care of your appearances (we are not exactly talking about a very high requirement here) so that your interviewers will not waste time on your appearance and can actually focus on what you have to say.

"If I am skilled, I should be getting offers."

Remember that you are actually in a competition, i.e. there are other candidates involved, and the company will pick the best one.

Your skills might be good, but unless it's the best of the bunch, you might come in second and not get the offer. If in every single interview you finished second, it means you have zero offers unless one of the winners turns the job down.

During the good times, there are many job openings and very few candidates on the market, so it becomes very easy to get offers even without lots of skills. But during difficult times, when there are many candidates against few job openings, it becomes the opposite, and you need to come across to the interviewers that you are the best of the bunch.

"There is an average acceptance and rejection rate I can use as a baseline."

There isn't such a thing, and it is not meaningful. The reason is that top people with great interview skills will consistently get more offers than rejections, and people without good skills or interview abilities will consistently get more rejections than offers.

The only meaningful rate is **your own acceptance and rejection ratio**. Work on building up your skills and interview skills to ensure your numbers go up.

"I have to answer correctly in my first attempt."

Nothing can be further from the truth. Some questions do not have a right answer, and some questions are designed so that you won't be able to get your answer right the first time. If you always try to get the right answer in the first attempt, you will fail miserably, and end up with the next misconception.

"It's better to think silently than say the wrong thing."

This is a corollary to the above myth. Since many people believe that they have to get the answer right on the first try, they sit and think in silence while appearing dumbfounded by the question during that time to the interviewer.

This cannot be stressed enough - **do not think silently,** at least no more than say 5 or 10 seconds. To know why – just imagine yourself on the other side of the table – what happens if you ask a question and are met with prolonged silence?

To be fair, this isn't strictly a myth issue; this is as much of a natural response to a tough question, and we are further educated to think silently during exams, and this habit easily spills over to interviews.

The key to overcoming this behavior is to understand that **interviewers are interested in your thinking process much more than just your answers.** Explaining your thinking process is the only way that can ensure that interviewers know how you came to the answer - even if it's the right one.

If you are well prepared, the chances are that you only get stomped by deliberately tough questions, and the interviewer knows you will have a hard time to answering them. Some of these questions might not even have a right answer. Encountering such a question is a cue for you to talk about your reasoning rather than just thinking silently.

Thinking silently takes away the exact thing interviewers are looking for from you. Let's repeat again for emphasis - **do not think silently.**

We will address how to overcome the problem of thinking silently in the Interview Body chapter (page 77).

Conclusion

Having misconceptions about interviews is natural - without knowing what it looks like on the other side of the table, it is easy for us to fill in the blanks ourselves, and often we end up thinking and imagining the worst.

By placing ourselves in the position of the employer, even just as a thought experiment, the misconceptions evaporate by themselves.

The sooner we can keep both sides of the equation in mind, the better off we will feel, and the better we can perform.

Chapter 5

Having the Right Mentality

> The right attitude and mentality will help, while the wrong attitude and mentality will harm. Let's see how we can build the right mentality.

Outcome is nothing. Attitude is everything. Obey your attitude!

Pardon the pun (for those too young to remember – search for "image is nothing" Sprite® ads), but your attitude, your outlook in life, will cause subtle behavior change in you that results in profoundly different outcomes.

When you are walking past a stranger, what is the first thing that you immediately think about?

If you think that this person can be dangerous – you will behave in ways that reflect your belief; you look anywhere but at the person, because you do not want to draw attention, and you have a "fight or flight" posture in preparation for the potentially dangerous situation.

If you think that this person can be friendly – you will also behave in ways that reflect your belief; you look at the person naturally and smile, and you have a relaxed posture in preparation for a potentially wonderful interaction with the person.

In the first case, the concern is what will happen to you. In the second case, the concern is about possible wonderful opportunities.

Although the outcome of encountering a stranger will most often be of little consequence, your mindset and reaction in interview settings (which are mostly with strangers too!) will be greatly amplified, and potentially be the difference that determines whether you get the offer. You want to make sure that you have the right mindset when going into interviews.

Locus of Control and Why It Matters

In psychological terms, people with the first reaction above (afraid of strangers) are said to have an "external locus of control," and people with the second reaction above (like to interact with strangers) are said to have an "internal locus of control."

Locus of control is a concept that describes what you believe to cause things to happen - either by yourself or by others. An external locus of control means that you believe things happen outside of your control – i.e. things happen, and you are the recipient; an internal locus of control means the opposite - you are the reason that things happen - you are in control.

One thing to keep in mind is that locus of control is a belief rather than a fact obtained via impartial observation. In other words, you might not actually have control over a particular thing happening, but you still believe so (vice versa as well). For example, during ancient times, people often conducted sacrifice rituals to appease the gods when they were mad, such as during solar eclipses or volcanic eruptions. Although the sacrifice rituals actually do not contribute to ending such natural phenomena, the fact that these phenomena did end helped ancient people internalize that their rituals helped appease the gods, and hence such rituals continued for a long time until new scientific knowledge was gained.

From our perspective, ancient people who held such beliefs were superstitious and not too bright, but what these rituals offered was an internalized psychological well being that that they were not powerless when these phenomena occurred - that they could do something about them, given the best of their knowledge at that time. Having an internal locus of control is important to our psychological well being, as the opposite means being powerless, which makes for a very unhappy living.

Keep in mind again that this is all about beliefs rather than reality - to see how it works, just recall a friend of yours who lacks confidence but is actually very capable. You know he can accomplish many things in life if he can just muster enough confidence to go along with his capabilities! Conversely, you probably also have a friend who is average in every sense of the word, but accomplishes so much because the words "no" and "not possible" don't exist in his dictionary. This is why we said attitude is everything at the beginning of this chapter.

We all crave controls in our lives, no matter whether we believe we have them. The ability to control our lives means living exactly the life we want, which leads to our happiness. Needless to say, people with an external locus of control are unhappier when compared to people with an internal locus, even if the first person is measurably more capable and more successful.

Interestingly, people who have an external locus of control also end up more self-centered. This is because a large part of their desire is to get their lives under control. Conversely, people with an internal locus of control already believe that they have their lives under their control, so they can afford to focus beyond themselves.

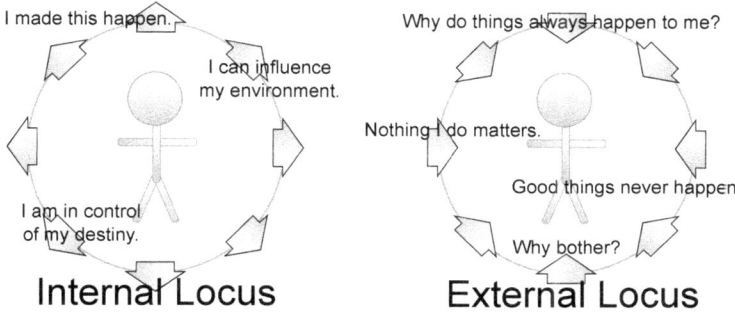

Figure 5.1 - Internal vs. External Locus of Control

Locus of control is only a belief - having an internal locus of control doesn't mean you will always succeed (or even succeed more than people without), but it allows you to cope with failures differently than if you have an external locus of control. Let's now see how a different locus of control can lead to different responses when experiencing failures.

Responding To Failures

One area where we can see drastic differences between people with an internal vs. an external locus of control behave is how they respond to failures.

A person with an internal locus of control will respond to failure in the following manner:

- I didn't do enough to succeed yet.
- I need to look to improve my weaknesses.
- Here's what I can do more for the next time.

A person with an external locus of control will, however, respond to failure in the following manner:

- I'm always so unlucky.
- Why do people not cooperate with me?
- It's someone else's fault!

As stated multiple times, the locus of control is a personal belief and has no bearing on reality. That means that you might think you need to improve yourself when the fault belongs to someone else. In a strict sense, that means that you are working harder than necessary, but this is the correct approach for both short-term and long-term, as it makes you happier to be in control of what you can do, and you are also more likely to overcome the challenge eventually:

- Even if it's someone else's problem, a person trying to improve might eventually win this someone over – a person blaming someone else might never get there.
- Even if it's random luck, a person believing a problem can be solved is more apt to try again and again, and the luck will work out one of these times.

An internal locus of control leads to persistence, and persistence leads to success. You want to have an internal locus of control if your goal is to be successful in interviews and in life.

How to Gain an Internal Locus of Control

Luckily, the locus of control isn't binary, nor does it apply universally to all situations for one person; it's instead a continuum where we have an internal locus of control for certain situations, and an external locus of control for other situations.

A software developer who is socially awkward has an external locus of control when it comes to social interactions, but has an internal locus of control when it comes to writing software. A project manager might be exactly the other way around.

The key to gain an internal locus of control is **mastery**. The more mastery you have over certain situations, the more of an internal locus of control you have. If you are a martial arts master, the chances are that you won't be very afraid of strangers.

Gaining mastery over interview situations gives you an internal locus of control needed for succeeding in interviews. You are well on your way reading this book.

Now let's take a look of the mentality you need to adopt for being consistently successful in interviews.

You Don't Need This Job

> **Yes. You. Don't. Need. This. Job.**

Repeat after me for yourself.

Chapter 5 Having the Right Mentality

I. Don't. Need. This. Job.

This is the very first, and the most important mentality for you to adopt. It doesn't matter what your actual situation is, even if you are six months past due on your rent and being served with a notice to vacate, even if your house is about to be foreclosed and your significant other is about to leave you.

Again.

You. Don't. Need. This. Job.

Why?? I'm about to lose my house and all things important! I need this job to pay rent! How can I not need this job!

If you think like that – you have an external locus of control. Things are happening to you, not you making them happen. To change to an internal locus of control, you need to believe – you don't need this stinking job!

If you really focus on wanting this job, you are creating a state of need, and a state of desperation. I am sure that I don't have to remind you whether desperate people are popular.

And finally, if you really need this job, your need will translate into nervousness, which will make you perform worse in the actual interviews. Your believing in needing this job desperately actually undermines your effort to land the job.

Conversely, if you are relaxed, you will be able to show the better side of yourself, and coming across more confident in the interviews. You will be more successful in interviews with this mentality.

Believe the following. You don't need this job because:

- There are always more jobs available.
- You will become a master in finding and landing jobs.

When you believe the above, you find yourself much more relaxed, because you are no longer dependent on the outcome that you must get this job. When you **must** achieve a particular outcome, you become tense, and even desperate, and perform much worse than if you are relaxed.

To relax yourself, you must get rid of the **"must"** and the dependency on the outcome. When you master your interview skills, the right outcome will occur more often than not, until then, struggling and tensing yourself to meet an expectation only deter you from getting the outcome you want.

You Are Here to Help

Since you don't need this job, you are applying for a job due to **your intense desire to help others**. You are here to know whether you are the best person to help them achieve their goals.

Your intense desire to help others will make you behave in ways that are congruent with your desire – your goal, words, and actions will all align and demonstrate your desire to help. You are no longer concerned about whether you get the job, nor will you be concerned about your performance – **you will place your focus away from yourself and onto the rightful target – the interviewers and the company.**

When you focus on others, you automatically become more relaxed, more natural, and less likely to make mistakes. You will perform better.

People also respond best to others who want to help them. A sincere desire to help others will come across to the interviewers – consciously or subconsciously – due to your coherent behaviors. Interviewers will interpret this as "self-motivated," "team player," "can-do attitude," which are the fuzzy qualities the interviewers look for.

All people look for is someone to help them. Your intense desire to help others will help you pin down and score the fuzzy criteria points!

You Are Happy to Walk Away If You Are Not the Right Person

Given that you don't need this job, and you are here to help, it follows that if you are not the right person to help, you are happy to walk away.

Walking away from a poor match is the best thing you can do, for both the employer and yourself. They will find some other person more closely matching their needs, and you will not be burying yourself at a job that you dislike. It's only win-win.

You Are Here to Learn and Grow

Although you place the others front and center, you know that an interview is a two-way street – you aren't here to just look for a paycheck, but also to determine whether it's the right place for you.

You have standards that need to be met as well – you know that your mission during the interview - besides answering questions - is to check the following off of your list:

- A place where you can learn something new.
- A place where you can continue to grow in your career.

- A place with values and cultures that you can belong to.
- A place where you find people to share your career with.
- A place where people value your skills.
- And any other things to add onto your checklist.

If you have this job – you will spend the majority of your waking time at the place. So finding the right job is of the utmost importance – you don't want just any job.

Interviewers Have the Same Goal as You

That is – to see whether you can be of help to them, which, if it hasn't yet been your goal, you will make it so for the next interview.

When you believe the above, your goal and the interviewers' goal are magically aligned!

Different interviewers do things differently – some will be friendly, others stern, but they all have the same goal in mind, and they love it if you happen to be that person, because that means that their search is over.

You want to know that too.

You Know You Can Get Better If You Keep Practicing

No matter what the outcome is from the interview – part of your goal is to verify where you are with your interview skills, and to know that you can continue to do better, whether it's your interview skills or your work skills.

You go in with the expectation that you will find out how well you do, as well as your areas of improvement, and you vow to yourself that your effort will be well rewarded if you continue the journey of your growth.

And it will be a journey worth taking.

Conclusion

Your mentality and beliefs affect your behaviors, and they affect at a subconscious level so you have little control over them. This is the reason why it's important for you to adopt yourself a new set of mentalities for your benefit.

Determine if you have an external locus of control and strive to convert into an internal locus of control. Go through this chapter as many times as you need to commit them to memory and burn them into your subconscious. Your new life is just waiting around the corner for you.

With proper preparation for the right mentalities, let's now move onto learning about how the game of interviewing works.

Chapter 6
The Interview Process

> What does an interview look like from the perspective of an end-to-end process?

The Interview Process describes the activities that occur when a prospective employer schedules an interview with you, all the way to when you hear the decision from the employer. Your effort during this timeframe determines your interview performance and the chance of you getting an offer. Let's look at the interview process to gain an understanding so we can optimize our result. The figure below maps out the overall interview process.

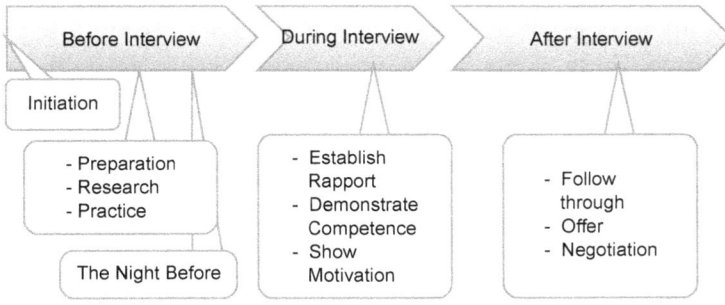

Figure 6.1 - The Interview Process

Being a linear process, the interview process can be nicely broken down into three stages based on the timeline – Before Interview (BI), During Interview (DI), and After Interview (AI). Let's quickly look at these stages from a high-level perspective below, and we will address them in greater detail in subsequent chapters.

Before Interview

For the lack of a better term, we will call the timeframe starting from the scheduling of the interview up to the interview itself, Before Interview (BI).

Your performance during an interview is dictated by your preparation during this timeframe. The more prepared you are, the more confident you can be of a good performance.

Your goal for this stage is to prepare as fully as possible for your interview.

Before Interview includes the Initiation event itself, the in-between time that you can utilize for Preparation, as well as The Night Before – the last minute preparation that you can do.

For each of the above, there are things for you to accomplish in order to optimize your preparation result.

Initiation

Initialization occurs when the company reaches out to you to schedule an interview, either directly or indirectly via a recruiter.

As soon as the company decides to interview you, they will schedule a time with you for either an in-person or a remote interview. In general, you can expect further interviews - pending your performance - if you were scheduled for a remote interview.

Your goal for the initiation is to allot enough preparatory time for you to adequately prepare for the interview. A week is generally adequate for most people. You can get by with a shorter timeframe if you are good at interviewing, or is currently interviewing frequently.

Sometimes, the recruiter will ask for an immediate phone interview during the initiation call. Being caught by surprise is never a good way to start an interview – you want to be at your most optimal state. Remember that it is always to your advantage to schedule for another time, but take note of the response from the recruiter to determine if rescheduling will jeopardize your chances for the position. Do not hesitate to reschedule as soon as you can determine that rescheduling does not jeopardize your consideration.

> **Desired Outcome – Schedule your interview with enough Preparation Time.**

Preparation

Preparation is what separates the bad from the good, and the good from the great!

Similar to exams, the amount of effort you put into preparing for an interview will turn into positive results, especially if you have a good handle on your own strengths and weaknesses.

One of the top complaints that interviewers have about candidates is that they show up underprepared. What it means is that your effort will not only reduce your fear of failure, but is an actual **competitive advantage**! Remember, only the winner gets the offer - prepare effectively!

We will dive into the Preparation phase in-depth in Part IV (page 147).

> **Desired Outcome** – maximize your readiness for the upcoming interview.

The Night Before

You might have gotten used to pulling all-nighters for exams back in your school days. Have you found that to be effective?

The chances are that you find that you need lots of caffeine to stay functional after an all-nighter. Even if you are a night owl, you will find that interviews are different from exams. With interviews, someone will be watching and observing you the whole time, and your energy level is a ranking criterion – implicitly or explicitly - for the interview. If you show up to the interview as tired as you feel in your college finals, you will get penalized.

Therefore, it is important to have preparations complete prior to the night before, and you use this time to unwind, relax, and work on your mental state for an optimal performance the day after.

The Night Before will also be discussed in Part IV (page 147).

> **Desired Outcome** – keep yourself relaxed and refreshed for an optimal performance during the interview.

During Interview

Depending on the company you interview with, the interview can take many different formats, but for larger companies, it generally can last a few hours to a full day, and you are likely to be meeting with multiple interviewers, often in a successive fashion.

For phone interviews, the number of interviewers and the rounds should be fewer, since phone interviews generally serve as the first filter for subsequent in-person interviews.

Interviewing for half a day to a day takes a lot out of even the most energetic person. This is why you make sure to rest well from The Night Before (you are well-rested, aren't you?).

For each interview, you can expect the following format:

- Meet and Greet (page 55) - the initial meeting with the interviewer - this is where pleasantries and small talks are exchanged.
- Opening (page 65) – the starting point of the interview - this is where the interviewer sets the context of the position.
- Body (page 71) – this is when the interviewer starts the question process. This is the bulk of the interview.
- Closing (page 91) – this is when the interviewer finishes questioning, and let you ask any last minute questions.

We will discuss these topics in-depth in Part II (page 43).

Opening

The beginning of an interview is often an exchange of pleasantries and small talks (page 55) since this is usually the first encounter between you and the interviewer. This can last around 5-10 minutes.

This is the time that you make a strong first impression. First impression lasts a long time and takes a lot to overcome, so make sure it counts.

The interviewer might also choose this time to provide you with the necessary job backgrounds to help orient the discussion. When the interviewer does so, it signals the end of the meet and greet, and the questioning phase will come afterward.

You are free to ask questions that you have prepared (page 161) if the interviewer does provide the context. Just make sure you are not being seen as stalling the interview by asking too many questions during this phase.

Some interviewers will skip the Opening and go straight into the questioning phase. Do not let that faze you.

> **Desired Outcome - Make a strong first impression, establish rapport, and set the context for the interview.**

Body

As soon as greetings and pleasantries are over, the Body part of the interview starts. The Body of the interview is the questions and answers, usually driven by the interviewer with questions, and you provide the answers. This is the bulk of the interview; expect it to last around 20-25 minutes for a 30-minute interview, and 40-50 minutes for a one-hour interview.

Depending on the nature of the job and the objective of the interviewer, you might be asked different types of questions. For example, in an interview with either the HR or the management, there will be a lot of focus on traditional and behavioral questions. If you are applying for a skilled-based position, you will likely be asked skill-related questions. If you are interviewing with multiple interviewers, the chances are that different people will handle different types of questions.

Given the importance of interview questions, we will delve into the types of questions and how to answer them in Part III (page 95).

> **Desired outcome** – demonstrate your knowledge, competence, and motivation.

Closing

As soon as the interviewer asks you "Do you have any questions for me?" it signals the end of the interview.

Always come prepared with questions!

Not having any questions for the interviewer at this stage not only robs you the chance to get clarifications on the job details, it also shows a lack of initiative and preparation to the interviewer. You will not compare favorably to the candidates who are prepared with questions.

After Interview

Do not think that the interview process is over just because you are done with the interviews. If you want to put your competition in the dust, After Interview is the best time to do it.

Appropriate follow-ups here will separate you from "just another candidate." You do not want interviewers to be "out of sight, out of mind" with your candidacy.

We will discuss After Interview in more detail in Part V (page 193).

Follow-Ups

Your job is not done as soon as you finish your interviews. Remember, your prospective employers are considering other candidates. To bring it home you should definitely do appropriate follow-ups to continue to build upon where you are.

See the Follow-Ups chapter (page 209) for more details.

Offers and Negotiation

If you received an offer, congratulations! You have finally achieved your goal. We will discuss how to handle the offer and negotiation phase to your advantage.

See the Getting the Deal You Want chapter (page 225) for more details.

Conclusion

Understanding the interview process is critical for you to successfully prepare for the interview. The remainder of the book will focus on diving into the details of each of the phases within the processes. Do make use of this chapter to keep track of where you are in the study so you can keep the high-level picture in mind.

Part II
Mastering Interview Flow

Although it might not seem that way when you are in the middle of it, there is an order to the madness that is known as interviews, and you will do yourself great favor learning how it all works.

We have already talked about the interview process in the previous chapter (page 37), now we will dive further into the interview itself, and see what things we have to do to be successful.

Interviews can be broken down into distinct phases. Learning how each phase work, and what you need to pay attention to, will be the main goal of Part II.

In Part II, we will cover:

- Making a great first impression (page 45).
- Understanding how small talk works to meet and greet (page 55).
- Opening - How an interview should appropriately start (page 65).
- Body - What you need to pay attention in order to help the interview flow (page 71).
- Closing - How to appropriately close an interview (page 91).

Chapter 7
First Impression Counts

Do you know that it takes as little as one-tenths of a second for people to form a first impression, and that first impression endures?

You might have heard that it takes seven seconds to form an impression, but according to the research conducted by Janine Willis and Alexander Todorov at Princeton University, apparently 100 millisecond was enough to form a judgment that doesn't change much even if more time is used. Scary, right? You never get to make a second first impression, and people basically immediately decide what they think of you even before they blink.

No matter what the actual number is, all these research studies do is to confirm for us what we have known intuitively for ages – that the first impression counts, and likely quite a bit. We've even tried the thought experiment of hiring a plumber earlier (page 11) – if the plumber looks like he just comes from dirt tracks, our initial impression of him will be unfavorable, and it will take him more effort to overcome the impression.

We try to look the best for dates, and we try to look the best for interviews. Our goal has always been the same – to impress the other party, at least to the point where the other party will be willing to hear what we have to say without having already written us off.

Although the above is straightforward to understand, in today's society, things somehow become a bit more complicated for some people, because they buy into the idea that "others have no rights to judge us," "we are free to do whatever we want," and "no one should judge a book by its cover," and they expect everyone to behave accordingly.

While the above are ideals that we should all strive for, the real world is anything but an ideal place. Ideally, we should be able to walk across streets blindfolded without fear of getting hit by a car, but anyone who tries that in reality deserves a Darwin award. The best and the surest way to influence the outcome isn't to act as if others will behave the way you want, but to be prepared for those who will behave the opposite of the way you want.

The golden rule in business is – **those with the gold make the rules, and customers are always right.** Your employer is your customer, and your prospective employer is your prospective customer – they will only dispense their gold when they like what they see.

If you do not have the tendency described above, great, you will not have issues with the guidelines in this chapter. If you believe that content is all that matters and packaging doesn't and shouldn't matter, then please give the following ideas a shot to help increase your odds.

For many of the things we will cover below, you will find that it's just common sense, and that you have been doing them on a daily basis. If so – great! As a matter of fact, the recommendation here is to try to integrate the advice into your everyday life, so it will be a second nature to you instead of you feeling weird when you need it. You can always benefit from making a good first impression in any situation, not just in interviews!

Appearances

It goes without saying that your appearance needs to be neat in any interview environment – casual or formal – no one wants to be near someone who seems like he hasn't taken a shower in a week.

Appearances include the following:

- Hair and beards should be well kept.
- Fingernails should be neatly trimmed.
- Teeth should be brushed and flossed to remove any food crumbs.
- Make sure that body odor (including breath) is eliminated or at the very least reduced; brush your teeth before the interview.
- Clothes should be fully cleaned; ironed and starched if applicable.
- Make sure the shoes are clean too.
- Cover up any body art if possible.

Having a neat appearance isn't only for the interviewers – it is for yourself too, as others' pleasant expressions when they meet you will boost your confidence for the interview.

> For breath - chewing gum can be a way to help with breath, but make sure you throw it out before the interviewer arrives.

Body Art

This doesn't apply to everyone, but if you have visible tattoos, try to cover it up with clothes or makeup, unless you are applying to jobs where having tattoos is a plus, such as a tattoo artist and a prison guard.

You are not obligated to disclose your tattoos during the interview. This is similar to your Miranda rights – "anything you say can be held against you in the court of interviewers..." The truths are:

- Most interviewers probably do not care whether you have tattoos, and quite a few places (where you do not directly interact with customers) do not care either, but you are better off to act as if someone does.
- If you are capable of covering up tattoos during the interviews, you are capable of covering them up when required, and thus will not be an issue for the employers.

If your tattoos are not coverable, like Mike Tyson's, hopefully, you are applying to a place where having a tattoo is really a plus.

If you find the need to cover up your body art offensive to your principles, you need to understand that no one is obligated to like your body art. If they are paying attention to your tattoos – even if just for being curious and without any bias or judgment - you have diverted their attentions away from your qualifications, and you will compare unfavorably with other candidates if what they can recall about you is just your tattoos.

> **Let them evaluate you on your merits alone – do not give interviewers reasons to divert their attentions.**

The Rules of Dress Code

It used to be that wearing business attire was all you had to worry about when it came to dress code for interviews, but times are changing, and with that comes a bewildering array of choices that can be hard for those of us who are fashion-challenged to figure out what to do.

That's why we focus on the whys instead of just being prescriptive - the more you understand the why, the more you will be able to make the appropriate choices.

Your dress code is influenced by the following factors:

1. The company's culture and norm, which is usually influenced by the industry's norm.
2. Your need to make a strong first impression.
3. Your need to be confident.
4. Your need to not distract the interviewer.

The first point - the company's culture and norm - will dictate the **category of attire** for you. For example, business attire is still expected in many of the conservative industries, such as banking and financing. Business casuals and (even) casuals, on the other hand, work for industries such as high tech.

The key thing to realize about the categories is that it works asymmetrically; i.e. it's better for you to **show up in business attire in a casual environment than the other way around**. You might feel a bit out of place in business attire in a casual environment, but it's easy for you to remove your jacket and ties so you blend in better; on the other hand, showing up in flip-flops in a formal environment is a nonstarter.

This means that if the culture is traditional, the acceptable categories of interview attires will be limited, and if the culture is more modern, you can work with more categories of attires. This is why consultants, who as a group often interview with new clients, have a general rule when it comes to dress code:

> **One-Up the Client.**

The second and third point - strong first impression and confidence - are about maximizing your personal choices for your benefit, just like keeping your appearance clean and neat (page 46). You want the clothes to make as good of a first impression as you can, and the same time you also want to be confident in them. The two might sound like exactly the same thing, and for the most part they will align, but some people are more confident in clothes that they are comfortable in rather than clothes they only wear for formal occasions.

So if your best clothes aren't the clothes you are most confident in, you should:

- Increase your confidence in the best clothes if possible. This means wearing the clothes more often so you reduce/eliminate your self-consciousness about it.
- Look for compromise in between - i.e. find the best clothes you are still confident in.

Confident is really the key to your interviews. The more confident you are, the better off you will perform.

The last point - not distracting the interviewer - is a tempering of your personal choices. Your best clothes overall might not be the right one for interviews. Although your goal is to make a strong first impression, it **should not** be so strong that your interviewer is still paying attention to your attire toward the end of the interview. Remember, if your interviewer is paying attention to something else besides what you are saying, he is not paying attention to you!

I.e. party clothes are not appropriate for interviews even if they make you feel like a million bucks.

Of course, even with the above guidelines, you are still left with bewildering combinations of wardrobe that will work for interview situations. You can do it as simple as wearing the most appropriate clothes currently in your closet, or as complex as hiring a fashion consultant to pick out and purchase your interview attires. We will leave the implementation details up to you, except to note the following additional points:

- Conservative colors, such as black, navy, and other dark solid colors will always work.
- Bright, flashy colors should only be used discretely with the goal to make a stronger impression, but be careful to have them overdone.
- A layered approach works well in all situations (i.e. have a jacket ready - take it off if not needed).
- Research by Professor Karen Pine has shown that tailored clothes make a stronger first impression.
- The same research has also shown that skirts make stronger first impressions on both men and women.

Posture

Having a good posture is not only healthy; it also does wonders for your confidence (when you need it) and others' perception of you.

When you stand straight, you appear taller and more in command of yourself. Standing tall projects confidence to others. If you stand hunched, you appear shorter and more uncertain of yourself and your surroundings, and others in turn will take you less seriously.

If you practice good postures on a daily basis, you should not have problems with your stances as well as sitting postures.

But if you haven't been doing so, it's time to get started - practice every single day from now on until it's a second nature to you.

For standing, the goal is for you to look as tall as possible but at the same time relaxed; i.e. not overly rigid (too much of a good thing is real).

One way is to imagine yourself as a puppet being suspended by a line that connects to the top of your head. Then, imagine that line is being pulled up, so you have to tiptoe a bit. Imagine that line is being slowly lowered so that your heels slowly come back down to the floor. The moment your heels touch the floor is the moment the line stops being lowered. There - your body's centerline is now lined up.

Next, imagine another line that goes into your left ear and comes out of your right ear. If you turn your head, the line will turn with you. Keep your head looking straight forward, and move your shoulders (for people who hunch, it will be moving back) until they line up on this line.

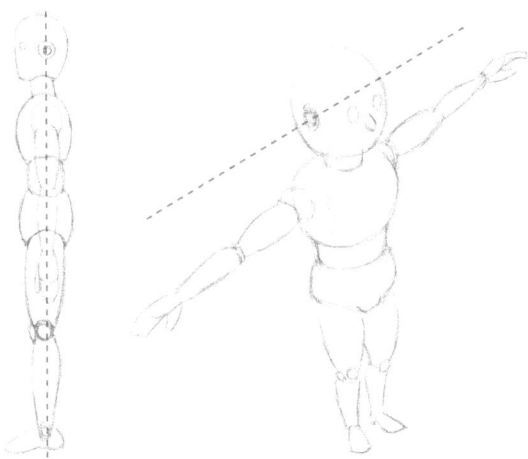

Figure 7.1 - Imaginary lines to help with posture

Don't expand your rib cage by breathing in though, you cannot hold that for long, and it will look too rigid if you do.

When you walk, just strive to maintain both lines. The lines will naturally move around a bit, but they should always go back to the same place.

When it comes to sitting straight, the approach is basically the same, but with a bit of forward lean, because forward lean indicates that you are paying attention and are highly interested in the conversation.

The easiest way to sit straight is to only use the front part of the chair, and lean forward around five to ten degrees. Still maintain both lines, with the legs no longer part of the centerline.

For interviews, you have more flexibility with sitting postures than just sitting straight the whole time. While you can appear relaxed and standing straight at the same time, sitting straight for a long period of time can come across as rigid. The only time you should do so is if you are sitting far away from a desk so the interviewer can see your whole body.

If you are sitting across the desk from the interviewer, you should leverage the desk as a prop for both your posture as well as your body language.

Lean on the desk and leverage the desk (for writing, etc.) as needed. Maintain the forward lean, but you can also try the mirroring technique described in the rapport chapter (page 84) as well, i.e. if your interviewer crosses his legs, you can consider doing so as well.

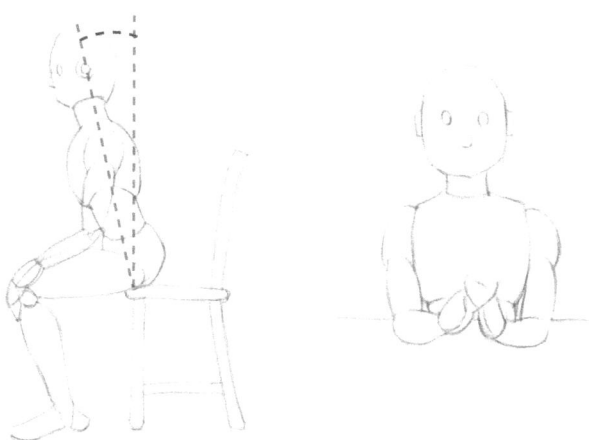

Figure 7.2 - Sitting Postures and leveraging desk as a prop

Eye Contact and Facial Expressions

Maintain a direct eye contact, but not staring.

Give your million-dollar smile! Everyone wants to be greeted by a warm person – show the friendly side of you!

See the chapter on rapport building (page 87) for more details on eye contact.

Handshakes

Nothing says confidence and makes a good impression like a firm handshake.

Although it seems like a firm handshake is about squeezing as hard as possible, it actually is not – your goal isn't to get into a squeezing match with the other party - the key to a firm handshake is to keep your hand in the "handshake shape" as hard and long as possible:

- Imagine that you are holding a two-inch steel pipe with your right hand, and imagine someone else with a bigger hand trying to squeeze your hand on top of it.

- Because the steel pipe is solid – you cannot squeeze it through.
- And if you let the bigger hand crush your hand between the bigger hand and the pipe, it will hurt a lot, so you actively resist the squeezing by the bigger hand.

Figure 7.3 - Squeeze a pipe and at the same time push out with your fingers to hold handshake

To try it – just hold your right hand like you are squeezing a pipe, and then use your left hand to squeeze down your right hand – your right hand should fight hard to maintain its shape.

The shape of gripping a pipe will allow you to grip the hands correctly, and the active resistance will generate force against the other persons' squeezing. This will give the perception that you have a firm handshake.

Here are some additional tips for handshakes:

- Keep your right hand free prior to the meet and greet – i.e., learn to hold things in your left hand if you have to hold them (better – put such things into your pocket or briefcase, so both of your hands are free).
- Be the first to extend your right hand – do so as soon as you see your interviewer.
- Shake hands for about three seconds – give one or two good squeezes and then let go.
- Maintain a welcoming facial expression – direct eye contact and a warm smile!

Sweaty Palms

For quite a few interviewees, there is a big topic about handshakes that we need to address in order to fully cover the topic of handshakes – and that is the sweaty palms.

For many, sweaty palms are caused by a case of nerves, but there are selected individuals who have excessively sweaty palms (yours truly included, but not severe compared to others) that are sweaty even when there are no reasons to be. This is a medical condition known as hyperhidrosis.

Having sweaty palms is an embarrassing situation when it comes to handshakes, doubly as embarrassing in an interview situation, since your goal is to come across as a confident individual, but having sweaty palms appears anything but confident. If you try to quell your sweaty palms through sheer willpower, you will only in fact exacerbate the problem. Your confidence is literally sweating out of your hands, even when you are actually not nervous!

Fortunately, many interviewers do know that interviews are nerve-wracking for all interviewees no matter what brave faces they put up, and will understandably overlook sweaty palms. You can take solace in knowing that at the very least, good interviewers will not hold your sweaty hands against you.

Depending on the severity of your sweaty palm situation, you can try out the following remedy:

- Short Term:
    - Keep an absorbent handkerchief in both of your pockets.
    - Use antiperspirants designed for sweaty palms.
    - Keep yourself calm and soothed - see The Night Before (page 185).
- Long Term:
    - Checkout iontophoresis devices (an electrical device that runs a mild electrical current through your palms) and see if they work for you – note that this is not something that works for everyone, and you should also seek competent medical advices for this particular treatment.
    - Botox is apparently another method that's been shown to be effective for the treatment - again, seek medical attention for advice for this particular treatment.
    - Seek medical attention and potentially surgical procedure.

Put in the effort to reduce and eliminate your sweaty palms if you have the condition – it will do wonders for your confidence.

Conclusion

Make sure that you keep your appearance neat – get a haircut, beard trim, nail trim, and cover up body art ahead of time as necessary. Put on your best attire appropriate for the dress code of the company, and remember to one-up. Be calm and relaxed before you meet the interviewer. Keep both of your hands free, especially your right hand so you are ready to shake hands with the interviewer. Stand tall but relaxed instead of being overly rigid.

Once you see the interviewer, walk toward him, immediately extend your right hand, and firmly shake his hand while maintaining direct eye contact, give a warm smile – remember you have an intense desire to help him and his company out!

Chapter 8

Meet and Greet - the Secret to Small Talks

Meet and greet is one of those things, for some it comes very, very naturally, and for others, it's worse than going to visit a dentist for a root canal.

If you are naturally outgoing and enjoy meeting new people, you are free to skip over this chapter. For those of you (yours truly included) who'd rather pull teeth out of an irritated alligator instead of engaging in small talks, this chapter is for you.

Small talks are basically informal conversations that do not cover any of the main topics to be discussed. This is exactly why it's irritating for some of us – we prefer getting to the meaty part, the main points, rather than "beating around the bush." And being more introverted doesn't help us liking small talks either, of course.

But even those of us who don't like small talks have at least heard that it's important, even if we don't know why. Small talks are conversation lubricants - they help to make the conversation smoother, especially when the parties don't know each other, as will be in the majority of interviews. The smoother the conversation, the more likely you will be perceived as articulate and skilled, and hence the higher you will score with your interviews. It behooves all of us to learn small talk skills, at the very least when it comes to interview settings.

Like any learnable skill, the more we do small talks, the more proficient we get and the more we will like it, which will move the locus of control for small talks internal.

The reverse is also true – the less we do small talks, the less proficient we get, which will cause us to further dislike it and move the locus of control for small talks external.

Remember the locus of control (page 29) – you want an internal locus of control, and you want to get proficient at small talks.

It's never too late to learn new skills. Small talks don't have to be hard, and we can learn specifically for interviews.

You Don't Need to Become a Small Talk Expert

The first thing to understand is, your goal isn't to become the best conversationalist, nor are you trying to be a standup comedian (unless that is the actual job you are applying for). You don't have to become a small talk expert, and certainly not overnight.

You just need to get good enough to keep things smooth until the actual interview starts.

Do Not Try Hard

One challenge for many of us who lack good small talk skills is that we try too hard. We rack our brains trying to come up with great one-liners and hoping to impress others so much so the conversation will flow itself automatically.

It will never happen. Trust me, I've been there way too many times.

Small talks are not jokes. You aren't trying to be funny. Your goal is to find some commonality.

It's Okay if the Small Talk Does Not Continue

Silence can be uncomfortable, but it beats becoming nerve-racking because you are trying to think about what you should say!

If you do not have anything else to say – just follow the interviewer and keep a warm smile on your face.

Start Off On the Right Foot

If you make a mistake in the beginning, you will start off with a deficit and it can take a lot of effort to make up the ground, especially if you also get nervous due to the mistake.

The one mistake you definitely need to avoid in the very beginning, besides everything we discussed in the first impression chapter (page 45), is to be on time for your interview.

Actually, make it earlier. You should arrive with time to spare.

Although this seems such an obvious rule, it is still a surprise that some people don't arrive on time. And there is usually a reason.

They didn't plan to account for the unforeseen.

There can always be some accidents happening to add to your travel time, or some interruptions to delay your start time.

Whether you plan for such possibilities is the difference between someone who is seen as a professional versus someone who isn't.

If you cannot be on time, it can be difficult for the interviewer to believe that you will deliver your work on time.

It's much better if you arrive too early than being late. Plan for it accordingly.

Accidents do happen, and shit can hit the fan so hard that your contingency plan is not enough. Your choice at this moment also makes a difference. Professional candidates inform the interviewer of the situation and agree on a new arrival time, instead of making interviewer wondering what is going on.

Your handling of such a situation will still be viewed as a microcosm of your performance. If you cannot inform others ahead-of-time of your progress in case of emergency, they will have difficult in expecting you to do so when you are hired.

> **Always plan for the unforeseen. If the unforeseen does happen, keep your stakeholder informed and updated regularly.**

Arriving fifteen minutes earlier is generally enough for the purpose of an interview (since you often have to check in at the reception and go through some processing), but it's okay if you do arrive too early. You can take some time for yourself to go through the relaxation drills (page 185) until the time you need to go inside.

Knowing that you won't be late does wonders for your nerves.

Listening (and Observation) is Key

If you feel that you are small talk challenged, the chance is that you will take solace with this particular point. Some people love hearing their own talking so much, they just don't know when to shut up, and completely missed the point of small talks. You don't have that problem right?

Listening is really **the** important part of conversations. If you are thinking of what to say next while the other person is talking, you are not really listening, and you are likely to miss the other person's points.

Observation is how you find things to talk about. For example, perhaps there is a nice painting in the interview room. That can be a conversational topic. Perhaps the interviewer is wearing some rarely seen adornment. That can be a conversational topic. If you aren't observant, you will not pick up these things.

The Goal

As previously mentioned, small talks are meant to be conversation lubricants. Their purpose is to bring the two people conversing closer together, so they can feel more comfortable with each other.

Another conversational tool serving the same purpose but for a larger group of people is the icebreaker exercise.

An icebreaker exercise asks people to share their personal information so people get to know each other more, and thus closes the distance among the group. Small talks do exactly the same thing, but in a less formal setting.

Your mission is to get to know the other person!

Stating the Obvious

For those of us who desire to be Jerry Seinfeld Jr., we need to tone down the goal of making the other person laugh and **just** state the obvious.

| **You** | The weather isn't so good these days, is it? |
| **You** | I am happy I left earlier; with the traffic out there I wouldn't make it if I didn't plan ahead. |

From a small talk perspective, statements like these are weaker compared to other conversation openers. But if you are struggling to come up with the great one-liner, try just saying whatever comes to your mind, without trying to embellish. You will appreciate the break of silence.

What Kids Can Teach You

Kids are the kings of small talks. Albeit not very skilled in conversations, kids are a curious bunch. When they encounter strangers, they pepper the strangers with tons of questions, including potentially embarrassing ones because they don't yet know about adult etiquette.

- What's your name?
- What are you wearing?
- Why are you wearing that hat?

- Why do you have a big booger on your nose? (This is when the adults shush the kid and look sheepishly at you)

Hopefully, you won't be asking the same questions as kids, but we can draw inspirations from them. We need to find and nourish our curious selves.

Remember again – you are here to help them, and in order for you to help them, you should already have a ton of questions in your head. Just let them out already!

What Everyone Loves

There are basically two things everyone loves – they love hearing themselves talking, and they love compliments, no matter how strongly they might appear to protest otherwise.

Compliments can be as simple as about a person's appearance or clothing. The stereotype is that women in general are better at complimenting each other's appearance, but with desire and practice anyone can do it.

> With heightened sensitivity toward appearance and harassment these days, commenting on appearances can be a sensitive topic, so if you are not comfortable doing so, it's okay not to - at least first practice it outside of interview settings.

All it takes is to pay attention to another person's appearance, and find one of the following:

- Something that the other person has obviously put effort into (the hair style, manicures, etc.)
- Something that you know is of high value (premium-brand handbags, a watch, etc.)
- Something unusual (a very flamboyant necktie, a new techno-wiz gadget, etc.)

What you need to do here is to practice on identifying something about the person's appearance or setting to talk about. You should first decide what you are comfortable doing - for example, you might be very comfortable talking about the other person's hairdo, so you decide to focus on that, or you might decide that you are more comfortable talking about unusual gadgets, or you might focus on handbags and watches if you have lots of knowledge about them. Make sure that you feel natural talking about the topic, and if it's a topic that you are also knowledgeable about, all the better, since if both you and the interviewer are knowledgeable and passionate about the same topic, you've just made a connection!

Once you decide on one or two topics to focus on, practice identifying them quickly in everyday life. This can be done by going to busy places such as shopping centers and watching people walk by. Try to quickly identify their hairdos, handbags, watches, or unusual gadgets that they have. Try to increase the numbers of things you can identify - you want to get to the point where you can identify something for everyone, but it's okay if you can only identify one thing out of ten people walking by. Just track them, and slowly increase the number.

Then, you just need to have stock questions or comments for them.

- I love your hairstyle. It looks great on you.
- Is that an LV bag (or whatever premium-brand it might be)?
- What's that watch you are wearing?
- Awesome looking tie. Is that Star Trek (or whatever the theme of the tie is)?

And let the conversation flow!

Compliments can also extend beyond their immediate selves – the offices, the buildings, the products and services. All these things are a part of one's extended self and all fair games for compliments. Anyone who is a passionate fan of a particular high-tech company's products applying there will have a lot of things to rave about!

Once you find something to compliment on, you can combine it with questions and fire away, and you will find the other person talking to exhaustion (or at least until the official start of the interview) and you can just sit back and "active listen" (that means asking more questions to prompt more talks from the other person).

The Bridge

Remember, you don't have to do small talks if you cannot find any topic, so do not struggle too hard with it.

But there is one sure-fire way to ensure you always have a topic to talk about – and this is my personal favorite method – and that is to start the main topic immediately. I call this technique the bridge, as in bridging between the small talks directly into the "main topic," yeah that will be the job you are applying for.

The way to do so is to switch from standard small talks into the main topic conversation as soon as possible, such as immediately after the introductions. From that point on, just start asking questions – you can ask personal questions or project questions, but you can ask them all as business-related questions.

Interviewer	Hi, my name is Doug.
You	Hi, my name is Bob. How are you doing?
Interviewer	Doing well. Busy. How about you?
You	Great! I'm very excited to learn more about the project – you say it's been busy?
Interviewer	Yes – we have an aggressive schedule and we are also short-handed! The interviews are consuming a big part of my time.
You	Oh wow, what's the current schedule?

Keep the Ping-Pong Going

It takes some practice, but your goal, should you find a conversational piece, is to keep asking follow-up questions, so the conversation keeps going.

In the bridge scenario above, you see that you first asked the project's busy-ness, and then asked about the schedule. You can continue to ask about other things, such as the interviewer's role on the project, and what other roles they need to fill on the project. Your goal is to keep the questions going.

If the interviewer initiated the small talk and asks you a question instead – you should then answer the question, but follow up with a question as well, so the ping-pong of conversation can keep going.

Interviewer	How was the traffic? Did you have trouble getting here?
You	Oh, the traffic was bad as usual, but I planned ahead so I arrived here without issues. Did you run into traffic on your way here?
Interviewer	No, I live really close by, so it's just local traffic.
You	Oh great, what neighborhood do you live in?
Interviewer	So and so neighborhood. How about you?

You	I live in this other neighborhood, but I've heard your neighborhood is quite nice, how do you like it?

The Conversation Flow

Generally speaking, if there is a power dynamic at play during an interaction (for example, a host receiving guests), the person with more power is obligated to start the small talk (the reason is because they are in charge of the conversation).

I.e. the interviewers are obligated to start the small talk in general. You just have to follow along and observe the Ping-Pong rules.

Once a while, you will come across an interviewer not making small talks with you besides the obligatory hellos. This can be due to:

- The interview is inexperienced.
- The interviewer is deeply in thought.
- The interviewer is simply not talkative.
- The interviewer wants to "test you" and see how you react. In this case, you should wait for a bit of time (like ten to fifteen seconds, which can seem like an eternity at the beginning of an interaction), and then initiate the small talk via one of the above methods.

If the interviewer responds to your initiation, continue with the Ping-Pong approach to keep the conversation going. If the interviewer appears to have other things in mind still, you should just wait until the interview starts. In any event, maintain a relaxed manner and smile at all times – if the interviewer is challenging you, being calm and relaxed is the key to pass the challenge (all interviewers want a candidate who remains cool under pressure).

One last thing – if you are offered a drink, turn it down unless you are really thirsty. You do not want to have a full bladder and having to run out in between interviews. If you do grab a drink, just drink enough to whet your thirst. The same holds true for most food items. You do not want to talk with your mouth full and having little pieces of food projectiles flying through the air and land on your interviewer's face.

Conclusion

Small talks can be very trying for some of us, but it's simply a necessity for two people to get comfortable talking with each other, especially between strangers.

Luckily, the time you need to do small talks should be quite short, and the interviewer would usually attempt to lead, so your job for small talks won't be too hard.

Identify things of interests to comment on. Be curious and ask questions. Listen, and ask more questions to keep the ping-pong going. No need to be a Jerry Seinfeld. Silence is okay too. And if you really run out of the topic, just bridge over to the main topic. You will safely slide into the first base and ready for the start of the interview.

Let's now look at how the interview opens.

Chapter 9

Interview Opening

Although arguably an interview starts the moment you walk into the company door, in this book, the Opening phase starts at the moment the conversation switches from small talks into business mode:

- The interviewer sets the context of the interview.
- The interviewer explains the background of the position, project, etc.

The Opening phase ends when the interviewer asks you the first official question of the interview. Note that for some interviewers, especially the very friendly ones, the separation between the Meet and Greet phase and the Opening phase can feel blurry, but once you are asked to share information about your qualifications, you have gone past the Opening phase.

Objective of the Opening Phase

The Opening phase serves the same purpose as going through the agenda in the beginning of a meeting. I'm sure you have your fill of poorly run meetings without agendas. Those meetings are a waste of everyone's time involved, as any topic can happen in such meetings, and there is nothing for people to focus on. An experienced interviewer will share the following information as the agenda:

- The background of the position or project.
- The goal for the role.
- What the interview will focus on – skills, experiences, the format of the interview, etc.

When such information is available, it helps you adjust your answers for relevancy and makes it more efficient for interviewers to get the information they seek. The only time that such information should be withheld is when a part of the goal is to test how well you respond to stress, and how resourceful you are in figuring things out in the dark.

If you are interviewing with multiple people in a row, generally speaking the background information will be disclosed by only one of the persons in the loop (likely the hiring manager), since each interviewer will likely focus on different areas of the interview. In that case, you should not be getting the same information repeated throughout the interview.

> If the interviewer doesn't appear to have a copy of your resume, this is the time to hand your printed resume over.

Missed Opening

Just like there are many meetings without an agenda, not all interviewers conduct an Opening phase to their interviews; i.e. some interviewers might immediately jump into asking you questions. This can occur due to the inexperience of the interviewer, or the interviewer is trying to be tough and throw you off your game.

You can just follow along with interviewer's script by skipping the Opening phase altogether, but if you want, you can also attempt to redirect the flow of the conversation:

Interviewer	Why don't you tell me a bit about yourself?
You	Definitely. But before that, is it okay for you to tell me a little bit about this interview for some context setting?
Interviewer	What do you want to know?
You	Well, I want to make sure of the goal for this interview, so I was wondering if you can share some information about the background of the project, the type of candidate you are looking for, and what area you would like to focus on, so I can make sure to focus my answers on what you are interested in.

The interviewer might or might not oblige your request. If he does so, you have just gotten information about the interview you would not have gotten otherwise. If not, it's okay – just follow along with interviewer's script.

Active Listening

When the interviewer is describing the project backgrounds, your job isn't to just sit there and nod along, you should make sure to do the following:

- Take Notes (page 67).

- Ask Questions (page 68).

Take Notes

A habit that you should develop for your interviews (if not for your professional career) is to take notes. I could have been rich if I got a dime for all the interviewees who do not take notes.

A good interviewee knows that taking notes is the only way to ensure that you did not forget any information. Although we've supposedly been taking notes since we were young, it seems that many of us rebel against taking notes as that seems docile and uncool (and of course the real reason is that we are also a bit lazy), and this carried over to the adult life where most people don't take notes - maybe taking notes make us appear "junior" or something.

It's important that we carry no such preconceived notion about taking notes – taking notes is productive, period:

- It shows that we are paying attention.
- It allows us to keep track of what has been said, and what not, and so you can reflect and utilize the information later.
    - Memory is unreliable, especially after your fourth interview in four hours - you probably don't even remember the first interviewer's name.
    - Nothing screams louder about you not paying attention when you ask a question late in the interview about something that has been previously covered.
- It comes in handy when you need to get contact information from the interviewer, but he doesn't have a business card handy.
- It also allows you to track action items for follow-ups post interview (page 215).

The key to taking notes during an interview is to jot down only the pertinent information. This isn't a college class, and you should not have your face buried in your notes. At all times, you should strive to maintain eye contact, and break off only jotting down necessary information, and then resume eye contact with the interviewer again.

It can take some practice to get this down – so make sure you practice taking notes during mock interviews (page 175).

If you find it awkward to whip out a notebook without informing the interviewer, just say "Let me jot down some notes" while you are doing that.

> **Note Taking with Digital Medium**
>
> Although we are in the digital age and are generally environmentally conscious, an interview is one place where a paper notebook is preferred over digital devices such as laptops, computers, or even worse, cell phones.
>
> The reason is that the interviewer might mistake you taking notes for browsing the Internet or texting somebody and not paying attention. Worse, the interviewer might think you are recording the session to post it later to YouTube.
>
> So if you really want to use a digital device, make sure to double emphasize that you are only taking notes digitally because you didn't want to kill more trees than necessary, and you are not doing anything else with it besides taking notes.

Ask Questions

The other key thing to do that demonstrates your active listening is to ask questions. Nothing demonstrates listening more than asking relevant questions about the current conversation topic.

Very few people talk nonstop, because there are always natural breaking points for even a small topic, so you do not have to worry about not having anywhere to add your questions.

Any questions relevant to the current conversation are good. For example:

Interviewer   We are hiring for this position because of the increasing demand for our customer services.

You   What does the demand growth rate look like?

Another Example:

Interviewer   The schedule on this project is very aggressive.

You   What phase is the project currently in, and how far to completion?

You can further insert commentaries that demonstrates your experience and knowledge while asking questions:

Interviewer   Our work with this external vendor has been going much slower than the project schedule dictates, so we are looking for specialists who know how to increase external vendor's productivity.

| You | Yeah, working with external vendors can be difficult due to a longer communication channel and lack of face-to-face rapport building – I've had to work on overcoming similar challenges in the past. Where are they located? |

Obviously, you want to ensure that your commentaries is appropriate for the context – i.e., do not be overzealous in inserting commentaries if you do not know all the information so that you do not end up giving a wrong commentary. But if you give appropriate commentaries, you are in fact selling your expertise and building credibility along the way.

How to Ask the Right Questions

Although we've heard that there are no wrong questions, in reality, there are definitely questions that are best asked differently.

When we ask questions, we need to be concerned about the following:

- Are we talking about a commonly sensitive topic?
- Are we saying things insensitively?
- Are we prying about something that should be a secret?

In an interview setting, the above mean the following:

- Anything that is commonly considered sensitive topics is still sensitive in interview settings. Steer away from such topics if you can. And that goes **both ways**.
- Always pay attention to what you say to make sure that nothing leaves your mouth will end up making you regret it later.
- Always preface the question with an understanding of the situation to show that it is up to your interviewer to decide whether to answer.

For example, let's say that you are asking about the percentage of the business (pertinent to your position's environment) the employer's vendor occupies. You can preface it with:

| You | I'm wondering… and **please do not feel obligated to share with me if it's information that I can't know until I join**… what is the rough percentage of the business the vendor owns for **our department**? |

The first bolded part tells your interviewer that you are experienced and sensitive to the potential that this might be something off-topic for now. And the second bolded part tells your interviewer to subconsciously consider you already part of the team. Your interviewer will know it's his discretion whether to answer you.

If you see a longer than normal pause, you can follow up with:

You Please definitely do not feel obligated. I am wondering because the number can make a difference in terms of management approaches - I'm just **brainstorming about how to solve this problem. We can definitely wait until later.**

The follow-up explains your position, and it subtly shows your desire to **help the employer**, as well as placing additional hints that **there is a future "we."** When you speak this way, you can disarm and sell at the same time.

The key to asking questions like above is to pay attention. And the key to paying attention is to have an intense desire to help others (page 34). By adopting the right mentality (page 29), you will be able to focus your attention appropriately and ask the right questions.

If you have the wrong mentality, as discussed in the Misconceptions chapter (page 21), then even if you have learned this technique, your application will likely come out wrong, since if the focus is on yourself, you end up trying "too hard" with this technique, and thinking about what to say while the interviewer is talking, instead of listening.

Conclusion

Although the Opening phase might seem like just a formality rather than a necessity, you want to make sure that you have a chance to be on the same page as your interviewer, and the Opening phase is the best time to do it. If your interviewer looks to skip over the Opening phase, ask for having the context set appropriately similar to setting an agenda. Ask questions sincerely with the desire to help them, and you will put yourself onto a great start for your interview.

Let's now take a look at the Body phase of the interview.

Chapter 10

Manage the Interview Body Flow

As soon as the interviewer is done with providing the context to the interview, the Opening phase is completed, and we are now in the Body phase. This portion of the interview is characterized with you answering questions to establish credibility about your candidacy to the interviewer.

From your perspective, this will be the most critical phase of the interview - the quality and the clarity of the information you provide here will be the primary factor influencing the interviewer's perception of your ability and fit. You want to make sure that this phase goes as well as possible.

Obviously, answering the questions well is a basic requirement, since the answers are what establish your credibility, but we need to be concerned about more than answering the questions. We also need to think about the "flow" of the interview.

What is the flow of the interview? It is the overall sense of how the interview goes. If you have a good flow, you will feel the interview went well; if it goes poorly, you might dread the outcome.

If we boil down the activities of an interview to a single true essence, we will find that it's about the exchange of information; the interviewer shares information about the company with you, and you share information about yourself with the interviewer.

This is most often done in the form of conversations. Yes, **interviews are simply conversations between people**.

Your goal for the interview, from a flow perspective, is to achieve a collegiate conversation; i.e. it should feel like two colleagues working together solving problems. That level of familiarity and comfort is the golden standard to strive for.

A large part of the flow of course depends on how well you answer the questions, which we will get into in Part III (page 95). In this chapter, we will talk about flow at a higher level - what you should pay attention to besides coming up with great answers.

Overall Flow

As stated previously, you want your interview to be, as much as possible, similar to a conversation you have with your colleagues exchanging ideas. Hence, recall a productive discussion with a colleague, and use that as your guide for an ideal interview flow:

- Both parties are focused on discussing the idea and share thoughts with each other.
- There might be one party leading the conversation, but the thoughts and ideas flow freely back and forth, without any strain or effort.
- The exchange rate is natural - there might be a few pauses here and there, but most of the time it's just a small pause, enough for a thought.
- Both parties ask questions and provide answers. If a question is ambiguous or difficult, the other party naturally asks for clarifications.
- The answers might or might not be long, but even if it's long, the other party is free to interject to make it a dialog instead of a monolog.
- Both parties reach for aids to help facilitate understanding as appropriate. Examples of aids include pen and papers, whiteboards, and computers.

Recall a particularly productive collaboration session you have had. Remember how great it felt to you when you bounced ideas with each other, sharing thoughts liberally, and saw things taking shape. Remember how great it felt when the problem seemed magically solved under the magic of collaboration.

That is the feeling that you want to strive for in an interview.

And if you recall it more vividly, you will see that this positive collaboration session of yours has at least some, if not all, of the elements above. Hence, you want to strive to achieve the above in your interviews.

Mentality and Flow

Yes, I know that you have read the Mentality chapter (page 29), but it's worth stressing here again, as having the right mentality will aid you in almost seemingly magical ways.

When you have **an intense desire to help others** (page 34), you automatically come across as more friendly, interested, and motivated. You will come across as more likable. And when people like a person, they are more likely to let go of small issues from that person.

Moreover, a lot of the techniques we describe in this book will automatically materialize for you when you are able to disregard concerns for yourself and just focus on the other party. Without such a desire, you will have to work that much harder to practice the techniques.

Your life just becomes easier with the right mentality.

When it comes to the interview flow, it's the same way. As stated above, you are looking for characteristics of a good conversation when it comes to interviews, and having the right mentality will produce a good conversation! See how that works?

Study the techniques. Make them part of your muscle memory. If nothing else, at least you will know whether you do well or poorly, so you can adjust. But go back to re-read the Misconception chapter (page 21) as well as the Mentality chapter (page 29) and commit them to heart; you will find your life just become that much easier.

Guidelines and Solutions to Flow Management

At a high level, below are the guidelines to keep in mind when it comes to managing interview flows:

- The interviewer has the lead in the interview until the lead is specifically passed to you.
- When the interviewer does not take the lead, it's your job to prod the interviewer to action.
- You want to keep your answer to a reasonable length. What the reasonable length depends on the question, but you definitely want to avoid a monolog.
- You can take some time to think before giving an answer. In fact, that's a great idea. But you want to make sure that you do not take too much time and appear frozen.
- Ideally, you would like there to be as much back and forth as possible. That means you should ask many, many questions along the way.
- Always pay attention to the interviewer. Make sure to pass the lead back to the interviewer as appropriate.

It's both simpler and harder than it looks above. Simpler, because the above basically paints the picture of a "regular conversation," so if you can do that, you do not need to worry about the details. On the other hand, it's harder because even though you know what needs to be done, executing a "regular conversation" in a pressured-filled situation isn't all that easy, or this book would not have been written.

Sometimes it's easier to look at the reverse situation - i.e. what makes a bad interview flow - in order to overcome them. Below are common interview flow problems:

- Dead Air (page 74) - the uncomfortable pause between topics.
- Talking too little (page 75) - you find very little to say for a given question.
- Talking too much (page 76) - you find it difficult to stop talking.
- Brain freeze (page 77) - all of the sudden you don't know what to say.

Let's look at them individually.

Dead Air

Dead air happens when there is an unusually long pause between conversational topics. Another issue - talking too much - is somewhat related to this issue (see below).

Given that interviewers are in the lead position for interviews, dead air occurs because of the following

1. The interviewer isn't prepared for asking the next question.
2. The interviewer is deliberately testing your reaction to dead air.

Although the first case generally only happens to inexperienced interviewers, anyone can get caught off guard.

Dead air can be uncomfortable, and it is made doubly so because the interview itself is uncomfortable. This is the reason why some interviewers like to use it as a test to see how candidates react. The theory is that if you are comfortable handling these situations, you are more likely to handle tough situations with calmness. Whether it's true or not, you will be expected to handle such situation well.

Some candidates, when encountering dead air, will continue their previous answer. Yes, they employ "talking too much" as a remedy to the problem of dead air. This is a no-no, because talking too much 1) is annoying, and 2) shows nervousness, which is the opposite of confidence.

The best approach to handling dead air is as follows:

1. Observe the interviewer, and determine the cause. If the interviewer appears busy doing something (whether nervously or not), wait calmly.
2. If the wait appears too long (generally anything over 30 seconds), ask, "Is there a particular topic you would like to talk about next?"

Basically, the solution to dead air is to wait calmly for a while, and then ask a question to the interviewer to remind him that the lead is back in his hand. Definitely resist the temptation to automatically elaborate without being prompted.

The above should address the problem in the vast majority of interviews. There are horror stories of interviewers who want to continue the contest of wills to see who can outlast the other with silent stares - hopefully you never encounter that. But if you do, practice the following gradual escalation steps:

1. Start with the two steps above.
2. If the interviewer responds, great. If not, wait calmly for double the time of the first wait.
3. At the end of the wait, ask, "I am not sure I understand the request here, do you mind telling me if you would like to discuss a particular topic?"
4. Repeat the calm wait - double the time again.
5. At the end of the wait, if there is still no response, ask "Right now I am getting the message that you would like to have a quiet time, although that's probably not the best way for us to know each other, I will follow suit for now. Just let me know if you would like to start the interview." And go ahead and wait for either the response or the end of the interview time.
6. If the end of the interview time comes, just say, "Thank you very much for your time. Although we did not get to know each other as much as I liked, I hope that my demonstrated professionalism here is what you are looking for."

No matter what happens, remain calm during the process even if you feel frustrated. You can always choose not to work for a company, but don't let them cause you to compromise your professionalism.

Talking Too Little

Unlike the dead air problem, talking too little is primarily the candidate's issue.

It can happen if one of more of the following issues is present:

- The candidate is nervous.
- The question naturally deserves a short answer.
- The question is poorly phrased so there isn't a lot to say.
- The candidate doesn't know the answer to the question.

In any of the cases, it's not a guarantee that the interviewer will arrive at the correct reasoning for the short answer and hence might attribute it against the candidate. Experienced interviewers might choose to help the candidate out in such situations by asking follow-up questions to get the candidate talking further. But it's not a good idea for the candidate to depend on the interviewer saving the situation. Hence, the best idea is not to give a short answer.

What exactly is a short answer? While there isn't an objective standard, single word answers, and likely single sentence answers are all short answers. Depending on the question, arguably answers less than a minute in duration might be considered short. Short answers are more likely to happen with definition questions (page 116) but are not limited to them.

Whenever you find yourself wanting to just provide a single sentence to the answer, resist the temptation to do so, instead, provide some additional elaborations to what you say.

The techniques we describe in Part III (page 95) will alleviate this problem for you if followed accordingly.

Talking Too Much

The reverse of talking too little is talking too much. As they say, there is such a thing as too much of a good thing.

As previously stated, talking too much often indicates a sign of nervousness, but for some people, it can also be caused by the love of hearing one's own voice - most people share that trait, but it isn't one you want to demonstrate in an interview setting. The thinking here is - if the candidate is so narcissistic even during a high-pressure situation like an interview, working with the candidate in a job setting might not be a pleasant experience.

We all love to hear ourselves talk - I love it so much that I'm making it book length. But in interview settings, keep it under wraps to enhance your chances. Remember - focus on the other party.

The challenge with talking too much is that the interviewer likely ends up with less useful information about you, since he wasn't able to direct the conversation flow as much as he would like otherwise. Not only is it a frustrating experience for the interviewer, it doesn't benefit you since he won't get to know you as well.

Some interviewers, either due to inexperience or due to having a very "nice" personality, exacerbate the problem by either being afraid or unwilling to cut off the candidate's monolog. It might not feel good being cut off, but it's better than wasting time on providing information the interviewer doesn't need.

So what exactly is talking too much? Basically, anything that can be called a monolog is talking too much. Giving irrelevant information is talking too much. If you find the interviewer getting fidgety while you are talking, you are very likely talking too much.

Being elaborate is not exactly the same as talking too much, however. As long as you are on the point and did not take a grand detour with your life story, it's generally fine, but of course better to be succinct and to the point. Also, although the duration is an indicator of how much you talk, it isn't the defining characteristics of talking too much. For example, answering a scenario question (page 118) or a brainteaser question (page 129) might take up the whole interview session, but as long as you are actively collaborating with the interviewer, you aren't talking too much. Monopolizing the airwave is.

If you have this particular issue, the following are keys to addressing the problem:

- Yes, have the right mentality (page 29) as stated earlier.
- Let the interviewer know ahead of time that he can interrupt you any time. This is especially crucial with the nice and/or inexperienced interviewers, so they feel fine about interrupting you and help you move on.
- Pay attention to the interviewer. Whenever you see the interviewer looking like he has something to say, it means that it's time for you to stop talking, and say "Yes, please" and pass the lead back to the interviewer.
- If the interviewer looks like he is restless, he is really not listening to you, no matter how eloquent your speech is. It's definitely time to cut the loss in this case.

Talking too much can be easily solved with the right mentality as well as paying attention to the interviewer. Don't let your reputation be the one who wouldn't shut up.

Brain Freeze

You know the feeling. You are caught with your pants or skirts down, and you are thinking furiously of what to do next, but nothing comes to mind.

It is one of the worst feelings in the world. The only thing that might come to your mind at this moment is to immediately jump through a window to vacate the premise, but you know that you can't. You are trying to find ways to get your brain working again. You need it to work again.

In the meantime, your interviewer just stares blankly at you. Without saying a word.

Your mind went blank. You are in a brain freeze.

Causes of Brain Freeze

If you take yourself back to a time when you had a brain freeze and replay it in slow motion, you will notice the following:

- You were asked a question that you cannot answer at that moment, whether it's due to not knowing the answer, forgetting the answer, or simply being caught off guard.
- You spend time trying to think, but found nothing there, so you think harder, only to watch the clock ticking away.
- The more time elapsed, the more nervous you get, and the more nervous you get, the more frozen your brain get, which took more time off the clock, which makes you even more nervous, and the cycle continues.

This is a vicious cycle, one that is extremely hard to break out of if you have no prior practices. Interviews are stressful enough as is, and if you happen to get a question that you don't know the answer to, it can be quite a nerve-racking experience.

And as you know, **unwanted, prolonged silence is a bad, bad idea in interviews**.

Mitigations for Brain Freeze

You need to observe yourself and recognize when you are in a brain freeze situation. Although it should be obvious, often we don't realize it until we've been in the cycle for a while. The earlier we detect it, the sooner we can start to break away from it.

You also need to be okay with not having answers to every question (this is not to say that you shouldn't try to come up with one). A big part of the reason for a brain freeze is due to us wanting to have an answer. By giving ourselves the permissions to not have every answer, we will be more relaxed, and more likely to break out of the cycle.

You should also know that you don't have to be the only one to come up with the answers! Too often, we think that we must be the sole person to answer in interviews. That is an absolutely false assumption. We can collaborate with the interviewer!

Example of Application

Let's go through a hypothetical situation so we can see what it would look like in interviews:

1. You were asked a question, and your mind goes blank. (Oh-oh!)
2. You quickly realize that your mind is now in a brain freeze situation, so you know you can't come up with an answer right now, and must break yourself out of the brain freeze mode if you are to have a chance. (Wait for it...)
3. You ask, "**Can you repeat the question again?**" (Yes, **talk** to the interviewer!)
4. Your interviewer obliges and repeats the question... if you think of the answer, great. But if not... (Wait for it...)
5. You said, "let me **paraphrase** this and see if I have it right..." and paraphrase the question back to the interviewer. Doing so will allow you to understand the question better in order to think of an answer. Ensure you get confirmation from the interviewer.
6. Repeat step five until you see your interviewer fully agrees. By this time, you might have the answer figured out, if so, great. But if not... (Wait for it...)
7. You said, "let's **brainstorm** on this a bit." Get to the whiteboard (or a piece of paper), and start throwing ideas out. As you write things out, say out loud what you've written, and **collaborate** with your interviewer by asking, "any ideas look good so far?"
8. Your interviewer will very likely to collaborate with you. Even if not, the steps you take above will likely generate thoughts in your head that you can follow on. If you still have trouble, you can still ask, "**Do you mind giving me some pointers?**"
9. Repeat the above until 1) you have an answer, 2) interviewer is okay with you not having an answer, or 3) time has fully elapsed.

The key, when you have a brain freeze, is to **actively collaborate with the interviewer**. The collaboration puts you into a working mode, and allows you to focus on the problem rather than on the situation (how nervous you are and how much time has lapsed), and it brings you outside help for you to find the solution.

Even if you did not come up with a solution at the end, it still allows your interviewer to see your thinking process, which is actually what the interviewer is looking for with their tough questions designed to trip you up. You will be able to show your thought process doing the above, rather than becoming a mime with a nervous breakdown.

Practice, Practice, Practice

Obviously, you need to practice in order to overcome this issue. This issue can be a hard one to practice for, because it might be hard to find that question that can cause you brain freeze during practices. Though if you are quite out of practice, ordinary questions can also cause a brain freeze.

So, first make sure you get enough mock interviews (page 175) done so ordinary questions will no longer trip you up.

After that, if you are still experiencing brain freezes, make sure you specifically practice for it by finding questions that will definitely trip you up. Brainteaser questions (page 129) are often good candidates - make sure you have a ton of these, since as soon as you solve them, they lose their power over you.

It is best to work with someone who knows how to observe and critique you, but if you cannot find that person, the next best thing to do is to find another person who is in a similar situation, and you both cross train each other.

This way, both will have the same motivation to help each other, and both can observe each other in making mistakes as well as coaching to overcome the mistakes. It would be a win-win.

Conclusion

Although the interviewer will primarily assume the lead in the interview, if you want to ensure a great outcome, do not leave it up to chance that you come across a great interviewer.

Pay attention to the interviewer, and pay attention to the flow of the conversation, and match it against what an ideal conversation would be. Monitor your own tendencies for answers, whether it's talking too little, too much, or a propensity to think silently, and guard against them.

Help your interviewer out by help manage the interview flow to be a collegiate conversation - this will end up helping yourself.

Chapter 11

Building Rapport The Easy Way

Ah finally – rapport, the magic word.
I'm sure that you've been told to build rapport, build rapport, and build rapport from all of your research on interview tips. Urban legends have it that rapport has the magical power that can transform an adversarial interviewer into your best bud and immediately offer you the job on the spot. Who doesn't want to gain a power like that?

But if something sounds too good to be true, it probably is. Rapport is just one of those things that interviewers evaluate when making their hiring decisions. It's an important consideration, for sure, but certainly not the be-all-and-end-all, i.e. all rapport and no skill does not a hire make.

We all know some high profile individuals who have communication challenges but yet continue to hold their jobs. We also know that many scientists and software professionals are very successful yet have some difficulties in social situations. People can be successful in spite of being socially inept. So if you truly have exceptional skills, some employer might just be able to look past the communication problems and offer you a gig.

But obviously for the rest of us non-Einstein, learning to interact with others well will vastly improve our chances.

And if you have been following the advice so far, you are already on your way toward building rapport.

Let's now see how to take it all the way home.

What Exactly is Rapport Anyway?

Although we often hear of the word rapport, we seldom hear exactly what it means. Maybe that's why it has such mystical powers.

Rapport is a state of the relationship between two people – specifically, rapport occurs when two people feel like they relate to each other well.

Other words that mean the same thing as rapport are "in sync," "on the same page," "on the same wavelength," etc.

If you say "Knock, knock," and the other person says, "Who's there?" you have a degree of minimal rapport (try it with people from another culture – they won't get it and you won't feel you have rapport with them).

If some stranger overhears your discussion of politics (now that's one topic you don't want to talk about in interviews unless you major in Russian Roulette), comes over and agrees with everything you say, shares his thoughts that also make you agree vigorously, you have just built a decently strong rapport with a stranger - you might even be on your way to becoming fast friends.

Conversely, you might love your family to death, but if when it comes to politics, you share very little common ground (e.g. he's red and I'm blue), then you do not have rapport with your family with regards to politics.

The first example shows how rapports are established (two people agree with each other), and the second and third examples show that rapport can be situational – i.e. you can have good relationship with people but not agree on everything.

The key takeaways here are:

- Rapport is about creating common understanding.
- Rapport can aid in building a closer relationship, but a relationship doesn't depend on having rapport on everything (i.e. disagreement is okay if the common understanding is to agree to disagree).
- You don't need to be friends to have rapport.

When two people (especially two who just met recently) have rapport, they are visibly relaxed and have smooth interactions. This is all made possible by the two of them "being on the same page." So rapport is a social lubricant that exists specifically between two people. This is why rapport is highly sought after – the less friction between you and the interviewer, the better.

Taking all the above into account, the goal of rapport building for our interview approach is clear – your goal is to achieve a common understanding with the interviewer that you are great and the best for the job.

That's it. You do not need to try to make the interviewer your friend. That wouldn't hurt of course, but do not mistakenly put the cart before the horse. Becoming friends during an interview won't guarantee that you get the job, and your friendship is very likely short-lived if you don't get the job anyway.

What does the above mean in concrete terms? It means – if you are to build rapport, make sure that you are building rapport on agreement about your capability and qualification for the job, and not about some other things, such fashion, sports or politics. Interviewers can find many others to build rapport with on those topics; they don't really need you for that. And you building rapport on other things won't give them a hint about your qualifications.

How to Really Build Rapport the Easy Way

Now that we've established why rapport is important and what exact type of rapport you want to achieve, let's take a look at how you can build rapport. Traditionally, the well-known rapport-building techniques are as follows:

- Mirroring (page 84)
- Parroting (page 85)
- Physical touch (page 86)

While knowing these techniques is important, what you need to realize is that the goal of these techniques is to induce a belief on your part as much as for inducing a belief in the interviewer -

> Rapport techniques are meant to make you like the interviewer.

How these techniques accomplish that goal is via an interesting phenomenon that even though our beliefs drive our behaviors, our behaviors can also drive our beliefs. By changing our behaviors, we can influence our beliefs to come in sync with our behaviors.

The colloquial term to drive belief via behavior adoption is to **act as if**, i.e., if you act as if you like someone even when you do not like the person yet, eventually your mind will become congruent with your action, and you will end up liking that someone.

Depending on whom you encounter, you might need to utilize the techniques in order to induce positive feelings about the interviewer. But if you enjoy meeting strangers and can be friends with anyone, or if by studying someone you can come to like them (another known phenomenon - familiarity breeds comfort and like), you can skip these techniques and still be effective.

If you have given yourself the intense desire to help, and act to show that you are here to help, all of your rapport-building problems will magically disappear. We've shown in the previous two chapters how this mentality helps, and a rapport technique's goal is to create this mentality in you so things become natural and smooth.

Although behaviors can influence beliefs, beliefs influence behaviors - more strongly - since it's at the subconscious level. So if you already have the right mentality, you do not need to focus on the specific techniques of rapport building to create rapport, as you will naturally perform these techniques without thinking in such a state. Nevertheless, it is a good idea to know and understand the techniques to supplement situations where you need them.

Mirroring

Mirroring is the primary technique behind rapport building. It is done when you are trying to mimic the behavior of the interviewees, such as in posture, speech speed, etc.

This is actually a naturally occurring phenomenon for humans, i.e. mirroring occurs a lot in real life, without us being conscious about it.

For example, when you are in a conversation, if one of you smiles, the other is likely to also smile. If one of you laughs, the other will be likely to as well. There, those behaviors are unconscious mirroring in action.

In conversations, if one of you leans forward to either talk or listen intently, the other is also likely to lean forward in response. This is another automatic mirroring in action.

Another example - one that we dislike - if one person in the room yawns, you will find yourself fighting off your urge to follow suit as well.

When two people are in sync, they often mirror each other without conscious thoughts. This is one of the reasons why we can easily identify couples - they act and behave similarly, and if they are together long enough, they might even acquire a "couple face" due to them frequently using facial muscles in similar ways.

All of the above mirroring occurs at a subconscious level. It makes sense for social animals to be in tune to one another's body language, both to imitate and learn, as well as for bonding purposes. We like those who act and behave similarly to us.

The idea behind mirroring as a technique then is to take advantage of what has been a subconscious behavior in an explicit fashion so you can create the rapport between you and the interviewer.

As we see above, it doesn't take a lot for mirroring to actually work. We are all programmed to mirror each other to a degree, especially when we are trying to be social. If someone is laughing, it is considered rude not to at least smile back to acknowledge a joke (this is a reason why outsiders always wonder what that party over there finds so funny - the joke isn't necessarily funny, but being in a group is fun).

And if that is the only technique you use - **smile a lot** - you will have quite a bit of success in building rapport. It is difficult to dislike a person who smiles; our mind-body link wants us to like what we smile about.

But you can obviously do more, you can mirror:

- Facial expressions
- Mood
- Movement
- Speech pattern
- Gesture

You can mirror to such an extent that the interviewer thinks that you are mocking him for a fool - don't do that!

Like all techniques, proper use is important. As mirroring is decently easy to accomplish, the key is to **be natural**, i.e. think of how mirroring naturally occurs and do that, instead of doing what would come across as unnatural:

- Do not mirror instantaneously. Most natural mirroring takes place after a small amount of time has lapsed.
- Do not mirror everything. It's okay to approximately mirror rather than getting it to be perfect.
- Mirror the positives, such as smile, forward lean (indicating interest), and hand gestures.
- Do not mirror the negatives such as frowns or slouch.

The best way to think about mirroring as a technique is to use it as **a corrective guide**, i.e., when you notice yourself out of sync, get yourself back in sync as soon as you can. Otherwise just act naturally.

Parroting

Parroting is a specialized mirroring directed for conversations. The idea is that you are not just mimicking the tone and the tempo of the other person; you are also saying back what was being said.

Obviously, if you reply back with only "exactly what was being said," it will sound robotic and a bit creepy, but the idea is to integrate the words in your conversations so that it flows more naturally and subtly.

You How are you doing today?

Interviewer	Not bad – **I was able to beat the traffic.**
You	**You were able to beat the traffic** – great! And the rest of the day so far?

Parroting is a technique for active listening, but specifically with the goal of repeating back words used by the other person. If you do active listening as described by in a previous chapter (page 66), you will be just fine without this technique, but feel free to try it to see if it fits your communication style better.

Also, realize that parroting is a technique to "pick up the words" used by the speaker. Speaking "their language" is a great way to enhance communication and connect with people; it shows that both of you have the same background and therefore can relate. When you parrot, you necessarily will use the other party's vocabularies. You don't need to parrot a full sentence - just a few keywords here and there will do the trick.

Be sure not to get carried away with this technique. It's cute when parrots echoing what you say, but when humans completely echo everything you say, it's called echolalia and can be extremely annoying!

Physical Touch

People feel closer to others when there are touches involved. This is one of the reasons why we have traditions of hand shaking. And this technique can be powerful if properly pulled off.

However, given today's climate, physical touch can be quite sensitive too and there is a possibility for this technique to backfire. And it creates an environment that people aren't used to be touched, and will feel weird if they somehow receive touches. If it's the opposite sex there can be more sensitivities.

Be careful utilizing this technique – the recommendation is that unless you are a natural "toucher," there are other techniques you can carry off more effectively.

> If you were a natural toucher, I would recommend you getting a good read on the interviewer to see if he is receptive to touching. I'm sure you would be much better at it than I will ever be!

And when you do decide to utilize this technique, make sure the touch occurs in "safe areas" such as arms or back – and do it "naturally" (if you have to ask how, you shouldn't do it).

Closing The Distance

Physical touch is wonderful for those who can carry it off. However, for those of us who are not natural touchers, there are other ways for us to reap its benefits by understanding the principle behind it:

> **People who are closer together physically will feel closer emotionally.**

Handshakes, physical touches, all these methods are simply extensions of this principle. The importance is to use it correctly - i.e. you should not willy-nilly violate other people's personal space (even without touching) just to close the distance, as that can backfire on you.

But correct usage work wonders.

1. Look for permissions. For example, handshakes are a time-honored tradition and that's why it's so powerful for closing distance. If you have the permission from the others, whether due to tradition or other reasons, you should definitely close the distance to increase the rapport.
2. Close the distance gradually. In order for people to feel safe about their personal space, they need to process it with time, and abruptly closing distance triggers the opposite response to what you are looking for.
3. Create opportunities for which the others will give consent. For example, bringing a handout that you can share reading together creates a tacit consent from the interviewer.

Eye Contact

Saying eye contact is important to build rapport is like saying water is wet, but it is important to discuss what makes effective eye contact for interview purposes.

The simplest way to understand how eye contact works is that it shows what you are focusing on. This is due to our biology; unlike animals such as rabbits or horses, both eyes of a human face forward at the same direction to form a binocular vision. Coupling with visible whites of the eyes, it is very easy for us (even other animals) to determine what another person is looking at.

If I'm talking to you, and you are looking at me, it shows that you are paying attention to me.

If you are talking to someone, and that someone is looking away, you will think that someone is not paying attention to you.

Hence, the rule number one for eye contact is very simple:

> **When the other person is talking, look at them.**

It doesn't mean that you cannot break away your eye contacts when they are talking, by the way. It means that if you are looking away, make sure you are looking toward something that doesn't make them think you aren't listening.

For example, looking down quickly at your notes while you jot things down is completely fine. Looking beyond the interviewer outside of the window to check out the hot person walking by is not.

When it comes to the speaker, the same rule basically applies, but in a slightly different manner and reason.

For example, if someone is talking to you but doesn't look at you, you will probably wonder, "whom is he talking to?"

And if he is constantly looking elsewhere while talking, you will probably think, "is he trying to end the conversation to go elsewhere?"

And if your goal for talking to him was to verify things, your thought will naturally turn to "why is he trying to end this - does he have something to hide?"

Hence, the rule number two for eye contact is also pretty straightforward:

> **When you are talking, look at the person you are talking to, as much as possible.**

Now, this rule is a bit different from the first rule because it is actually pretty hard to always look at another person when talking. We have natural eye movements when we are thinking. For example, most people will naturally look toward their upper left corner when recalling something from the past, and toward the upper right corner when thinking creatively (like solving a problem). So our eyes naturally move around when we are the one doing talking. But having your eyes wandering around too much (it shows your brain is context switching) cause other people to wonder about your sincerity, so it's something to watch out for.

The best way is to practice taking more time to gather your thoughts (your eyes will wander during this time), and then speak (your eyes will be focused during this time). That way it gives a firm clue to the interviewer that you are focused on the task at hand.

How To Look

You are very unlikely to go wrong by just focusing solely on listening to the interviewer, thinking your thoughts, and talking to your interviewer in distinct phases. The right level of focus will generally naturally bring out the appropriate eye contact.

But things can go wrong sometimes - we don't want our eye contact to be misconstrued for staring, for example - and it's good to know how to avoid and fix the problems.

The way to look without appearing to be staring is to look in the reverse triangle area that is formed by the other person's eyes and the mouth.

Figure 11.1 - Area for eye contact focus

When you look in this area, it allows you not to look directly into the other person's eyes for a prolonged period (that is **staring**) but still "maintain" the eye contact; i.e. you can be more relaxed without worrying about losing eye contact, at the same time without coming across as aggressive.

> Keep in mind - do not look above this area. It will make the other person think you are being condescending.

The Sweetest Sound

The sweetest sound to anyone's ears is the sounds of his own name.
-- Robert C. Lee

Last but not least, do not forget to make ample use of the interviewer's name!

From a rapport building perspective, nothing makes it clearer that you remember the interviewer well as using his name.

Obviously, depending on the culture of the company, you might need to either address the person formally or informally, sometimes you might need to use solely titles. In any case, a liberal use of the situationally appropriate address is warranted in any situation.

Conclusion

As previously stated, techniques are great to know, but they are putting the cart before the horse. If you have gotten the right mentality, and know how to actively listen by taking notes and ask relevant questions, you do not have to worry about techniques such as mirroring or parroting, because the goal of mirroring is to induce the right mentality so you can actively listen. Half-baked techniques actually take your mind away from the active listening.

Moreover, your goal isn't to build general rapport, but rather to build rapport specific to your qualification and credibility for doing the job, and that means you gain more dividend by paying deeper attention to the questions and answer them correctly than worrying about how to induce the interviewer to match your posture.

So – learn the techniques if it piques your interest, but unless you are already practiced, prioritize having the right mentality and active listening above and over everything else.

Chapter 12

Interview Closing

So far we have covered the interview Opening phase (page 65) and the Body phase (page 71). The last step in the interview is the Closing phase. As soon as the interviewer asks you, "do you have any questions for me?" or anything else to signal the end of the interview, you are officially finished with the Body phase and entered into the Closing phase.

Hopefully, it's clear by now that the wrong answer to the above question is, "No, I do not have any questions."

Your Questions

With the questions you prepared before the interview (page 157), as well as the questions generated during the interview, you should have a good list of questions built-up by the end of the interview, i.e., you should not have problems finding questions to ask at this time.

Hence, the only time "No, I do not have any questions" is the right answer is if you have been able to squeeze all of your questions in during the interview, so you can follow it up with, "you have already answered all of my questions."

Keep in mind that you can ask the same questions to all the interviewers in a given interview loop – not that you have to – but as different interviewers are likely to give you different perspectives, it will actually be to your advantage to ask the canned questions multiple times.

But even then, you should still have three more questions you can ask. Unless these questions are covered during the interview itself, you should consider asking them for your own benefit.

The three questions you should always have with you are:

- Can you give me some feedback on how I did? (page 92)
- Is there anything else I can answer for you? (page 93)
- When can I expect you to make a decision? (page 93)

Let's take a look at them in detail.

"Can You Give Me Some Feedback?"

Very few people ask for feedback in an interview. Maybe people are concerned about breaking some interview protocols, or maybe they are just afraid of rejections, but others' loss is our gain.

What could be the worst possible outcome to ask for some feedback?

Could they end up not hiring you due to your asking this question?

Obviously, it's not possible to say that such a possibility does not exist, since there are all types of people out there, including crazy ones, but any place that will reject you solely due to your asking for feedback is a place you do not want to work for anyway. You might as well find out as soon as possible.

The chances are that the worst possible outcome for you asking this question is that the interviewer might say "no."

By the way, this might be the only time you will hear direct and unfiltered feedback. Once you leave the room, you might not get feedback at all, and if you do it will be filtered. If you crave feedback, this is the time to do it.

But as usual, unless you ask, you will never get the feedback in the first place. As feedback is critical for you to actually know how well you perform so you can further improve, you do yourself a big favor by asking this question.

Do keep in mind that depending on how this question is phrased, the interviewer might interpret the question differently than you intended. He might think you are asking whether or not you are the best candidate for the job, and he might hesitate to over commit his statement, since he might not know until he has a chance to regroup with other interviewers on the actual outcomes, so you will need to make sure he understands that you are only interested about the feedback from an improvement perspective, i.e., does he think you have met the standard (with the understanding he has then to compare other candidates) or failed miserably, and are there additional things that he think can be of help for you to improve on.

As long as you provide the necessary caveats, it's unlikely to be misconstrued and make the interviewer uncomfortable.

Ask genuinely. Show him that you are sincere in wanting to improve and better yourself, regardless of whether you get the job. Good interviewers will oblige and give you pointers. Take copious notes if you do get the feedback, so you can use the information for your improvement next time.

"Is There Anything Else I Can Answer For You?"

After you have gotten feedback from the interviewer, and if there is still time left – asking if the interviewer still have questions for you - this will be an opportunity for you to do an additional pitch for yourself.

This is especially a good question to ask if you feel like the interview only covers a part of your strengths and qualifications. In that case, you should amend this question with lead-in like, "perhaps about my background in this particular area" to help direct the interviewer toward the appropriate topic.

Without an additional lead-in, the chance is that the interviewer will not have more questions for you, since that's the reason why the interviewer signals for the end of the interview in the first place. So it is better if you have a lead-in. In either case, if the interviewer declines to follow through, the interview is effectively over, so you should move on with wrapping up the interview.

But if the interviewer does ask more questions, you have just been given permission to continue to make your case, so do make sure you answer them with the same intensity, desire, and skill as you have demonstrated so far.

"When Can I Expect a Decision?"

You might or might not ask this question, depending on what the interviewer's role is, since if there is more than one interviewer, each will share different roles, and not all of them are in charge of the timeframe. Ask this question to either the HR or the manager.

If you do not get the answer to this question throughout your interview loop – ask this question as a part of the After Interview phase.

Conclusion

Once all of the questions are done, it is time to wrap up the interview, and it is important to continue to demonstrate desirable traits such as attention to detail, organization skill, and ability to follow through and get things done diligently.

The best way to do so is to provide a summary to the interview back to the interviewer that includes the following:

- At a high level, what has been discussed during the interview.
- What action items (page 209) you have taken away from the interview.

- And when you will follow up with the interviewer with the action items.

And if you have not gotten the contact information from the interviewer, make sure you ask for the information at this particular point so you can actually follow up with the interviewer later on.

Congratulations, you have just successfully concluded your interview. You can carry on small talks with the interviewer as appropriate for him to lead you to your next interviewer or out of the door. Thank the interviewer, shake hands, and conclude on a high note.

Part III
Ace The Interview Questions

Questions are the meat of the interviews and are the primary means for interviewers to access the skills of the candidates. We use the term "question" to refer to all techniques used by the interviewer to access the interviewees, as it is the predominated format. But not all questions come in the format of a question; it can be a request, a written exam, or a task/drill to be performed.

In this section, we will cover the following types of questions commonly found in interviews:

- Questions that have been asked traditionally in interviews (page 97).
- Questions that are designed to ask for your detailed experiences (page 107).
- Questions that assess your skills (page 115).
- Questions that assess your "smarts" (page 129).
- And finally, a technique you can leverage as the "ace in the hole" (page 139).

> We will use the pronoun "she" in these chapters.

Chapter 13

Traditional Interview Questions

Traditional questions, as previously mentioned, are questions that have been asked in interview settings since time immemorial. That means that we are all familiar with them to some extent, but these questions can still be difficult to answer.

The focus of traditional questions is on you, the individual. They are designed to probe your background, experiences, future goals, and aspirations. They do not focus on your skills and capabilities (page 115), nor do they address your past work behaviors (page 107).

Traditional questions should be straightforward to answer, but for many of us they are still difficult. This is due to:

- We are naturally uncomfortable with being under the spotlight.
- We are also naturally uncomfortable with talking about ourselves with strangers.
- We do not put in the effort to practice these questions.
- We are unaware of the objectives of the traditional questions and hence provide unsatisfactory answers.

You cannot afford to answer these questions unsatisfactorily, however. Traditional questions are designed to let you provide most of the context for further probing by the interviewer, so a poor showing leaves few clues to the interviewer and results in a jarring interview experience for you. Given that these questions are still used by many today, a poor showing also comes across as under-prepared, and that is not the trait you want to convey.

Although behavioral questions (page 107) have been replacing the usage of traditional questions, these questions are unlikely to fully disappear, so you should definitely be prepared and knock them out of the park.

How People Fail to Answer Traditional Questions

Here are some of the frequently asked traditional questions:

- Tell me about yourself.

- What are your greatest strengths?
- What are your greatest weaknesses?
- What do you see yourself doing in five years?

Unprepared candidates stammer something similar to the following answers:

- I have been working in the industry for X years, and at Y Company for 2 of the years, and Z Company for the remainder.
- I am a natural leader, a great team player, and...
- My biggest weakness is that I work too hard.
- I see myself moving up into management in five years.

Put yourself in interviewer's shoes (yes – this is something we will drill into you), are you impressed with the answers above?

Let's now try the following answers for size:

- I have been working in the industry for X years, most recently at Y Company, where I have been overseeing the production process. I have optimized the production process at Y for a 30% productivity increase. I believe I can help your company improve your baseline productivity as well.
- One of my strengths throughout my career has been my ability to be the glue of the team and bring everyone together during tough times. I'm versed on how a highly dynamic environment places stress on teams, and I believe my strength can be an asset.
- I've had challenges working with people who don't pull their own weight before, as it brought the whole team's productivity down. But I've since learned that we are all in the same boat together, and put in additional effort to help mentor and guide those who need help to raise their productivity.
- My goal has always been to add more and more value to a company like yours however I can. I believe that the more value I add, the more valuable I become to the company, and everything else will take care of itself.

What are the differences between these two sets of answers?

- Obviously the second set of answers is **longer.** One of the biggest problems with unprepared people is that they often have very short answers, which end up leaving many periods of dead air in between.

- But the second set of answers is **not too long,** either. Some people have ways of talking without stopping, and that's a problem for the interviewers as they won't be able to ask questions to their satisfaction.
- The first set of answers provides facts from with the perspective of the candidate; the second set of answers provides **facts tailored to the perspective of the interviewer**.

In a nutshell, the second set of answers is designed to be **sales pitches.** The product is **you.**

Goal of Traditional Questions

Giving you a chance to pitch is the goal of the traditional questions. Interviewers are waiting for you to sell them on why you are the greatest thing since sliced bread. You have to pitch with your answers to these questions, including the negative ones. Any answer provided without a tailored perspective is a wasted answer.

If your interviewer is only interested in your recitation of facts, she could have just read your resume instead of conducting an interview.

The trap of traditional questions is that they are designed to sound like two people just chatting in a bar, and interviewee's "guard" is often down implicitly, and the goal is forgotten.

This is very similar to some salespeople who buy prospective customers drinks, and talk about their interests, families, but never remember to sell the customers on their products before the happy hours ended.

You must **A**lways. **B**e. **C**losing.

Let's work through the above questions again to see how you can structure your answers for traditional questions.

"Tell Me About Yourself."

This, or a variation of it, is very often the first question (technically a request) asked in the interview since it's the natural starting point. Even skilled interviewers will need to start with knowing your background, and they are very likely to start with this question.

Because this question occurs so often, there is no reason that people are unprepared for this one. Use this question to start with a bang!

This is your elevator pitch time!

As we've seen above, unprepared candidates do not provide satisfactory answers here. They most often just recite a laundry list of their experiences in an abbreviated format (for those who are aware of time) or go into a highly detailed monolog about every sordid secret of their career and suck the patience out of the interviewer.

Now that we know that traditional questions are sales pitches in disguise, what should we do instead?

1. Ask yourself, what experiences do you have that are relevant to the job you are applying for?
2. Which part of those experiences provides the highlight that will wow the interviewer?
3. Organize these experiences reverse chronologically, with the most recent experience first since that will be the most applicable.
4. If you have lots of experiences, you can quickly allude to that in the beginning (I have been working in the industry for X number of years, and hold similar positions in the past), but then quickly move toward the most recent experience.
5. If your experiences aren't directly relevant, that's okay – look for what's transferable from your past experiences, and work your angles from there.

Let's take the previous example and see how it works:

You 1) I have been working in the industry for X years, 2) most recently at Y Company, where I have been overseeing the production process. 3) I have optimized the production process at Y for a 30% productivity increase. 4) I believe I can help your company improve your baseline productivity as well.

1. You have a lot of experiences, so you mention it quickly.
2. You then focus on the most recent experience.
3. You further focus on your accomplishment that's relevant to the company (in this case, a productivity increase).
4. You finally make the pitch on your experiences being transferrable to the interviewer's situation.

Stating the Obvious

Some candidates might have done step one through step three above, but will fail to make the pitch in step four.

That is a wasted effort. You cannot count on your interviewer making the connection for you, no matter how obvious it may seem to you.

As a matter of fact, the more obvious it seems to you, the more you ought to state it out, because what seems obvious often comes from the perspective of being close and knowledgeable about the issue, therefore the assumption cannot be applied to someone else further from the issue like the interviewer.

Furthermore, even when it's truly obvious to the interviewer, it doesn't mean it's necessarily applicable, especially if you are coming from a different situation:

- When you are jumping industry.
- When you are changing role.
- When you go from a large to a small corporation, or vice versa.
- When you go from a full-time position to a temporary contract, or vice versa.

When the experience isn't directly equivalent, you cannot assume that the interviewer will agree with your assumption that your experiences are fully transferrable. You should make your own case.

Let's now look at the next example.

"What Is Your Biggest Strength?"

Well – talk about asking you to pitch. How much more obvious can it get?

Interestingly, some people still fail this question by only iterating their strength(s) without pitching. You often hear:

- I'm a team player.
- I'm a natural born leader.
- I'm blah blah blah.

Without hearing how these strength applies to the job.

Let's try again:

You I have always been known as a team player, and to me it means more than just blending in with the team. I excel in team collaboration during the forming stage when people are still trying to figure out their roles, well before a distinct culture is formed.

In my past roles as a facilitator, I worked with management to identify role confusions and conflicts on the team, and implement team exercises to improve the team bonding.

The before and after surveys show an improvement of more than 30% on morale. Based on my understanding of your environment, a fast growing company will have quite a bit of role confusions and conflicts. I believe you will be able to take advantage of my skills and backgrounds.

In the above example – you state your strength, but you then:

1. Explain how this strength is unique (your unique selling proposition).
2. Back it up with your past experience where you get to apply this strength.
3. Demonstrate the value you added.
4. Pitch on how your skill can be transferred to this job!

Always close your pitch by talking about how what you said applies to the interviewer's situation.

> Given that traditional questions - especially ones like this - are designed for you to make sales pitches, it is easy to mistake flowery languages as a pitch.
>
> In an interview setting, the important thing is to have as normal of a conversation as possible with your interviewer, i.e., it should be no more formal than how you would talk with a colleague during normal business hours.
>
> The reason to make the conversation as normal as possible is because you want to be perceived as already part of the team (a bit of a psychological trick here) instead of as an outsider who are here to make a sale (even though that is what you are doing). The more you sound like an insider, the less you will trigger natural defense mechanisms people have when they meet a salesperson.
>
> Although that means you should not use flowery languages, it does not preclude you from using jargon as long as it is accepted (and can signal you as an insider) in the particular environment you apply to.

The previous two examples show the following:

- There isn't a single format for answering to traditional questions.
- However, there are still similarities:
  - Answer the question asked.
  - Back it up with some level of detail as necessary.
  - Demonstrate your competence and value.
  - Apply the relevance toward the job you are applying for!

Let's work through another example.

"What Is Your Greatest Weakness?"

You might have heard and think that this is a trick question, but this is no more of a trick question than other traditional questions, as soon as you understand that every single traditional question is asking for a pitch.

So the issue with this question is — how can I pitch with this question? How would a weakness be an asset that you can pitch?

As soon as you ask yourself that question — the clue would be right in front of you. The interviewer isn't really asking you for your greatest weakness, she is asking to see if you have worked on your weaknesses so you can turn them into assets.

Many people opt for "safe" answers that disguise strengths as weaknesses:

- I am a perfectionist.
- I often drive people crazy with my attention to details.
- I work too hard.

The rationale here is that paraphrasing strengths into weaknesses tricks the interviewers into thinking that the problem isn't a big deal. Interviewers are, of course, wise to the move (and heard the above plenty of times... I would have gotten rich if I get paid one dollar to hear every person giving me these answers) and discount the answer, which makes this interaction useless and wasted. Interviewers don't get useful information from you, and you didn't score any points.

> Due to the high ratio of ineffective answers for questions like these, traditional questions are being replaced with behavioral questions to obtain more precise answers from the candidates.

Let's take a look at a better example:

Interviewer   Tell me about what your greatest weakness is.

You   I used to have a tough time dealing with aggressive personalities, as I grew up in households that value civility and respect.

In the past, when some of my past colleagues were being aggressive with me, I had a hard time handling them calmly and successfully.

But that just emboldened them to be more aggressive. So I decided to overcome this weakness.

I read all the books on this topic I could get my hands on and took classes and training on how to deal with bullies.

Since then, I have no more trouble dealing with my aggressive colleagues. Not only did I not get bullied, I was able to point out the flaws of their ideas and proposals in a matter of fact manner without getting aggressive myself. From that moment forward, no one bothered me anymore. My boss noticed the change in my demeanor and the increase in my confidence and had valued my contribution much higher. All in all, I would say I have successfully turned myself around on this issue.

Demonstrating your ability to overcome challenges is **the asset** employers look for, so let's focus on turning this question into a pitch opportunity:

- Find what weaknesses you once have that you have turned into an asset.
- Describe how you have done so, and how much value it has added to you and the company you were working for since then.
- Pitch on how it would be relevant to the new company.

Always be pitching!

"Where Do You See Yourself In Five Years?"

Let's go through the exercise one more time - what is the interviewer looking for in such a question?

Imagine yourself as the interviewer. What would be the perfect answer someone could give you for this question?

It won't be "what the candidate wants." Any answer that is only from the perspective of the candidate can automatically be disqualified.

What you are really trying to ask is – "how do you expect to continue to help me in five years?"

This is definitely another question that has lost its favor, especially since there are less loyalty between companies and employees these days, and this question simply doesn't really apply toward a temporary contract position.

But loyalty is still a quality that employers like, even if they don't reciprocate. After all, from the perspective of the employer, they will be incurring additional costs such as training that they would like to see as much return on as possible.

What you want to do is to paint the perfect scenario for the what-if question - what would you do if everything turns out well with the employment?

As loyalty is still a valued attribute, sell that with something like the following:

You   I love to continue adding value and grow with the company if things work out. I have always valued loyalty, and my staying with a company for seven years demonstrated that. There are not many things more rewarding than to participate and see oneself as a part of a larger whole and help it become successful. If I'm able to add value to the company until then, I believe that everything else will take care of itself.

Since this is a what-if scenario, you do not need to rely on past information to make a point, but if you have been at a company for a long time (5+ years), then it's certainly a strong support to your words as we've seen in the above example.

Selling on flexibility is also an important thing, since there is no way that the company can actually guarantee you anything such as a promotion (or even a position in five years), your pitch then is to say that you're focusing on adding value to the company, rather than any other objectives (such as a promotion) that focuses on yourself.

> The smartest way to cast the spotlight to oneself is to cast it onto others.

"What Salary Are You Seeking?"

Strictly speaking, this question, and its cousin - "what was your previous salary?" - are not interview questions per se, but rather "filter questions," i.e., they are used as a filter to know whether or not you are in the ballpark of their budget for them to pursue further. This is often asked in a "preliminary round," but can also come up again during interviews.

If your number appears too high, they would think they couldn't afford you and terminate the conversation. If your number is too low, they might also filter you on the belief that your experience isn't comparable to what they seek - i.e., it's a no-win situation if you provide a number.

Therefore, the right answer to the question, "what salary are you seeking?" is not a number. You can answer in the following ways:

- A vague answer. For example - "I'm seeking a market competitive salary" is a perfectly valid answer, and one difficult for the interviewer to object or counter.

- A delaying answer. You can delay answering by saying something like "we can work out a reasonable agreement once we determine we are the right match for each other."

The key point here is - **do not discuss salary until you have an offer in hand**.

The same goes for your previous salaries since those are often used as a guide to gauge your current salary. If asked, decline to answer with the following:

- Focus on the current position. "For my current position, I'm seeking a market competitive salary".
- Decline to answer. "My past salary information is irrelevant to this current position."

We will discuss salary negotiation techniques in Getting The Offer You Want chapter (page 225).

Conclusion

Remember, traditional questions are about letting you pitch yourself to the interviewers, so you should make sure your answers are designed to pitch. Beyond just talking about yourself, be sure to talk about why hiring you will benefit the employer. Always tie your answer back to the employer's needs. If you are asked a negative question like your weakness, make sure to demonstrate how you overcome that weakness so it is now an asset.

With the guidelines in this chapter and diligent practice, you will ace traditional questions in no time.

We will next take a look at the successor of traditional questions.

Chapter 14

Behavioral Interview Questions

Traditional questions have been slowly phased out as being ineffective for determining how the candidate will actually behave and perform on the job. After all, traditional questions are passive in that they let you pitch to your heart's content, and it can be difficult to determine the degree of embellishment. Behavioral questions are designed to mitigate the downside of traditional questions.

Behavioral questions are based on the premise that your past behavior is the best indicator of your future behavior. As most people seldom make drastic changes in behavior, understanding how you have behaved in the past provides a pretty good glimpse into how you are likely to behave in the future.

Another advantage of behavioral questions over traditional questions is that they are much more specific in comparison. Instead of dealing with high-level concepts such as strengths and weaknesses, the interviewer will be dealing with the detail of your past actions for her to draw her own conclusions.

Compared to traditional questions, behavioral questions put the interviewer in a stronger position to drive out the information she looks for, and reduce your chance to embellish.

Furthermore, behavioral questions can also serve as skill questions (page 115) for certain types of jobs, specifically those that are heavily dependent on soft skills such as communications and management.

So behavioral questions are the favorite questions of HR personnel and managers who have learned modern interviewing techniques, and you are likely to encounter them at least as much as traditional questions if not more, so you should definitely be prepared to answer these questions, and knock them out of the park.

Jobs that require lots of human interactions also lend themselves well to this format, so if you are applying for customer service, management, or sales jobs, expect lots of behavioral questions.

Format of Behavioral Questions

Behavioral questions roughly follow the following format:

> **Tell me a situation in which you <fill in the challenge>. Tell me about the situation, and what you did.**

The challenge can be anything that's relevant to the role, such as the below:

- Working with difficult co-workers.
- Working for demanding bosses.
- Dealing with angry customers.
- Presenting a proposal to the senior management.
- Negotiating a deadline extension with stakeholders.
- Ushering in an organization-wide process change.
- Implementing a web application from scratch.

As you provide your answer, expect that the interviewer will dig further based on your responses to ensure that:

- They can form a mental picture about what happened.
- They can ensure that the mental picture appears realistic.
- They can verify to their satisfaction that what happened corresponds with their experiences of what would happen.

What the above means is that their probing are meant to **verify you on the coherence of your story,** so be sure you are not making things up on the fly (if you do - make them up very good!). If they discover a discrepancy, it can impact or even discredit your candidacy.

How to Answer Behavioral Questions

The general model of dealing with behavior questions is called the STAR model, which consists of four steps:

1. What was the **S**ituation?
2. What were the **T**asks that need to be accomplished?
3. What **A**ctions did you take?
4. What **R**esult did you achieve?

The above provides the general template for your answers to behavioral questions.

Keep in mind that while behavioral questions differ in format and scope from the traditional questions, there are no differences in terms of the aim. Your goal is still to pitch the interviewer that your answer is relevant to her needs. You just need to do that within a different context.

That means that you have to be mindful and choose answers that are actually relevant to the position, and make the connection explicitly for your interview.

Let's quickly work through one example here:

Interviewer   Describe a situation where you had to deal with conflicts in the office, and tell me what you did.

You might provide the following answer:

You   In my past position I had two reports that were constantly bickering with each other, and often came into my office to talk about how much of a problem the other person was. I ended up physically sitting both of them down together, and had them resolve their differences. Afterwards, the infighting has been drastically reduced, and the team has overall better morale.

Good answer? Yes, not bad. But we can do even better:

You   In my past position, I had two reports that were constantly bickering with each other. The challenge was that their roles were not well defined due to the changing environment, so they were constantly stepping on each other's toes.

Okay – here we further explained the environment – this is one place that you can use to leverage the relevancy of your answer:

You (cont.)   The ambiguity and the animosity that resulted from the situation had caused the whole team's morale to drop. This is an often-observed situation in dynamic environments like my last job and your company.

Makes the connection here! What you did going forward is now relevant to this company.

You (cont.)   I worked closely with both of them to help them get on the same page and made them realize that they were on the same team. I helped set and manage the changing roles and expectations so both of them stay in sync with each other.

> We met on a weekly basis to monitor the progress, as well as identifying any changing conditions so they can adapt accordingly.

Yes, some more details of what you did exactly upfront will help tremendously. Less information here can make the scene looks "fake" and might cause the interviewers to dig deeper:

You (cont.) Once they realized that their conflict came from missed-and-under-communication and that everyone had the same interest at heart, they literally became best friends. The rest of the team was pleasantly surprised by the change, and the overall morale became much improved.

The above answer basically makes the clear connection on this particular experience being relevant to the company, and the additional details on what you did make it much more credible.

Your interviewer might be satisfied with the above answer, or might still dig deeper. But if your interviewer did not immediately go into additional questioning, you can further extend your response with a sales pitch like you would with traditional questions:

You (cont.) As stated earlier, ambiguous roles in fast-paced environments such as yours are very common, and when things are not diagnosed early they can spiral out of control. I believe in helping everyone finding their way in even the most challenging environment, and it is my goal to ensure that I provide that support wherever I go.

How to Answer Further Digging

Whenever there is a further digging, it is due to either a lack of clarity or missing information.

For a lack of clarity – ensure that you understand the question first.

For example, your interviewer might say:

Interviewer I am not sure I understand what you said there – why do they have conflicts again?

It might seem like she didn't hear you correctly, so there would be a natural urge to respond with exactly what you have said.

But what you should do here is to **provide more details,** rather than "repeat what you say." Because the chance is that the lack of clarity is caused by lack of details rather than the interviewer mishearing things.

In other words, don't get into the following:

You   It's a plane.

Interviewer What did you say?

You   I said it's a plane.

Interviewer I don't understand. What did you say again?

You   I said, IT'S A PLANE.

Much better to:

You   It's a plane.

Interviewer What did you say?

You   I said it's a plane. I mean I just saw a plane that flew through the window (and point to it).

Interviewer Oh, I see. I was wondering why you mention a plane all of the sudden.

So – **always answer the objection by providing more details** instead of just saying the same thing again but louder. Let's continue.

For this particular objection of the office conflict, you could then follow up with:

You   Well, before I got onto this team, it never had a clearly defined division of labor for the team members. And the two colleagues were both interfacing with the same prospective customer, but at different times, so neither of them knew what the other was doing, and they were both suspicious that the other person was trying to steal the account.

They were also seldom in the office at the same time, so they never had much time communicating with each other – as you know, email and telephones just don't work as well as in-person conversations, especially for tough conversations. So the animosity basically came from not being on the same page.

Providing more details will never hurt. But don't stop there – keep going and paraphrase your Action, and the Result as well unless your interviewer interrupts you.

You (cont.)   As soon as I got onto the team and realized what was going on, I quickly scheduled a face-to-face meeting with both of them, and asked both of them to debrief each other on their progress with regards to this particular account. Although they complied, at first it was as clear as day that they were very concerned about what the other person is doing behind their backs. I took the chance to get debrief from them, and have them compare notes to show that neither of them were working effectively alone on this account, and it's much better to work together.

You (cont.)   I got them to gauge where they were in the sales cycle, and asked them to share their plans with each other. As they talked through their plans, they realized that both of them were thinking more alike than not, and they might actually complement each other. John was much better at the initial phase, while Jim felt more natural at the closing phase. So with a little prompting they decide to work with each other. I then got them to come in on a weekly basis to debrief with me on the progress. From that point on, they were a team. A very good one, too. They are now on their third account together.

As long as you are not stopped, you should go through the STAR steps with more details until your interviewer is satisfied with your answer.

Note: Can You Talk Too Much?

The short answer is yes, even following a prescription like the above. Sometimes the interviewer is too polite to interrupt, so if you tend to be on the wordy side, you should look for the following signs:

- The interviewer looks like she has something to say.
- The interviewer is shifting around in her seat.
- The interviewer's eyes are looking away from you more than looking at you.

The key is to **pay attention to the other person while speaking**.

If none of the above occurs, simply speak until you have discussed the outcome of your response, and pause for a second or two for the interviewer to see if she moves to the next question. If she appears to want more infor-

> mation, ask her if there is anything specific that she would like more details from you.

And each furnishing of the answer should be provided with reasons and justifications of your thinking process and operation philosophy. Your interviewer will love the sharing – they will feel like they know how you think! If they agree with your thinking process, you will be making a very strong connection. If they disagree with your thinking process, as long as you can justify it, knowing how you think gives you much more leeway than otherwise.

There is one thing that you can skip the detail phase though. You don't need to make another explicit relevance connection or sales pitch after the first shot (and you might not be given the time anyway). Once it's made, you are good for the remainder of the question.

Gotchas for Behavioral Questions

Behavioral questions are designed to probe the details that traditional questions wouldn't uncover, so the interviewers can get a better gauge on you.

That means that the candidate has less room for embellishment than with traditional questions. Yes, it means that if you are into "exaggerations" in interviews, you can get caught with an interviewer who knows how to drill deeper with the questions. Many HR personnel are specifically trained to probe as deep as they can to verify the answer.

It goes without saying that it's never a good idea to lie in interviews to make oneself more favorable. I know that this doesn't apply to the vast majority reading this book, but got to make sure that the very tiny minority gets this friendly advice.

Conversely, the Miranda rights apply equally well to behavioral questions as they apply to traditional questions. Honesty counts, but not all skeletons need to be cleaned out of the closet during interviews. As long as the issue has no material impact to the job at hand, you are free to pick milder stories.

Obviously, sometimes the dangerous skeleton must be aired out because the chance is that the interviewer will find out somehow, and you want her to find out from you personally. This is when you must come clean, and you should make sure that you stay on this point for as long as possible to answer everything to the interviewer's satisfaction, because any such detail discovered through another channel will basically eliminate any chance of you being hired.

Use your best judgment.

Conclusion

Behavioral questions are an improvement over traditional questions in that they allow the interviewer to probe you deeply about your past behavior and use it as a predicator of your future behavior.

Behavioral questions, however, are still similar to traditional questions in that they are both designed for you to pitch to the interviewers, so tailor your answer with an eye on making the case for yourself as the best candidate for the job. Use the STAR system to help bring the point home.

We will next examine skill interview questions in detail.

Chapter 15
Skill Interview Questions

We shall now look at skill questions. Skill questions attempt to directly verify your job-relevant skills, as much as possible. If you are applying for a bagger position in a grocery store, you might be asked to lift a fifty-pound bag over your head to show that you are physically strong. If you are a software developer, you are very likely to be asked to write code. If you are a cook, making an omelet might be in the order.

Not all interviewers will test your skills directly, since not all interviewers interviewing you are qualified to verify your skills. This is one of the reasons that interviews are often conducted as a team, where each person is responsible for a specific part of the assessment. You should certainly prepare for being tested on your skills. Not preparing for it is to leave your interview outcome to chance.

Not all skills are easily verified via the interview process, especially for positions such as management, unless a more costly approach such as simulations is used. As a simulation will often last a least half of a day, if your interview is scheduled for less time, you generally do not need to worry about walking into one.

> Behavioral questions are often used to verify soft skills in the absence of simulations.

Types of Skill Questions

Skill questions can roughly be categorized into two buckets:

- Fundamental/Definition questions – these questions test the foundation and the knowledge of your skill:
    - Physical drills for professional athletes.
    - Computer science concepts for software developers.
    - Project management methodologies for project managers.
- Scenario/Design/Case questions – these questions test your ability to apply the foundation to a particular situation:

- A management consultant might be asked to devise a business model for an emerging market.
- A software architect might be asked to design a conceptual architecture for an ecommerce platform.
- A software developer might be asked to write code to implement a particular algorithm.
- Project Managers might be asked to produce a project plan.

For physical skills such as lifting fifty pounds overhead, it's straightforward for the candidate to follow the instructions. We will focus on dealing with knowledge-based skill questions for the remainder of the chapter.

Fundamental/Definition Questions

Fundamental or definition questions test your basic knowledge or ability required for the particular job.

You might need to lift fifty pounds over your head. You might need to demonstrate that your physical condition is in top 0.01% of the world. You might need to explain the differences between the role of a Project Manager and a Scrum Master.

For knowledge-intensive fields, however, asking questions on fundamentals isn't as useful for gauging actual skills. The reasons are:

- Memorizing definitions isn't a difficult thing to do.
- Memorizing definitions does not equate to having the ability to apply them.
- Conversely, not knowing some particular definitions also do not signify a lack of ability to do the work.

Hence, fundamental questions for those fields do not work well, but you will still find interviewers use them, so you will still need to prepare for them. You just need to make sure you do not spend an inordinate amount of time doing so - it's easy to fall into this trap because it feels similar to preparing for exams back in schools and can be mistaken as a productive activity. As we have seen so far, there are quite a few other things to prepare for, so make sure you do it sparingly:

- Refresh what's required for your role's knowledge, but no more.
- Refresh the definitions to see if you still understand the concept, but do not try to memorize.

Chapter 15 Skill Interview Questions

- **Do not try to acquire new concepts**, as it will be a waste of time - you might not remember it or understand completely, and you might not be asked.

Let's now look at how we should answer fundamental questions.

How to Answer Fundamental Questions

When you are asked a fundamental question, utilize the following strategy:

- Do not recite word for word for the definition. Instead, **describe the concept**.
- Describe the application of the concept, its pros and cons - if any - to show that you have the appropriate experience.

Some fundamental questions will, however, be so simple that you wouldn't really have much to say about it. That is okay.

Since it makes no sense to prepare for all concepts, you probably will come across a question you don't know. This is where you need to practice the following answers:

- I don't know that one. What is it?
- I have heard of ...(the concept)... before, but I'm not familiar with it. I'm sure that I can pick it up quickly though.
- I don't know that term, but maybe I know it by a different name. Do you mind describing it a bit more?

Your interviewer can then choose to:

- Move onto the next question.
- Give you her answer.
- Stall and try to dig further.

You might be penalized for not knowing the answer (this depends on the interviewer), but you will be penalized more if you "fake" the answer (you won't be able to fake it unless your interviewer doesn't know it herself, in which case, you are doomed anyway).

If your interviewer gives you her answer, then you can either:

- If you knew the concept but didn't remember the name, now is the time to launch into your understanding of the concept as previously described.

Remember – your interviewer can tell if you are faking it. So do not just say –"Oh, I knew that" – that will be interpreted as you are faking it, and you WILL be penalized for this response.

- If you didn't know the concept – say, "thank you - I love learning new concepts, and this is great."

Definition questions are pretty much the only interview questions that you are allowed to answer, "I don't know." So practice it judiciously.

> The other questions that you can answer with "I don't know" are ones that start as "do you know <such and such>"? These questions might come up during interviews, but they are not really interview questions (they are in general used to guide interviewers the types of questions to ask subsequently).

Scenario/Design Questions

Scenario or design questions, along with brainteaser questions (page 129), are the questions that "scare" people about interviews. These questions, outside of actually running simulation interviews, give the best indicator of how you can perform on the job.

The following are the different varieties that we categorize under Scenario questions:

- Professional athletes - participate in mini-drills that simulate parts of the game, or play in a shortened game.
- Cooks - cook a new dish based on available ingredients, Iron Chef® style.
- Project managers - solve a particular project management problem, such as missing deadlines.
- Architects - design a conceptual architecture based on requirements.
- Software developers - write code to implement a particular algorithm.

Scenario questions are often open-ended, but they usually have at least one solution. Many are basically a "mini-simulation" of tasks that you will perform on the job; some might even be exactly the problem you will need to solve for the job (many jobs, especially short-term contracts, evolve around dealing with a very specific problem). Smart employers want to make sure that you are exactly what you advertised and know that these questions are best way to find out, so it's prudent that you prepare for them.

What Interviewers Look For

Make no mistake – Scenario questions are **hard**. They are meant to be hard, as they are designed to determine where your skill levels are, and an easy problem will not be able to test your limits.

With hard problems, they can verify:

- Your thought process, demonstrated (this is where your interview skill comes into play).
- How you handle a stressful situation.
- Can you think on your feet?
- Have you dealt with similar problems before?
- How sound is your logic?
- How much of an answer can you formulate in a short amount of time?
- How well do you communicate?
- How quickly do you give up – do you persist to challenge yourself or do you let it go quickly?

As you can see, coming up with the right answer is only a small part of the target. Sometimes the interviewer doesn't even know the answer herself. But it's all the other things the interviewer looks for that determine whether you fit the needs.

Don't fret about having to come up with the right answers. Let's make sure that you check everything else off, and your answer won't be too far off.

The Whiteboard is Your Friend

When you are given a scenario question – get out of the chair immediately and get to the whiteboard! Many candidates seem reluctant to get onto a whiteboard, even with multiple prodding by the interviewer. It's unclear whether it's due to arrogance ("I can solve the problem in my head." False – most people cannot), feeling being slighted ("I'm so much better than this question." "This question shouldn't be directed at me"), or having a fear of the whiteboard ("I don't know what to do with a whiteboard. I hate presentation and am scared of whiteboard.").

Whatever the reasons, the whiteboard is your friend and savior – if there isn't a whiteboard in the room, you should request one.

- The whiteboard allows you to write down your thoughts, so you can actually park them instead of trying to keep everything in your head,

which you will find that you cannot, as interviewers will *add more to your plate until you overflow*.
- The whiteboard allows you to verify your thought process – you can actually inspect what you have written down to see if they are correct, and backtrack as necessary.
- The whiteboard allows you to visually share your thoughts with your interviewer. If you cannot keep your thoughts straight, neither can your interviewer - make things easy for her.
- The act of writing things down gives you the pause necessary for you to verbalize your thought process.

In other words, you are much better off using a whiteboard than not, especially for these hard questions:

- Do not think you can solve these problems in your head, and even if you can, that's not the only thing the interviewer look for.
- Do not think that these questions are beneath you; they might be, but why did you look for this job in the first place? Is the job now beneath you as well?
- Do not be afraid of the whiteboard – you need it to survive and pass these types of questions. If you are not given one – be afraid of your chances.

The worst case is you are in a room without a whiteboard. And if your request for a whiteboard cannot be fulfilled (either denied or simply unavailable) – use the notebook you have brought with you as the whiteboard.

How to Answer a Scenario Question

The following steps will help guide you through answering a scenario question successfully, especially when you do not have the final answer on the top of your head:

1. Gain an understanding of the question (page 121).
2. State your assumptions (page 122).
3. Formulate your hypothesis and approach (page 124) (state how you would solve the problem).
4. Test the hypothesis by solving the problem (page 125).
5. Backtrack and repeat the above as necessary (page 126).
6. Convert the solution into the final format (page 127) as appropriate.

Let's now go through the process to answer a scenario question. Let's work through a hypothetical example here:

Interviewer   Design me an ATM.

> This, by the way, is a common classic design question for entry-level programming positions.

Remember, you are now standing next to the whiteboard, or if you are not, get up now and go to the whiteboard. **Do not wait** until your interviewer asks you.

If you find getting up from the chair awkward, just say the following "looks like this problem requires a whiteboard," and proceed to get up. And if there isn't a whiteboard, again, ask for one.

Paraphrase the Question

The first step in dealing with any non-trivial question is to paraphrase it yourself, so you can fully understand it.

You   So you want me to design an ATM, like the ones we see outside of the bank?

Interviewer   Yes.

You now proceed to write down the words *Design an ATM* on the whiteboard.

You   So I assume it looks and acts like the ATMs we see in the banks today, is that correct?

Interviewer   Yes.

You   Is it used by one person at a time?

Interviewer   Let's start with that.

You then write down *one person at a time* on the whiteboard.

You   And I assume this ATM can take my bank debit cards?

Interviewer   Yes.

You then write down *bank debit cards*.

You	And is it just for withdrawing, or also for depositing as well?
Interviewer	Show me both – what would it be if it just handles withdraws, and what would it be if it could also handle deposits?

You now write down *Withdraw* and *Deposit* on the whiteboard as well.

You	Does it do anything else?
Interviewer	Let's start with this.

Congratulations – you have successfully paraphrased the question into a list of requirements.

This set of requirements isn't complete, but it's enough to start with for you to dig deeper.

Successful candidates **will come up with a variation of the above**. The time it takes to write things down on the whiteboard as well as paraphrasing the question will allow you to think about and analyze the question. This process will be used until the answer is found.

Unsuccessful candidates will stare silently at the whiteboard during this time, or starting drawing a bunch of stuff on the whiteboard without verifying any of the above with the interviewer.

State the Assumptions

As you proceed from the previous step, you start to formulate a design and a response in your head. But then you realize that in order for the design to stick, you need to clarify some assumptions on your part.

You	Okay, these are my current assumptions for the problem. Please let me know if you disagree with any of them.

You write down the word *Assumptions*.

The interviewer nods.

And then you proceed to write them down while you speak about them.

You	First – we are designing an ATM used outside of banks. The exact placement shouldn't matter too much as long as the bank personnel can service it easily, but to simplify the discussion, we'll say that this is a standalone unit in front of banks.

You write down *standalone unit in front of a bank*.

The interviewer stays silent.

You Second – in order for us to make withdrawals, we need to know how much money exists in the bank account. So the unit must have some sort of network connection.

You write down *network connection required*.

You But the connection might get interrupted – so we'll need to deal with that. But for now, let's assume that if the network goes out, the system will be inoperable.

You write down *without a network connection, the ATM is down*.

Interviewer Okay for now. We might revise this assumption later.

You We said earlier that the ATM needed to be serviced by bank personnel. We want it mostly to operate without maintenance, but we'll need to move money in and out of the ATM, especially if the ATM does handle withdrawals.

You write down *secure box for money holding* and *periodic bank personnel service*.

You We obviously also need a user interface for the customer to interact with. These days, it means a touch screen.

You write down *user interface; touch screen*.

You We obviously need to ensure that the customer is authorized to withdraw money and also withdraw only from the account he owns.

You write down *authentication*, and *authorization, user account*.

You I might have more assumptions, but these are enough for us to get started – is there anything here you disagree with?

Interviewer No, go ahead and continue.

Congratulations – you have just accomplished step two. With this step, you have added both additional clarifications, and also solidified the constraint for your design, so now you actually can proceed with a solid design.

Formulate Your Hypothesis and Approach

In general, formulating a hypothesis and a starting point for design can take a while, but since you have been taking the time to state the problem and define the assumptions and constraints, you have been thinking so far. You might not have the right hypothesis, but you probably have thought up a few already.

Whether you think they are the right starting point, do not dismiss them right out of the gate, and certainly not silently.

What you want to do now is to state the hypothesis and approaches that you have come up with, no matter what you think of their potentials.

Let's continue with our example.

You	Okay – it looks like I can try a couple different approaches here. I can design from the outside in, or I can start by designing the architecture stack.
Interviewer	What are the differences?
You	Designing from the outside in means to start from the user, defining the scenarios, and then define what the user experience will be based on those scenarios, so on.
Interviewer	Well – don't we already pretty much know those things? We are talking about an ATM here.
You	So you are not looking for those definitions?
Interviewer	If you were applying for a product management role, I would emphasize those more, but for now we can assume a "regular" ATM until further notice.
You	Okay – so I'll start with the conceptual architecture then.

See – not too hard, right? The key, again, is to hold the conversation throughout the process – your interviewer wants to move things along, and will help prod you toward the right direction.

> **Your goal is to make this a collaboration effort with your interviewer!**

Attempt to Solve the Problem

Once you have your hypothesis formulated collaboratively with the interviewer, you are now at a point where you can try to solve the problem at hand with the hypothesis you have laid out. The effort you put into collaborating with the interviewer will ensure that your hypothesis is a solid lead, since most interviewers will work with you (that is after all, the goal of the interview) to see what you can do.

We will now try to solve the problem.

You   Okay. Given what we have seen here, we know that we need a network layer.

You draw the network layer.

You   And the network will connect to a central server that has the account information.

You draw a central server and indicate a user with a bank account on it.

You   On the other side is the ATM itself.

You draw the ATM.

You   There will be a user using the ATM.

You draw the user. And then you start to connect the user to the ATM, then connect through the network to the central server.

Interviewer Now drill into the components you have drawn out – what do we need for each?

You look at the requirement and assumptions again.

You   We need to have a secure deposit box, and we need the service personnel on this diagram as well.

You added both.

You   We also need a cash dispenser at the ATM, a touch screen module, a bankcard reader module, and an authentication and authorization module over on the server side.

Slowly, you added each of the components onto the diagram, and the ATM architecture takes shape.

Backtrack if Necessary

You might make a couple of missteps here and there which require you to backtrack. You might also have to adjust assumptions along the way (your interviewer will help you do that if you go through the process in this fashion). It might even be possible that what you came up with falls short of the actual solution.

Even without mistakes on your part, it is likely that after you solve the problem, your interviewer will add more requirements to the plate to see how you handle them. Some of the new requirements might conflict with previous requirements, and thus requires you to backtrack.

For example, in the case of the ATM, your interviewer might add the following:

Interviewer Let's now make it so that the ATM continues to work even when the network is disconnected.

With the new requirement in hand, you need to "go back to the drawing board" to make sure everything is fitted in.

To systematically backtrack, you should:

1. Evaluate the new requirement against the current requirements, and see if there are any conflicts between the two.
2. If there are no conflicts, you should be able to address the new requirement without changing the existing solution. Go ahead and do it.
3. If there are conflicts, track back to the underlying constraints to see if we can reconcile at that level, and if so, repeat step two.
4. If not possible, continue to repeat step three at a lower level, until the original hypothesis have been reached.
5. If the original hypothesis does not work with the new requirement, you will have to start over and redo the whole thing.

Although the steps above appear tedious, it in fact just spells out how we humans solve problems instinctively. With some practice, you will be able to quickly go through the above steps without thinking. You do want to take some time though, just to ensure that you do not miss things - that is often how we end up with a wrong answer.

Convert Into Final Format

One thing about whiteboard collaborations is that you will likely create a lot of "draft writing," i.e. the work you quickly scribble down without worrying about how it looks or whether your writings are legible.

That's what brainstorming sessions look like. People are focused on creating the right content without worrying about the presentation. When you have a good level of collaboration with the interviewer, she will not be too picky about whether what you have created look right.

But remember that you are still in an interview setting, and presentation matters. If time permits, you should attempt to put in the extra effort and make your final result presentable.

All you have to do is say "Let me format this a bit to make it clearer".

If the interviewer is pressed for time, she will tell you to not worry about it and move to her next question.

If not - you now have a chance to make it a bit more presentable. That includes cleaning up unnecessary marks and straightening out some writings and some graphs. Your taste will dictate how much effort you put into it, but make no mistake, attention to details matters in interviews, and this will add points to you if you answer the question correctly.

Once you are done, just say

You I think **we**'ve got it. Is there anything more?

Use the word **we** to emphasize the fact that this has been a collaborative effort, and it subconsciously places you as on the same team as the interviewer.

The interviewer will then decide either to conclude the question or add additional requirements for you to repeat the process. Repeat until the interviewer is satisfied.

Conclusion

Fundamental questions and scenario questions make up the bulk of your skill testing. Depending on the exact job you apply for, these questions might range from close to non-existent to having it fully dominate your interview sessions. Your previous experience should tell you how much to prepare for (unless it's your first time, in which case you should prepare as much as possible).

If you answer these questions as described in this chapter, your interviewer will be able to know your thinking process, your knowledge, and your ability to communicate and collaborate.

By showing all of the above, your interviewer will get to know you much better than even if you are able to answer the question correctly in the first try, but did not show how you think.

Practice this process. Have it down cold. And you will succeed in answering skill questions.

Chapter 16

Brainteaser Interview Questions

Brainteaser questions, a.k.a. puzzles, are the really, really scary interview questions.

These questions are meant to test your general abstract reasoning faculty, your ability to perform under pressure, as well as your communication skills.

Often when these questions are asked, the interview will turn into a stretched-out uncomfortable silence, during which the interviewer looks at you blankly, possibly giving you some hints, but there are still no answer popping into your brain.

According to William Poundstone in *How Would You Move Mount Fuji?*, Microsoft more or less helped popularized this type of questions, although it is not the first company to use them. If you are applying to companies that are more "modern" and "high tech," like in technology, consulting, or even finance, you can reasonably expect to come across brainteaser questions, especially if you are applying to junior positions - young candidates have less relevant experiences and these questions act as a substitute for experiences to let them demonstrate their intelligence.

There are also debates on whether these questions actually test your general abstract reasoning ability, since these questions are similar to IQ tests, which also have controversy surrounding their claims.

If you are a relatively new job seeker applying for a job that requires quite a bit of intelligence but not necessarily a lot of credential (software development, management consulting, etc.), you are more likely to come across these questions. Otherwise, your chance of encountering them is much lower.

Regardless of your personal stance on these questions, you should be prepared for them if you have a reasonable suspicion that you might come across them. The reason is because of your confidence – these questions can eat away your confidence like nothing else if you are caught off guard.

And "I don't know" isn't a good answer to these questions, because you are not supposed to know the answers.

> Why should you practice brainteaser questions?
>
> Brainteaser questions test one's ability to deal with unknown problems. The more you practice, the better you get at them. Critics say that these problems are too abstract. But solving abstract problems is a great way to exercise your brain.
>
> The ability to think on your feet is important!

Objective of Brainteaser Questions

Unlike fundamental skill questions (page 116), which you can get away with not knowing the answer, your interviewer actually expects you not to know the answer of brainteaser questions yet expects you to answer.

This is because the objective of brainteaser questions isn't to see if you know the answer. If you can come up with the answer, great, but interviewers don't expect that, as some of the questions are quite hard, and some of the questions don't have a right answer.

> The biggest problem with brainteaser questions is that they can only be used once with a candidate, since they usually rely on some tricks that will lose their magic once you know the answer. These questions are also difficult to design, so often interviewers rely on stock questions created by others. What it means is that if you practice solving them frequently, it's possible that interviewers won't come up with something you haven't seen!

Instead, the goals of these questions are to:

- Understand your reasoning.
- See if you can think on your feet.
- See if you can think outside of the box.
- See how well you handle pressure.
- See how well you communicate.
- See how persistent you are in trying to solve the problem.

Notice a similarity with the scenario skill questions (page 118)? Brainteaser questions are, in a way, scenario skill questions with a twist - how well can you solve problems if you have never encountered them before?

Instead of solving problems that you ought to be familiar with, you are now asked to solve problems that you are not familiar with.

And you are **expected to put in the effort to solve the problem instead of just saying, "I don't know."** The goal here is to see how well, and how much effort you are willing to put into tackling the question. This is in a way a microcosm of work today — you're constantly asked to take on work that you have no previous experience with, and if you give up quickly, for the interviewer it translates into you giving up quickly at work.

Luckily, while these questions are difficult, the actual criteria above gives us a good way to tackle the problem so you can knock it out of the park, even if you didn't come up with the right answer.

So — get ready for the rough and tumble ride of brainteaser questions!

Types of Brainteaser Questions

Brainteaser questions roughly fall into two categories:

- Logical puzzle questions (page 133) — these questions often have a right answer.
- Open-ended questions (page 135) — these questions are much more open in format, and generally the answers are unknown.

Logical puzzle questions are called as such because the questions are designed as puzzles to be solved. You are presented with a situation, a set of constraints, and asked to arrive at a right answer. They are tricky because they usually play on faulty assumptions that people usually have that can lead them toward either a wrong answer or even no answer.

Logical puzzle questions are generally longer than the open-ended questions. This is because it takes quite a bit of effort to explain and set up the needed context of the question so it can be solved. If the interviewer takes more than a minute describing the question, you can expect that this is a logical puzzle question and has an answer.

Here are some examples of the logical puzzle questions — notice that they are longer than the next set of questions.

- You drive a car around a one-mile racetrack one time and averaged 30mph; how fast do you need to go to average 60mph if you go around the track once more?
- We have three switches in the hallway; one switch controls a light in a room at the end of the hall. You cannot see from the light from where the switches are because the room door is closed. You can only make one trip to the room. How do you decide which switch controls the light?
- You hire a contractor to work for you for seven days. You will pay her with a gold bar, and you agree to 1) pay at the end of every day, and 2) pay an equal amount everyday. You can only make two cuts to the gold bar. How do you make it work?

- There are 10 bags of coins, and each contains 10 coins inside. All the coins weigh 10 grams except for one bag that contains coins weighing 9 grams but otherwise look identical to the 10-gram coins. How do you find out which bag contains the 9-gram coins by using the scale only once?
- How many places on earth can you 1) go south for 100 miles, 2) go east for 100 miles, and 3) go north for 100 miles and end up back at the same place?

Open-ended questions are called as such because, unlike logical puzzles, they usually don't have a single right answer, and they usually don't have the same elaborate setup that logical puzzle questions have.

- How many gas stations are there in U.S.?
- How many piano tuners are there in the world?
- If the Star Trek transporter were for real, how would that affect the transportation industry?
- Why does a mirror reverse right and left instead of up and down?
- If you could remove any of the fifty U.S. states, which would it be?
- Why are beer cans tapered on the ends?
- How long would it take to move Mount Fuji?
- How would you weigh a jet plane without using scales?

We will cover the logical puzzle questions first, and then we will take on open-ended questions.

Before we dive into them though, there are a few more points worth making

> **Logical puzzle questions aren't about having the solution. It's about showing the process of your particular solution.**

If you are able to answer these questions in under a minute – you have heard the answer before, and your interviewer knows it. It's better to let your interviewer know that you have heard the answer before prior to answering it, so you can get honesty scores, rather than "pretending" to solve the problem

> **All the positive approaches that we have discussed from the skill questions apply here.**

Logical Puzzle Questions

Logical puzzle questions usually rely on our faulty assumptions. It means that the first answer that you come up with will often be wrong (or you might be "stuck" without an answer).

To answer these particular questions, it is exceedingly important to follow the process that we have outlined in scenario questions section (page 120):

1. Paraphrase the question.
2. State the assumption.
3. Determine the hypothesis/approach.
4. Solve the problem.
5. Backtrack if necessary.
6. Converting the solution into the final format as necessary.

With logical puzzle questions, the chances are that you will be doing more backtracking than scenario questions because part of the "fun" with these questions is that people often make faulty assumptions. Given their nature, you are also less likely to get immediate help from the interviewer compared to scenario questions. So make sure that you backtrack as soon as you realize something is wrong.

Let's go through an example.

"You drive a car around a one-mile racetrack one time and averaged 30mph; how fast do you need to go to average 60mph if you go around the track once more?"

Upon hearing the question, you immediately say, "Let's whiteboard this out – it would be easier to see," and rise up and walk to the whiteboard.

You   Okay – so we have gone around the track once, and we are going to go around it again.
              The first time is 30mph.
              We want to average 60mph with the first and second laps.
              Did I get the question right?

Interviewer   Yes.

You	It seems like the answer is quite straightforward, since 60mph for 2 miles means that I am going 120mph, so 120mph − 30mph means that I should be going 90mph.

Thinking you have the problem solved, you are about to sit down again, but you see the interviewer's corner of mouth twisting up, and you remember — this is a logical puzzle question, and the first answer is most likely wrong. So you catch yourself and re-examine the board again.

> When encountering logical puzzle questions, many people's first try is usually done without stating the assumptions. This occurs because of the way the question is often designed to hide the faulty assumption. That is okay, but when we backtrack we need to revisit our assumptions.

You	But that doesn't seem right — there is something off about what I just said… what could it be? Let me check what my assumptions are with that answer.
	What did I do there?

Thinking through how you answered the question…

You	So this was my equation. I average the speed of the first mile and the speed of the second mile to get to the desired speed.
	The assumption here is that I can get to the average speed with the above equation.
	Is that not valid?

And you stare at the problem for a bit… uncertain whether that was valid, then you think maybe you ought to approach the problem from another angle to see if you come up with the same answer…

You	Maybe let me try to see if I solve this problem from another angle, would I come to the same result.
	Another way of solving this problem is… figure out the exact time it takes to go through the first lap, and the time it would take to go through two laps at the speed that we want, and then see how much time it would take at the end.

The interviewer is biting her tongue — you didn't notice it though as you are busy solving the problem.

You	So since I'm doing 30mph for the first mile, it means that it took 2 minutes to finish the mile.

Chapter 16 Brainteaser Interview Questions

And since I want to average 60mph for two miles, it means that I have to get through two miles in 2 minutes! Ah ha!

There it is – it's impossible to average 60mph under this setup!

Your interviewer's eyes light up – you have solved the problem! But you are not done yet!

You But why did I come up with the first answer? What tripped me?

Obviously, my thought of averaging the two is incorrect – does that mean that I cannot calculate average using the formula above?

Then the light bulb goes off in your head.

You Ah – it's exactly because we are supposed to be able to average the speed that we often will neglect that some average speed would be impossible to achieve under a particular scenario! I get the trick now!

Congratulations – you have just successfully passed your first logical puzzle question!

Again, the key to understanding logical puzzle questions is that you are very likely to have faulty assumptions, and your initial answer is likely to be incorrect. So definitely temper your enthusiasm when you come up with a quick first answer.

Some of the logical puzzle questions are so hard that you will fail to come up with an answer unless you have persisted in trying many different approaches. You will know these ones right off the bat, as you couldn't solve them easily.

In either case, make sure you do not stumble once you realize you didn't have the right answer! The psychology here is important – the interviewer wants to see if you are tenacious, and how you would react under adversity

Open-ended Questions

Open-ended questions are questions that appear to be impossible to answer at the first glance:

- How many gas stations are there in the United States?
- How many golf balls can you fit into a 747?

- How much does the Empire State Building weigh?
- How many piano tuners are there in Chicago?

Note that these questions are generally short in nature, and they often ask you to come up with a number that seems outrageous to figure out. When you see both it's basically a giveaway that this is an open-ended question.

The key to answering these questions though is to understand that:

- The interviewer likely does not know the answer either, even if there is a right answer.
- The idea behind answering these questions is to "guesstimate" – i.e. determine your assumptions, and then based on the assumptions to come up with an answer.
- The goal for these questions isn't to actually get a right answer since there often isn't one, but rather for the interviewer to see and understand your reasoning and thought process.

> Open-ended questions are also known as Fermi questions, named after physicist Enrico Fermi, who is noted for making good, approximate back-of-envelope calculation with little or no data.

The approach to solve open-ended questions is actually not that different from solving logical puzzle questions - the main difference being that instead of trying to trick you with a faulty assumption, you are simply expected to come up with the assumptions in the first place.

Use the following approach to tackle open-ended questions:

1. Know immediately that in an open-ended question, the goal isn't for you to come up with the correct answer, as there often isn't one (or if there is, it's either constantly changing or too difficult to actually determine).
2. Since there isn't a single right answer, your goal is to come up with a defensible answer by laying out your assumptions and deriving the answer based on your assumptions
3. The way you pass the question is to successfully defend your assumptions.
4. Remember - the interviewer wants to see how you arrive at the answer - your best strategy is to collaborate with the interviewer and spell out your thought processes!

Let's go through one such question as an example.

Chapter 16 Brainteaser Interview Questions

Interviewer	Can you tell me how many gas stations there are in the United States?
You	Eh, I don't know the answer to that question.
Interviewer	Well, why don't you humor me and try to think through how many gas stations there might be?
You	Sure, let's see. I know that there are roughly 350 million people in the United States.
Interviewer	Okay.
You	And I don't know what the actual car to people ratio is, but I believe it's something north of 1 to 1. So let's say that there should be around 350 million cars in the U.S. as well.
Interviewer	Okay.
You	So all of the gas stations in the United States ought to be able to fulfill these car's gas needs, potentially with some capacity to spare, since I know that although some gas stations are backed up, most of the time they are not, so I'm likely to underestimate if I guess the number of gas stations operating at full capacity.
Interviewer	Go on.
You	But most of the time, cars aren't waiting in line to get gas. I think I might get gas once a week. That means gas stations should be able to sustain all of the cars filling gas around once a week.
Interviewer	So everyone always gets gas once a week?
You	Well, some people might fill it up more frequently, others less, but if most cars are used for commuting purposes, I believe once a week is a good average.
Interviewer	Okay.
You	I think my average time at a gas station, without waiting, is about 8 minutes, so that means a single pump ought to be able to serve 24 * 60 / 8 = 180 cars a day, if it's operating at a full capacity.

And because we fill gas only once a week, that means at any given day, only 1/7th of cars will be going to a gas station, and for 350 million cars, that means 50 million cars go to a gas station per day.

So given that a single pump can serve 180 cars a day if operating at a full capacity, it means that in order to serve 50 million cars a day, we will need to have 50 million / 180 = around 278 thousand pumps.

We obviously need more since not all pumps operate at full capacity – I think it's probably busy 1/3 of the time. Let's say that pumps operate at 33% capacity, so that means we have around 834 thousand pumps.

So we just need to figure out the number of pumps a gas station has on average. Based on my past experience, I've seen as few as 2 and as many as 16, but I've mostly seen 8, so I'm going to guess that 8 is the average.

So 834 thousand divided by 8, that should give us somewhere around 104 thousand gas stations in the United States.

Interviewer Not bad.

Answering open-ended questions is all about making assumptions, stating them, and making sure that you can logically combine all of your assumptions to derive the final answer. Whether the answer is correct or not (most often the interviewers do not know the answer even if there actually is one) isn't the point – if you can come up with a logical way to derive the answer and defend your rationale, you have successfully answered the question.

Conclusion

Being asked a brainteaser question can be a nerve-racking experience for those who have not encountered them on a daily basis. Oftentimes candidates freeze up when encountering these questions, which unfortunately is exactly the opposite of what interviewers are looking for.

Luckily, as you can see from this chapter, you can learn to tackle brainteaser questions in an organized, methodical fashion, and it surprisingly is very similar to scenario questions. As long as you understand the nuances and have some practices to challenge your built-in assumptions, you will find yourself mastering brainteaser questions in no time. Check the companion site for more practice tips and questions.

Chapter 17

Ace in the Hole – Presenting Your Big Idea

Although the above strategy and techniques described will work well for your interviews, depending on the type of the job you apply for, there is one additional approach that can be added to your arsenal.

This method doesn't work for all job types, nor does it work for all interview situations, but when it's suitable, it can be very, very effective.

The way to think about it is that when you answer questions, you are often, though not always, in a reactive mode. And this method turns it around so that you are in a proactive mode instead. The best defense is a good offense, so they say. This is the ace in the hole.

What you do is to prepare and bring a **presentation** to the interview, and present your presentation to the interviewer. Yes, we are talking about PowerPoint decks, slides, or physical brochures.

Instead of waiting for the interviewer to ask you the questions, create a presentation that will answer the questions.

Not all jobs lend themselves to this approach. For some jobs, having a presentation is simply not applicable. For some other jobs, you might not know enough about the job to actually be able to put together an effective presentation. Yet for some other jobs, presentation alone won't answer all the questions that might be asked.

Yet for some jobs, you will be explicitly asked to interview this way.

For jobs that match, a presentation can be very effective. Business deals are made through presentations. Salespeople made sales through presentations. Consultants secure their projects through presentations.

Given that the majority of candidates will not have a presentation, you showing up with one will be quite a differentiator in and of itself. It immediately speaks to your initiative, motivation and other great qualities.

Obviously, the downside of a presentation is the effort involved. Interview preparation is time-consuming without adding in the effort involved in creating a presentation. If you have to prepare one for every single interview, you are quite unlikely to utilize this technique.

Thus, the ideal circumstance for utilizing this technique would be:

- You specialize in solving a particular set of problems, and every job you apply for basically involves these problems.
- Your solution can be packaged and described in a consumable way by prospective employers.

The more specialized you are, the more likely you will be able to apply your solution uniformly. There will always be some variations, but you should be able to frame the problem and the solution in a way that will apply to the situations you will encounter.

If the above describes your situation, you can create a presentation, and reuse it for many, many times. You might still have to put in a bit of effort to adapt against a particular job, but it will be a variance that you can easily handle.

The nice thing about being a specialist as described is that you will be able to solve the same problem many times, so you can continue to hone and fine-tune your solution and presentation over time.

We witness this phenomenon in political campaigns. The candidate has a plan on how to make our lives better, and her plan and pitch gets better over time (that is, if we agree with the her position – otherwise it's the opposite because we disagree more and more as the candidate becomes better at her plan). If we focus on a single type of job, we can achieve the same outcome as well.

Preparing a Presentation

A presentation for a job interview can be thought of as a "sub-presentation," since it isn't a complete sales presentation that salespeople utilize. The main differences are:

- Your resume would have traditionally been part of the presentation, and it is already available separately to the interviewer.
- You also would not include any "pricing" type of information that can be found in sales presentations.

Your presentation will simply be a description of the problem that you solve, and how you would go about solving them. Think of it as a regular PowerPoint presentation for a meeting.

Below are the topics to include in your presentation:

- What are the types of problems that you focus on.
- What are the challenges people have with these types of problems, and what are the business impacts of these problems.

- How do you go about tackling such problems:
  - Processes
  - Designs and architecture
- Benefit of the solution
- Past experiences and outcome
- Testimonials (if applicable)

Such a presentation, when well formulated and targeted (i.e., making sure this is at least in the ballpark of the job's needs), will serve as the conversation piece for the interview. The interviewer will likely ask you questions based on the presentation, and you can then knock those questions out of the park since the questions are now tailored toward your expertise!

Execution

A presentation is very effective in a larger setting like a panel interview (page 17). Its power, however, isn't reserved to just larger settings.

A presentation can be equally effective in an intimate setting where you are sharing your computer screen with another person. Sharing a screen also has the added benefit of making the situation more casual and less stressful. Furthermore, in order to share a screen the interviewer will have to get closer to you and huddle together, and as we know, a closer distance builds rapport (page 87)!

Fine-Tune Your Presentation

The key about the presentation is that you need to relate it to what the interviewer looks for. Hopefully, your preparation work (page 157) has gotten that part covered so that you know what the interviewer wants and can target your presentation correctly. But unless you know for sure, the first thing you need to do is to figure out where the gaps are, so that you can tailor your presentation during the interview.

In order to determine that, you need to start with a few questions before you launch into presentation mode:

- Questions about the problem space that the interviewer is tackling.
- Questions about the challenges currently faced by the company that needs your help to address.
- Any specific details that will help you fine-tune your presentation.

You can certainly ask these questions while you are presenting, but what you want to avoid is to presenting some information and having the interviewer objecting to its relevance. Relevancy is what you are looking for when you are in presentation mode, asking questions first will help alleviate potential objections later.

Interactive

You want to be prepared for people asking you questions while you are presenting. That's what interviews are all about - people asking you questions - a presentation won't change that. So if you are used to making presentations where people don't ask questions until the end, you will need to adapt to a different way of presenting.

If you are very comfortable with doing interactive presentations, you can safely skip the remainder of this section. If you are not used to doing interactive presentations, the following tips should make your life easier as a presenter.

- Set the stage - tell the interviewer to ask questions anytime she wants. She will do so anyway, so you might as well take charge of the process.
- Answer the simple question immediately - for small questions that can be answered quickly, even if it's something that will be covered later in your presentation, you should go ahead and answer it. This makes you seem flexible.
- Park the complex questions - For more difficult to answer questions that will interrupt your presentation flow, you can ask to park the questions by saying that your presentation will cover the question (if it does) later and request the interviewer to wait until then. Do so confidently, and 99.9% will acquiesce.
- For the 0.1% of the times that the interviewer insists, what you should do is to go ahead and skip to the section that address the question, and go ahead and talk about it. You can add additional transitions as appropriate to smooth out your presentation.
- In the case when the question isn't covered by your presentation, the same rule above applies, except that "parking the question" now means you will say something to the effect of "my presentation doesn't cover that particular point, but I'm happy to address it after my presentation is over."

One point about "parking the question" - it is important that when you park a question, you are able to refer back to it successfully, and that means **writing it down**, and **writing it down visibly so both parties can see them**. Generally that means writing the question down on the whiteboard, or at least on a piece of paper. Parking the question "in your head" is not acceptable.

As previously mentioned, the best part about a presentation is that you are now in charge of the flow of the interview, and that means that you should take advantage of the situation to be in command. Instead of discouraging participation, you should proactively encourage participation:

- Set the stage for interactions as previously mentioned.
- Proactively ask questions to the interviewer to ask for his thoughts and opinions throughout the presentation.
- Place emphasis on discussions and collaborations, rather than just the presentation.

Most interviewers have their shares of dreadful meetings and presentations that can serve as powerful anesthetics for brain surgeries, so they will welcome any well-run interactive presentations. A great, refreshing interactive presentation will make you the talk of the water cooler for days to come.

Put On Your Sales Hat

Although it's a no brainer that presentations are pitches, it's interesting that people often actually forget to make the pitch while in the presentation. This issue is very similar to answering traditional questions (page 97) - most people forget that it's their opportunity to pitch.

The same rules applying to traditional questions applies here. You should make as many references and tie-ins to **how you can help the company** as you can. Do not expect the other party to get it - your assumption here is your loss.

For example, if you are making a presentation on how you would implement a new sales procedure and your slides are about the details of the sales procedure, do not directly launch into a discussion about how the sales procedure works. Instead:

1. Ask about the current sales procedure, and let the interviewer explain it to you.
   - Whiteboard it out while the interviewer is explaining!
2. Ask about the issues with the current sales procedure, and what they would like to see improved.
   - Again, whiteboard is your friend.
3. Talk about your sales procedure, and **answer explicitly** about how your sales procedure will improve the current procedures.

4. If you have examples of where this is previously applicable, all the better.

   It could look something like the following:

   You   Since we are on the topic of the sales process, **do you mind sharing a bit of your sales process with me so I can address it in my presentation?**

   Interviewer   Sure, our sales process is pretty straight forward, ... (the interviewer gives the detail of the sales process)...

You draw out the interviewer's sales process on the whiteboard as she provides the detail. There is a bit of back and forth for correction.

   You   Thanks for the details, **I have seen that in a few other places as well,** and I generally get the feedback that they are looking for a more streamlined approach. What are your experiences so far, and do you find issues with it?

   Interviewer   Well, although we are happy with what we have, we are always looking to improve our revenue so we're looking for better ways, and what we've found is that our sales process is not fully effective when ...(the interviewer gives the details of the problems)...

You write down the detail of the problems on the whiteboard as the interviewer describes them, and adjust them to her satisfaction.

   You   Yeah that's very much the issues we've found as well, which is the reason why I want to talk to you about the sales process in my presentation, **we've had successes with this new approach**.

                  ...(You go into your sales process presentation)...

                  As you can see, this new sales process is designed to deal with the types of challenges you mentioned. We were able to see immediate improvements and increase our revenue by 20%. **I believe it can work well in your environment as well.**

   Interviewer   Your idea is very interesting. Can you tell me more about how it has worked for your environment?

By having an interactive session and asking the appropriate questions, you will be able to find the information you need to tailor your presentation and turn it into your best sales pitch.

Conclusion

Although a presentation isn't something that you can employ in all situations (yet mandatory in some other situations), if it's applicable, you can find it to your advantage to do so, as the cost of preparing a presentation is large enough that this is a technique that many will not use.

Make the presentation relevant, make it address the employer's pain point, and make it interactive and fun, and you will have an ace up in your sleeve.

Part IV
Practice Makes Perfect

No performers will walk onto a stage without practice. Neither should you.

The key to a successful performance, as every performer knows, is practice, practice, and practice. An interview is a performance, one that can decide your future. You should put in as much effort as possible during the timeframe of the Before Interview phase (page 38).

We will cover the following:

- Smart Planning (page 149) - failing to plan is planning to fail.
- Research (page 157) – find out as much as possible about your "enemy" in order to strategize.
- Refresh and Synthesize (page 165) – the other half of research – find out all about yourself that you have forgotten.
- Mock Interviews (page 175) – the drills and simulations of the interview.
- The Night Before (page 185) – how to get yourself into the optimal state before the big day.

Chapter 18

Craft Your Winning Plan

If you want to succeed in any nontrivial endeavor, you need to have a good plan to track and tackle the moving pieces.

Our strategy so far has been to first understand the game of interviewing, and then maximize our score by doing what matters in an interview.

Having a plan allows us to see and track what all needs to be done.

Luckily, interviews, including the preparation, form a linear process with few dependencies, so our planning won't be that difficult.

The type of planning we are talking about here for interview preparation falls into the category of project planning – interview preparation is a **project** itself. If your expertise is in project management, great – what is described in this chapter will be second nature to you; if not, the information here will help you on your way to becoming a competent "mini" project manager.

Luckily, you do not have to get certified as a Project Management Professional™ by the PMP Institute® to conduct interview preparation planning, as interview preparation is not a complex project and doesn't take years of experience to run successfully. But interestingly, we all are better at managing other people's tasks than managing our own. This is due to a few reasons:

- We often **keep track of things on top of our head** instead of writing them down.

    We are often our own worst enemy. We don't forget things because they are too hard, but because we have too many things to remember. Do you have a task list? Do you know what you are supposed to get done today, tomorrow, and a month from now? If not, you are keeping everything on top of your head. And depending your energy level, what other things you have on your plate at the time, you will forget things.

- We do not have **a commitment to others** when we manage ourselves.

    When others manage us, or vice versa, it creates an expectation and a commitment feedback loop. We do not like to disappoint others because not meeting other people's expectations makes us feel worse about ourselves.

When we manage ourselves, we lack such a feedback loop, and it becomes very easy to miss the commitments since we are only dealing with ourselves.

Due to human nature, it is much easier to have others manage us if we want certain tasks done. Unfortunately, there is one large drawback with this approach – project management professionals don't come cheap. Alternatives such as friends or family members are unlikely to be real project management professionals, and you also might not be on speaking terms for long if one of them has to manage you for an extended period of time.

Since you are unlike to hire someone to help you with interview preparation and monitor your progress, it means that for better or worse, you have to manage yourself.

How do we overcome the challenge of managing ourselves? This is a huge topic in and of itself and literally thousands of books and professional courses have been written about it. A detailed treatment of the whole topic is beyond the scope of this book, but we will boil it down and talk about the essential approaches:

- Create a detailed project plan (page 150) – having things written down ensures that you are not tracking things in an ambiguous state in your head.
- Monitor yourself regularly (page 153) against the project plan to track progress.
- If you can, find people who care about your project plan and ask them to help you review and (page 155) create commitment. Join an interview focus group if there is one around you.

Let's look at the steps in more details.

Create a Detailed Project Plan

Writing things down makes things clearer than if they stay in your head.

A detailed plan is created in stages. Just like anything complex, you will not immediately produce a finished product; you will start from the highest level, and flesh out the details as you go along:

1. Identify the objective (page 151) – determine the goal that you want to accomplish.
2. Task breakdown (page 152)
    - Identify a list of tasks that needs to be done in order to achieve your goal.

- With each of the tasks, break it down into a list of subtasks that need to be accomplished to support the tasks.
- Repeat until the tasks are broken down to a granular enough detail for you to carry out.
3. Prioritization (page 152)
    - Determine the priority of the tasks so you can prioritize them accordingly.
4. Timeline matching (page 153)
    - Lay out the tasks against the timelines – you want to ensure that you can fit the tasks within the timeline.

Identify the Objective

For interview preparation, you want to *achieve maximum preparation you can under the timeline constraint you have*. That is your goal; arguably, everyone has the same goal with regards to interview preparation.

Your objective will be how you plan on achieving that goal. For example, if you already know the company inside out (maybe you have previously worked there), you can safely skip that portion of the preparation. If, on the other hand, you know that you really need help on your small talk skills, you should make sure to prioritize practicing small talks.

Make sure to keep your objective short and to the point, and make sure it's focused - if you focus on everything, you have focused on nothing.

Below is a good objective for interview preparations:

> *Improve my communication skills, my skill question answers, and steady my nerve.*

And this is not a good objective for interview preparations:

> *I want to improve everything about my interview skills, including the meet and greet, the rapport building, managing the interview flow, answering the interview questions successfully, etc.*

> While you should make sure that your objective is short and focused, it doesn't mean you do not do some of the tasks that are required no matter what the focus is, i.e., just because you want to focus on practicing communication skills, it doesn't mean that you do not research the company. It just means that you will prioritize improving your communication skills over researching if you have a shortage of time. Objectives will tell you how you should prioritize.

> You might have noticed we did not call out a timeline for the objective. Since the interview date is the deadline for the preparation, it is up to you whether you want to explicitly call it out. The chances are that you will not forget it either way.

Having the right objective will give you the needed focus for you to create your project plans.

Task Breakdown

Below is a general high-level breakdown that you can use to adapt to your project planning. You can find a more detailed plan on the companion website.

Table 18.1 - Sample Task Breakdown

Category	Goal	Sample Tasks
Research - The Employer	Find out as much as you can about the job so you know what to expect.	Research the company, the industry, their products, and the interviewers involved.
Refresh - Yourself	Review what you have done; see if you can match your experience with the employer's needs.	Review your resume and past accomplishments.
Synthesize - Interview questions and responses	Go through interview questions and plan out the answers.	Design your interview questions. Answer your interview questions.
Practice - Mock interviews	Practice the questions and answers in interview formats to work out kinks.	Identify mock interviewers. Provide information to mock interviewers. Conduct mock interviews.

Prioritization

Depending on how practiced you are in interviews, how recently you have gone through interviews, and the particular type of job you are applying for, you might have a different priority assigned to the high-level buckets above:

- If you haven't gone through interviews in a while, getting some mock interviews will be a high priority for you.
- If you have been going through interviews recently, getting mock interviews will be of lower priority, and researching the company/interviewers will be higher prioritized to get you the edge you are looking for.
- If you have been struggling with a particular type of interview questions, prioritizing practicing those questions will give you a better return for your time. You can do so on the companion website.

Prioritization is especially important when you have limited time for preparation. You want to make every second count.

Timeline Matching

Finally, you want to ensure that everything in your plan can fit into the preparation timeline you have. Depending on your timeframe, you might need to revise your plan. For example, if you are notified that you have an interview tomorrow, it doesn't leave you a lot of time to prepare, and you might have to trim quite a few activities that you would like to include.

Some of the activities might also depend on others being available (for example, running a mock interview), so mapping your tasks to a timeline will help you see when you need to reach out to secure other's time.

You can download a sample project plan from the companion website and use it as a starting point for your planning.

Monitor Your Progress

It can seem weird to monitor one's own progress since you should already know quite well where you are and how you are doing. Unfortunately, if it were that simple, books wouldn't be written about it.

The best way to think about this is to imagine yourself going to a place that you have not previously gone before. It doesn't really matter where or how far, but let's just assume for the sake of the argument that it's about a 3-hour drive from where you are. It's a small town that you have never been to before, and you are going for the first time.

What do you do? You get a map, and you map out the direction from where you are to your destination, and you drive toward it.

While you are on the way, the chances are that **if you do not regularly check your progress against the map, you will get lost**.

Running a project is the same way:

- Determining your objective is equivalent to finding the destination.
- Crafting the plan is equivalent to planning out the route.
- Monitoring your progress is equivalent to regularly checking where you are on the map.

A lot of people drive with a map right next to them, so they can steal a glance against the map to constantly see where they are. That is also the best way to monitor your progress against your plan - yes, have your plan right next to you all the time.

Obviously, people have succeeded without having a plan right next to them all the time as well. Many drivers only look at the map at regular intervals.

People who don't read maps again are simply betting that their memory will serve them well enough. That might be possible in a short-drive situation where there aren't a lot of street changes, but it will be very difficult in an interview preparatory situation that spans multiple days while having other things on your plate.

How to Monitor Your Progress

The simplest way to constantly monitor progress is to set aside a small chunk of time on a recurring basis - like every day or every two days - for progress reviews. A natural time block is either the first thing in the morning before your day starts, or the last thing at night before you go to bed, but any time works, as long as you can secure and allocate it for reviewing purposes.

It doesn't need to be an elaborate process either since only you are involved in the review. Going through the following will be sufficient for most people's needs:

- What was accomplished during this period?

    Verifying what was done gives you a sense of satisfaction, which is a great positive reinforcement for you to stick to the routine.
- What do I need to accomplish for the next period?

    Going through what you need to tackle for the upcoming period prepares you mentally for what you need to do - the more clearly you can see the tasks in your head, the easier it is for you to work on them.
- Are there any issues that I need to pay attention to that might block me from proceeding?

The ability to anticipating issues ahead of time is a hallmark of a good project manager, as it ensures you to have ample of time to deal with the problem.

Issues often occur as a part of external influences. For example, you might need to track down the HR to ask questions, but you know he will be out of town until a couple of days right before the interview, so you will either have to rearrange your project plan or find a way to address some of the questions without him. It can also be your other commitments, such as needing to attend a friend's wedding and hence will take away your time for preparation.

By calling out the issues, you will be able to formulate your plan with them in mind.

The above process can be done in a very short amount of time, especially if the period of review is short, like on a daily basis. It can be finished in 10-15 minutes. Spending 10-15 minutes a day is a great way to ensure that you are on your way toward total preparation.

Create Commitment Feedback

As stated before, one of the primary reasons self-management is harder is because we lack a commitment feedback loop coming from having others involved.

This is a very well known phenomenon. For example, many people become much more motivated and more likely to stick to an exercise routine when they workout with others. Peer support groups are also built on the same idea - seeing yourself as part of a group and having you making a commitment to others makes you more likely to stick through the process.

Needing that feedback is one of the reasons, if a subconscious one, why people go to work. Having to make the commitment and the subsequent follow-through is how most people organize their days.

It is, of course, possible to do everything by oneself. There are plenty of successful people who shun the above approach. But you should evaluate yourself candidly and think about whether you benefit from having others help holding you accountable versus going at it alone.

The way to have others holding you accountable is as simple as the following:

1. Find someone who is willing to do so for you.
2. Go through and create the plan (page 150) with the person to arrive at a workable plan.

3. Determine an agreed-upon interval for you to set up a recurring meeting.
4. Meet at the regular interval, and report the progress (page 153) to the person.

That's it. You still do most of the heavy lifting, what you need is just another person being your sounding board. You can even make it simpler by creating the plan and the reports separately, and just show the person the finished plan. Either way, it will make you feel that you need to stick to the plan because you are now accountable to another person.

> Do keep in mind that unless you are paying the other person to do so, you cannot expect that person to actually drive you through the project plan.

This can be done by anyone who is willing to spend a bit of time listening to you, unlike in mock interviews where the choice of the person can have qualitative impacts. It can be friends and family or a complete stranger. The choice is up to you as long as you are comfortable.

> A potential source of a sounding board is the job interview interest groups. These groups probably meet at a slower pace than you need (like once a month), but since they are all interested in interviews, you might find people there willing to spend more time with you outside of the meetings.

Conclusion

Preparing for an interview, although straightforward, is a complex enough endeavor that you benefit strongly by following project management principles and approaches. Identify your objective for the preparation, craft your plan, monitor your progress, and leverage external influences to help you with your commitment, and you will be on your way to a strong preparation.

Chapter 19

Know Thy Enemy - Research, Research, Research

By now, if you are not yet tired of the cliché "knowledge is power," you should have at least gotten the theme of this book. The more you know about "thy enemy" (okay, employers are not your enemies per se, but you get the drift - make sure you don't tell it to their face), the more prepared you will be.

Your mission, should you accept the challenge, is to find out all you can find about the job you are applying for.

The Order of Things

It might seem like that if we have done our jobs appropriately, we shouldn't have to do any research during the interview phase since research should have occurred prior to you submitting your resume to the company. Ideally you should have a deep understanding about the company and the position by the time they reach out to you to schedule interviews.

But the chances are that you still have to do more research:

- Depending on your resume submitting strategy, your research might have been just enough to decide whether you are interested in applying for the job; if so, there is a lot more to do.
- In the case where the employer finds you through other means rather than you submitting the resume, you might not even be aware of the company prior to them contacting you (this is obviously a good problem to have), so you have to research.

As stated before, we can never have too much knowledge when it comes to interviews, and the research phase is when this phrase applies the most – you want to strive to find out as much information as possible!

Curiosity Saves the Cat

Although it might seem like researching the job is a straightforward task, there is actually more than what meets the eye. For example, do you know what is the best way to do research?

With the above question, you might be thinking – in this day and age, the Internet (and pick your favorite search engine) is your friend. I will go online and search for information about the company. Done.

Well, if it's that easy, then all the candidates will all be well prepared. Who doesn't have access to the Internet these days? Why aren't all candidates well prepared?

Primo vs. Secondo

Researching on the Internet is what's called a "secondary research." It's called a secondary research because you are collecting information previously generated for other reasons instead of specifically for your research. A primary research generates information (from interviews, surveys, etc.), and a secondary research gathers information.

> Primary and secondary researches are related but different concepts from primary and secondary source, which you might have heard of. A primary source means the information comes from the originator, and secondary source means source other than the originator. You can conduct secondary research against a primary source, and vice versa.

Incidentally, **an interview is a primary research method.** So when employers interview you and other candidates, they are conducting a primary research for the best candidate to fill their vacancy. When they are going through tens if not hundreds of resumes to filter down to the list of candidates to interview, they are conducting a secondary research.

Here we see things mirrored – you are conducting a research on the employer while the employer is conducting a research on you!

So how does knowing the difference between primary and secondary research factor into our discussion here?

- Secondary research is always cheaper to conduct – because they are going off of available information.
- However, for certain decisions (such as hiring) – primary research is required in order to make a decision. This is because a primary research, although more expensive, is a superior method compared to secondary research.

- You knowing the difference between a primary and a secondary research will help you categorize and organize your effort.

If you have done research prior to resume submittal, chances are you have done just a secondary research – now you know the option of a primary research!

How to Research Successfully

Since we can categorize an employer's hiring process as a research process, let's look further into it and see how employers conduct "their research" – do they just say "we need to hire someone," and then find bunch of random resumes and randomly select people to interview and hire?

What actually happens is that the employer goes through the following process:

1. Assessing their needs. They will look at their specific workload, existing people's skill set, and available capacity to determine whether the need justifies a hiring.
2. Once they are certain of the need, the next step is to formulate the requirements for the position. It can be a particular skill set (such as accounting or legal), and/or a specific amount of experience (being in the industry for 5+ years, for example). Some of the requirements are mandatory while others are optional.
3. The position requirement initiates their hiring process. This can be ad hoc, such as posting the requirements on some job posting site, or formal, with a full workflow automation system driving the process, and involving external staffing agencies to fill the role. The opening is passed through as many hands as their hiring channel allows. This also includes internal referrals (some companies look internally first before going external).
4. Resumes start to flow into the hiring channel for the position, and they might be filtered in stages:
    1. If external staffing agencies are involved, they usually do the first level filtering, before submitting the resumes to HR.
    2. HR also performs some filtering as well via automation and keyword filtering, before passing the resumes to the hiring manager.
    3. The hiring manager and others who will be involved in the interview loop filter through the resumes themselves, and compare resumes against each other to determine which ones they want to interview.

5. The filtered resumes are the ones that made the cut to be interviewed. HR starts the process to schedule the selected candidates for interviews.
6. Once all the candidates have gone through interviews, everyone involved in the hiring process will jointly make decisions. The decision is usually the hiring manger's to make, with others providing input.
7. The successful candidates are checked for references to ensure that they pass the checks.
8. An offer is made to the strongest candidate. If it doesn't result in a hire, continue to the second candidate, so on, or if all candidates fall through, start the process all over again.

Step one and two formulate the criteria on which all the rest of the steps are based on. Resume scanning (step three, four, and five) is a secondary research process. Candidate interviews (step six) are a primary research process, and reference checking (step seven) is also a primary research process.

> The prevalence of social media also gives another dimension to an employer's research on you. They can conduct this during any time as soon as they are aware of you, i.e. they might have seen your social profile before giving you a call.
>
> You can find many stories of people who are barred from consideration or even lost jobs because of being caught in unflattering, compromised positions via social media.
>
> Needless to say, it is important to be careful about what you say and do online. It's impossible not to make mistakes, of course, but it's extremely important to assume that anything you write online is public and will be seen and read by someone at some point, i.e. if it isn't something you would want seen by a prospective employer, do not put it up.

The key to an employer's successful research starts with them having a set of criteria to base their research on. Before they decide to look for candidates, they must first decide what type of candidates they are looking for, and what skills the candidates must possess. The criteria narrow the research's focus to help guide the company's effort in finding the right candidate.

If they have a list of incorrect criteria, they will end up with the wrong candidate. The same goes for your research - you need to make sure you have a list of correct criteria for your research to succeed.

Your Research Criteria

Depending on how much prior research you have done on this company, you should research for some if not all of the following information:

- Industry – does this company operate in an industry that you want to work in?
- Products and Services – do this company's product and services interest and excite you?
- Project – will what you work on in this company with this company interest you?
- Role – are you excited about what you will do in your job?
- People – will you get along with and like the people you will be working with?

The above are the targets for research for all jobs, whether the job is a profit or cost center (a profit-center job is directly related to the product and services offered by the company; a cost-center job is a support function for the company).

For the job, you should prepare to research the following categories:

- The company
    - Its products and services
    - Its history
    - Its future direction and roadmap
    - The industry
    - The customers
    - The problems and challenges unique in the industry
- The Interview Loop
    - Who are the interviewers – what are their functions

Ask Questions!

The best way to formulate research criteria is to **ask questions** - that's why you should be curious! As we've seen, interviews are actually a primary research method, and interviews consist of questions. A smart interviewer will have a list of questions pre-prepared, and so should you.

Ask yourself this first and foremost - what do you want to find out about the company, the industry, the position, and the interviewers?

- About the company

- How long has the company been around?
- What are the company's main products and services?
- Who are the leadership and the management team of the company?
- What industry(s) does the company compete in?
- What are the directions of the company for the next six months, one year, and three years?
- About the industry
    - Who are the main competitors of the company?
    - Who are the customers of the industry?
    - What is the trend of the industry?
- About the position
    - What are the roles and responsibilities of the position?
    - Which department will the position belong to?
    - Who will you report to?
    - Who are your peers?
    - Who will you interact with on regular basis?
    - Will you be expected to relocate?
    - Will you be expected to travel? What will be the frequency of traveling if it's expected?
    - How will this position add value to the company?
    - Why is this position needed for the company? How vital is it that the company fills the position?
    - What growth potential and career prospect will be available in this position?
- About the interviewers
    - Who will be on your interview loop?
    - What are the interviewer's positions and role within the company?
    - What type of backgrounds do they have?
    - What type of interviewers are they?
    - Will you be interacting with the interviewers on a frequent basis on the job?
- Resources in the company
    - Who do you know in the company besides the HR personnel who reached out to you?
    - Does the company conduct an informational for the position?
    - Can the people you know in the company talk to you about the position?

- Do you know people who know people in the company, i.e. the six degrees of separation?

By going through the steps of asking yourself the above, you will be able to formulate a list of questions, from which you can then expand upon by trying to **answer them yourself.**

Some questions are easily answered through secondary research such as via the Internet. You should capture the answers and write them down.

Some questions will not be answerable without talking to someone from the company, and you should park these questions to the side for now until you have a certain numbers of them accumulated. Once there are enough questions accumulated, you should reach out to the company, either through the formal channel (the recruiters), or informal channel (people you already know in the company) to gain answers for those questions.

> Anything that is interview specific will have to be answered by the recruiters.
>
> Anything non-position specific can be answered by others you know who work(ed) in the company.

Phrasing research in the form of questions naturally demands and begs answers to be found. While you are gathering the answers - you will likely come up with more questions in the process. Repeat the above - capture the questions and try to answer them again. Anything not fully answered during your research phase automatically become the questions you will bring with you to the interview!

See how easy it is to generate questions for the dreaded question "So do you have any questions for me?" (page 91) This is why interviewers frown upon interviewees who do not have any questions at the end of the interview – it shows that they did not do their homework (Note – the only time you are excused for not having questions at the end is if you have been asking questions throughout and clearly demonstrates that you have been researching).

How Resourceful Are You?

As stated above, some of the questions you come up with cannot be answered through secondary research, and must be gathered through primary research - i.e. reaching out to the company.

For example, you won't find out who will be in your interview loop via the Internet, and this question must be answered by your HR contact since they are most likely the person to actually schedule the interviewers. You must not be shy to ask for the information – the worst you will receive is "I cannot tell you."

Although some HR personnel might be protective of such information before they are ready to share it with you, given that the candidate will eventually know the answer, this isn't exactly some classified information that must not be shared until you show up on the interview day. Knowing the answer ahead of time simply allows you more upfront time to do research about the interviewers through other means.

Your ability to find out information will set you apart from other candidates who cannot gather such intelligence ahead of time.

It is possible that HR might not be ready to share the information since it takes time for them to schedule the interviewers and won't know who will actually be in the interview loop until a day or two before. In such a case, you will have to find information through other means if you want to gain an advantage through intelligence gathering.

Do you know anyone in the company? Anyone through your LinkedIn contacts know people in the company? Be diligent and try finding more information about the people in the company - any additional information that can come from you buying someone coffee to understand more about the company, the department, and expectations for any of the positions in the company, even if generalized, is immensely useful.

You should shoot for talking to at least one person from the company outside the interview channel as a test for your resourcefulness. If you have achieved it, just know that at the current moment that puts you above other candidates. But in the future when all candidates wise up, it will mean the opposite - the person who cannot do it will be behind other candidates.

Conclusion

By finding out as much as you can about the company, industry, position, and interviewers ahead of time, you put yourself in an advantageous position to prepare for your interview. Not only do you come across as much more knowledgeable, you also come across as interested and self-motivated, which are the characteristics that the employers look for.

We've just accomplished "Know Thy Enemy." Now let's take a look at "Know Thyself."

Chapter 20

Know Thyself - Refresh and Synthesize

It might seem like we know ourselves well, but the chances are you might not know yourself enough for interview purposes at this moment.

Depending on the amount of experiences you have, you might not recall all of the details of the work you've done six months ago, let along six years ago. And if you cannot vividly recall what you have worked on, how well can you possibly pitch yourself to your prospective employer?

Hence, for most of us, a refresher about ourselves is in order. You might have updated your resume prior to sending it out, but it never hurts to go through your accomplishment again.

The following steps outline the process for refreshing your memories:

1. Ask yourself a question (page 165).
2. Go through your resume (page 166) to find answers to the question. Yes, there are likely multiple answers.
3. Map out the details of your answers (page 168).
4. Map against the job requirements (page 170) to tune the relevance of your answers.

Let's go through each of the steps in detail.

Ask Yourself a Question

As we've seen from the Know Thy Enemy chapter (page 157) – **asking questions is the most effective way to research**, so we will do the same here – ask yourselves the following questions:

- What would be the three-minute summary of your career experiences?
- What are your major accomplishments?
- What are your major strengths?
- What are your weaknesses?

- What are some of the challenging situations you have gone through in your career, and what have you done about them? Give a couple of examples.

You probably have noticed and say, "Hey – these are interview questions!" Exactly! Instead of aimlessly reading through your resume and hope that some light bulbs will be turned on at the end of the exercise, the best way to refresh yourself on your experiences is to put yourself in the shoes of an interviewer, and ask yourself interview questions and practice your answer!

> **The best way to refresh your own memory is to ask yourself interview questions!**

Not only is asking yourself interview questions the best way to refresh your memory, it also allows you to formulate great answers that you would otherwise find difficult to formulate on the spot. Obviously that can be rectified with mock interviews (page 175), but 1) you might not necessarily conduct mock interviews, and 2) the more you do ahead of the time, the more efficient and productive the mock interviews will be.

This is why refreshing your knowledge of yourself is separated from mock interview practices, even though they have some overlaps. Ask yourself questions here, and you stand to be more successful whether you do mock interviews.

Go Through Your Resume

No matter how well written your resume is, the chances are that they are not written in a way that will readily provide answers to interview questions.

Even for some of the simplest questions, such as "tell me a bit about yourself," only some resumes can readily answer them. For the more difficult questions that talk about particular circumstances (page 107), you probably won't even find a mention of them in your resume.

Unless the answer to the question is a very recent experience, or you have a photographic memory, what you track in a resume remains your key to unlock your past experiences to the answers.

Because you won't find ready answers to the questions you ask, going through a resume is necessarily an indirect process:

1. Go through the descriptions of your work.
2. Based on your work, recall details that relate to the question, even if the detail isn't directly related.

Chapter 20 Know Thyself - Refresh and Synthesize

3. If you only find something indirectly related, use that as a launching point, and see if you find thing else closer.

At this stage, your goal is to refresh your knowledge of yourself, with an eye toward answering the question, but not yet worrying about answering it.

When you look at the list of the accomplishments, try to put yourself back at the time of the work, and vividly recall the experiences.

Let's run through a quick example. Let's say that the following are your experiences as a customer service representative:

- On average handled 60+ customer service calls a day.
- Excellent customer feedback - 4.5 out of 5 - on a consistent basis.
- Service Rep of the Month five times, Service Rep of the Year once.
- Taking on team lead duties after six months on the job, taking up a backup supervisor role after one year.

When you read the above, you should be able to recall your time at the bullpen handling the incoming calls, answering customer inquiries, and dealing patiently with irate customers. You should also be able to recall sharing a laugh with co-workers, helping them out with their frustrations, and getting recognition from the management.

The more vividly you can recall the past, the more you can find answers to your questions, and by going through the exercise with every question, the recall will come easier with every try, which further enhances your answers.

Sometimes it can be difficult to immediately recall what has happened. For example, even though you might have been a Service Rep of the Month five times, it doesn't tell you what happened to the other months when you weren't a Service Rep of the Month. That might not necessarily indicate an issue - after all, it's difficult to be a Service Rep of the Month with all the competitions - but you would want to know the answer.

The way to further recall what isn't written on the resume, again, is to **ask more questions**. In this case, ask yourself the following

- What happened to the other months when I wasn't nominated?
- Was I was a near miss at these other months?
- Are there some months when my performance was far below my personal norm?

> Experienced interviewers are trained to ask detailed follow-up questions to dig information and analyze candidates. You might as well practice digging information yourself to get used to them.

You might recall that the reason you weren't nominated more is because the company has a policy not allowing one person winning more than once per quarter, and you were actually able to win it in five straight quarters! Or you might recall that while you didn't win the other times, you were almost always part of the finalists (you know that because that was announced by the management as part of announcement of the winner).

By continuously asking yourself questions against your resume, you will be able to not only remember details that are related to what you write down on the resume, but also what aren't written down, as well as the why. And by asking yourself enough questions, it will give you the necessary coverage and repetition to prepare you for coming up with answers for the actual interview questions.

Map Out the Details of Your Answers

As you recall the details from your resume, you should start "mapping" them out - by that, I really mean drawing them out on a map, like a memory map.

By mapping them out, you can see more clearly of the details - what's available and what's missing. Moreover, since you are likely to recall more information than needed for the current question, by mapping them out, you will have done some legwork for additional questions.

When you are mapping, you want to make sure you categorize the items - this can be done either explicitly (actually using different color, shapes, fonts, or areas) or implicitly (just keep track of the categories in mind):

- **People** - coworkers, boss(es), underlings, customers, etc. They can either be specific (a particular co-worker), or general, like customers.
- **Roles** - the functions you and others perform. This usually (but not always) equates to the job title. In the above example, you the customer service rep actually have three roles - customer service rep, team lead, and backup supervisor.
- **Relationships** - co-workers, boss, etc. Often drawn as annotated lines between two people.
- **Tasks** - work performed on the job, including work that is above and beyond the call of duty.
- **Situations** - particular circumstances of note. For example, a particular tense moment between you and a coworker.
- **Outcomes** - any specific outcome that are tied to the situation and tasks.

If we take the customer service representative example above, we map out our current information as the following diagram.

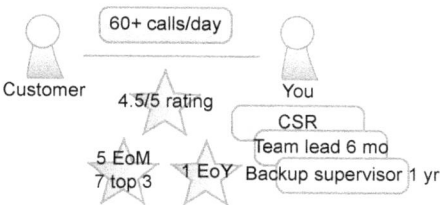

Figure 20.1 - Mapping of the resume detail

As more information is recalled with additional questions, come back and fill out your diagram.

For example, maybe the next question is "What is an example of your having conflict with a coworker, and what do you do about it."

As you go through your resume again, you recalled a situation where you were having issues with Jimmy over the handling of customer escalations, because Jimmy almost never allowed customer escalations and became rude the moment a customer wanted to talk to a supervisor.

Your mapping diagram will now look like the following:

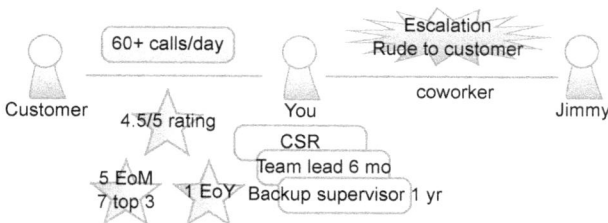

Figure 20.2 - Mapping with addition of Jimmy

The conflict did not last long because of your ability to remain calm. You understood Jimmy's perspective (he felt disrespected by the customers when they asked to talk to the supervisor) and calmed him down by listening to him. You further were able to get him to see that customers just needed their issues fixed, and some of the issues required decisions of the management. Your explanation was able to get through to him on why it made no sense to be mad at customers who asked to speak with the supervisor.

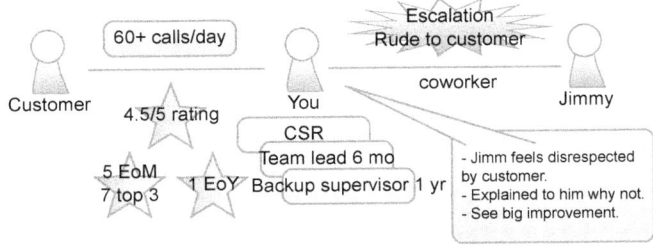

Figure 20.3 - Mapping with addition of resolution

By going through this process, you gain a clearer and clearer picture over your past experiences, and at the same time tailor them toward answering interview questions.

> Note on the name of your coworkers, bosses, and customers.
>
> Yeah, I know you noticed the name of the coworker, Jimmy, on the diagrams. That's done on purpose so we can have this sidebar here.
>
> Make sure these diagrams, however you create them, are for your eyes only if you are to use real names.
>
> That means if you write on paper, shred them afterward, and if you use a computer, encrypt or permanently delete the file. You don't want any personally identifiable information leaked from you.
>
> Another way is to use code names instead of real names. You are very likely to remember the stories correctly even if you don't use real names. This way, you can show the diagrams to others (like your interview coach) for the purpose of helping your practice.

Although this process can seem a bit tedious, mapping things out is actually pretty fast once you get the hang of it. You can leverage diagramming software or draw them on paper. Once you draw them out, you will be amazed at the clarity that it will produce.

Make sure that you do this for every past job that is relevant to the question.

Map Against The Job Requirements

Up to this point, we have been refreshing our past experiences to make them more vivid and organized, but that alone won't produce great answers. We must also make sure that our answers are relevant to the job opportunity at hand.

Answers require more work often due to one of the following:

- Out of the multiple applicable experiences to the questions, some are just more relevant, interesting, or impressive than others.
- Some questions are about a summary of experiences rather than individual experiences.
- Some experiences, although relevant, requires additional elaboration to clarify the relevance.

Therefore, we must take additional steps to make the answer as relevant as possible.

The way to do that is to compare the job requirements against your answers and see whether your answers address the job requirement well.

Let's continue with the customer service representative example. If you are applying to another service rep job, by default the degree of relevance will be high since the nature of the job function is likely to be very similar. But if you are applying for a job as a customer service rep supervisor, while some of your experiences are relevant (being the backup supervisor when the actual supervisor is out), you will now have to work harder to make sure the relevance sticks.

The more gaps there are between the jobs you've had and the current job opportunity, the more work you will need to put into mapping your experience across.

Some of the gaps you will have to overcome are:

- Different level of experience - a junior position vs. a senior position.
- Different level of accountability - a staff vs. a team lead vs. a manager vs. an executive.
- Different industry - finance vs. government vs. entertainment.
- Different function - a project manager vs. a system architect.

You might have to overcome multiple gaps at the same time. This is the main reason why mapping out your resume in a visual format provides tremendous help - you can quickly glance at the map to see the gaps and what you need to do.

Make sure your answers always addresses the gaps even if you aren't asked explicitly.

Different Level of Experience

Mapping a senior level experience to a junior level experience is generally easier since people usually get to the senior position via a junior position. As long as your experience at the junior level isn't too far in the past, most interviewers would not think they are no longer applicable.

Mapping from junior to senior is more difficult. You will need to qualify why your experience is the equivalent of the senior experience when you are a junior. The way to do so is to understand the differences between the two levels - seniors have more responsibility as well functioning with more autonomy.

Mapping out your experience with your supervisor - that will help you tell whether you have been performing with the responsibility and autonomy of a senior position, and what additional effort you need to achieve that.

Different Level of Accountability

Individual contributor roles and management positions have a different level of accountability. This is independent of the concept of dual tracks (one technical and one managerial). Management has to be accountable for others, and senior management has to be accountable for profit and loss.

Going from a management position to an individual contributor position is again, similar to going from senior to junior position, easier than the other way around, since you likely have individual contributor experiences before you got to a management position.

Going from an individual contributor position to a management position will require you to show that you have been involved with if not performed management functions, i.e., when you are a staff member, you have been involved in mentoring team members; when you are a manager, you have been involved in P&L business decisions. Make sure that you map those out.

Different Industry

Going across industries, depending on the particular position you seek, might be a non-issue, a showstopper, or somewhere on the continuum in between the two extremes.

For example, if you are a web designer, the work of designing a website is basically the same in any industry. But if you are a mechanical engineer, you basically won't find mechanical engineering work in the finance industry. If you are a project manager, you will find that while your project management skill is transferrable, your lack of specific industry experience can cause you to have lower performances i.e., construction project management looks very different from software project management, even though project management skills work in both.

Be certain to accept the effect of industry-specific knowledge and do not downplay it. Obviously, make sure to leverage your transferrable skills, but also demonstrate learning about the new industry, such as taking classes, having related hobbies, etc.

Different Function

Similar to going across industries, going across functions requires you to determine the gap of the skills.

For example, your skill as an accountant is very unlikely to land you a human resource position, and vice versa. On the other hand, many people can move into sales, as there isn't much prerequisite for becoming a salesperson (obviously succeeding is a different story).

Determine what applicable skills you currently have - leverage these as your selling point, and determine the gaps of what you still need and come up with a plan to address the gaps.

Conclusion

Going through the process of refreshing your memory of your experiences completes the second half of the "know thy enemy, know thyself" equation. This step is often overlooked because we think we know ourselves well enough to "wing it," but that usually turns into a serious case of underselling, if not an outright disaster.

No one will be pitching you except you in an interview. By taking diligent effort to refresh yourself on your past, you not only put yourself in the position to come up with better answers, you might also come up with completely forgotten gems that would be pertinent to your unique selling proposition. Every effort you put in at this phase will show up in your mock interview preparations as well as the actual interviews.

Let's now move onto how to practice for interviews.

Chapter 21

Practice! Time for Mock Interviews!

With all of your research done, it is now time to put things into practice, and by that I don't mean you stay at home and read out the questions and answers by yourself – I mean mock interviews.

The central premise of this book is that you should do whatever is in your power to maximize your interview skills, and that means if you are choosing between mock interviews where others are practicing with you, versus you staying at home reviewing the answers, you should do mock interviews.

Even real interviews aren't necessarily better than mock interviews for improving your interview skills. The reason is that with real interviews you only have limited feedback. So even if you have already gone through a string of interviews, you do yourself a favor by continuing to do mock interviews.

Types of Mock Interviewers

Chances are you will ask your friends and family to help you practice your mock interviews. But they are not the only option. The following are the types of the mock interviewers.

Friends and Family

The best thing about friends and family is the cost – they are your friends and family and will do things for you for free. They can potentially be more available than other types of mock interviewers as well, although that's not necessarily a guarantee since you didn't pay for their time.

But the disadvantages with friends and family as mock interviewers abound; your friends and family are not necessarily good at interview skills, and they are also unlikely to be good at mock interviews. Furthermore, the existing familiarity doesn't always work well in mock interview situations.

Since this is the most likely option you will end up using, do realize that with friends and families you will have to do more handholding in order for them to be helpful to you, i.e., you need to show them how to mock interview you appropriately in order for the mock interviews to be productive.

Colleagues

Since it can be weird for you to tell your current colleagues that you are interviewing elsewhere, this is generally a less-likely option; more likely are ex-colleagues who have become your friends and trusted partners.

Colleagues are likely to be more competent mock interviewers than your regular friends and family since they are likely to have similar professions and experienced similar interviews.

However, they aren't necessarily more experienced than you are at interviews, and hence will still require some guidance on how to appropriately conduct mock interviews.

Further, their availability is probably quite likely very limited, so you might have to supplement with other types of mock interviewers in order to get as much practice as possible.

Professional Interview Coaches

These are people who make a living on helping others improve their interview skills via mock interviews. They are generally called interview coaches. You can certainly expect that they need no handholding to conduct mock interviews for you (if they do, you should ask for your money back).

> We use the term "mock interviewer" in this book because not every mock interviewer is an interview coach.

You should be able to find general interview coaches as well as job-specific interview coaches, although specialized interview coaches do not necessarily exist for every job out there. General interview coaches focus on general interview skills that are applicable to all jobs, whereas job-specific interview coaches focus on interview skills specific to a particular type of job, which can involve a lot of practice on skill questions.

The obvious downside to professional interview coaches is the cost involved. Depending on your current financial situation, it might or might not be something that you can afford. A good interview coach who can help you pinpoint your weaknesses quickly and guide you toward fixing the problems obviously is worth the money spent.

If you do decide to utilize professional interview coaches, make sure that you get good references so you increase the odds that the coach will work out for you.

Mock Interview Interest Groups

If available around your area, mock interview interest groups can be a great way to get you some mock interview practices. If not, you can certainly use this book as a blueprint to set up a mock interview interest group.

> A mock interview interest group is likely to be a part of a job-hunting interest group. Students can find them on college campuses, possibly ones that target specific professions.

The quality of the mock interview group obviously depends on the people involved. Since many people only look for such groups when they are looking for jobs, a mock interview group's staying power depends on the people's willingness to volunteer. The longer they volunteer, the more likely they have built up good skills, and the shorter people volunteer, the less likely the group is well run.

If you can find a good mock interview group, you can potentially reap good rewards. Just realize that it's more likely the group will focus only on general interview skills rather than skills specific to your job.

Another drawback of a mock interview interest group is that you might not find one that meets your specific needs, be that the quality isn't good enough, lack of job-specific expertise, or that the group do not meet frequently enough for your purpose.

Structure of a Mock Interview

A mock interview generally has the following structure:

- Goal setting (page 178) – decide the goal and the focus of this particular mock interview session, so both the mock interviewer and interviewee know what to do.
- Runs and feedback (page 178):
    - Initial run – the mock interviewer and interviewee run through the decided script. Potentially the initial run can be stopped immediately in order to point out the issue.
    - Feedback – the mock interviewer provides the feedback to the interviewee on the issues and how to improve.

- In-between runs – the runs are repeated as many times as possible within the preparation timeframe to gain competence.
- Final run – the goal is to have a perfect run at the end without the need for further correction. If time allows, a couple of final runs are preferable.

• Repeat the above for every single script you have.

Depending on the length of the session, it is possible for a mock interview to work through multiple scripts.

Let's examine the steps in detail.

Goal Setting

The objective of the goal-setting phase is to ensure that both the mock interviewer and the interviewee know what to do. Depending on the mocker interviewer you choose, you might need to do a lot of handholding and explanation during this phase in order for you to have a productive session.

For example, you might feel like you need brushing up on one or more of the following areas:

- Handshakes
- Initial meet and greet
- Running through scenario questions
- Answering traditional questions

Having these specific areas agreed-upon before starting ensure the mock interviewer and you are on the same page.

You need to prepare your own mock interview scripts for any of the interviewer types except for a professional mock interviewer. But you should still ensure the professional mock interviewers know what you would like to work on during the session.

Runs and Feedback

You should shoot for getting to the point where you can run through a full script without finding any issues. However that's not realistic in the beginning, and getting feedback is after all the whole point of going through mock interviews.

You have a couple of choices on how you receive feedback - you can receive feedback throughout the session, or all at once at the end. Both approaches have their own advantages and disadvantages.

The advantage of giving feedback at the end of the run is that it allows a more continuous flow for the interviewee so the interviewee feels like something got accomplished. Some people perform worse if constantly interrupted.

The disadvantage is that the feedback is separated from the issues. When feedback is decoupled from where the issues occurred, it can make the lesson more difficult to understand and absorb. The separation can also make the mock interviewer forget about the feedback as well.

If you receive feedback immediately, the advantages and disadvantages above are reversed.

Also, inexperienced mock interviewers might have difficulties keeping track of the issues and waiting until the end to provide the feedback. If you do choose to work with inexperienced mock interviewers, you should let them provide immediate feedback. For experienced mock interviewers, waiting until the end should not be an issue.

Numbers of Mock Interview Sessions to Conduct

You should have as many mock interview sessions as your preparation timeframe, mock interview budget, and interviewer availability allow.

Obviously one of the reasons is because the more mock interviews you do, the more practice you get and hence the better you get at interviews. But another reason is that you are unlikely to get through all of your practice needs within one single mock interview session, as mock interview sessions can be quite intensive and mentally draining, you are not likely to run a single session long enough to cover all your needs.

The minimum recommended number of sessions is two – one for initial practice, and one more for verifying that you have absorbed all of the feedback.

Improvement Areas

As we've seen, there are quite a few distinct skills one need in order to perform well interviews. You should therefore ensure to target the particular areas you need for improvement.

Below are additional notes on a few of the areas of improvement.

Appearances

Often people don't spend as much effort on appearances for mock interviews as they do for the real ones. This is natural since most people don't have a lot of issues with keeping their appearances neat. But if you find dressing for interview a challenge, do not hesitate to make this into an improvement area for the mock interviews. In this case it might also make sense to involve fashion consultants.

Meet and Greet

If you are practicing for the meet and greet phase, you are probably practicing for the initial steps like how to properly shake hands (page 51). Follow the tips given in the First Impression Counts chapter (page 45) and practice until both your mock interviewer and you are satisfied with the result.

Small talks (page 55) can be difficult to practice since as soon as you get to know your mock interviewer the challenge with small talks usually disappears. If you want to practice small talks, you might be better served to seek out specialists in this area.

Traditional and Behavioral Questions

Both the traditional (page 97) and behavioral (page 107) questions are straightforward enough that they can be asked by just about anyone, including your friends and family. Professional interview coaches can give better assessments of your answers, but with some training you can get value out of the assessments from your friends and family. If you choose friends and family, do a few dry runs with them to show them what they should look for, including and not limited to the following:

- Eye contact
- Smoothness of the delivery
- Nervousness
- Passion and motivation
- Coverage of all the main points
- Relevance and pitch

Skill Questions

Depending on your specialty, the skill interview questions (page 115) might require a specialized mock interviewer. The reason is that even if you write down both the question and the answer in a script for a regular mock interviewer, it won't simulate enough of the pressure generated in a real interview for it to be effective.

Definitely seek out specialized mock interviewers, or have a colleague in the same profession as you to come up with skill questions for your mock interviews.

Brainteaser Questions

Brainteaser questions might not be applicable to your interview, and once you have heard a particular brainteaser question it ceases to have power over you, so it can be quite difficult to practice.

As stated before, brainteaser questions are best practiced on frequent basis. But for mock interview purposes, if you choose to practice brainteaser questions, you should find a question that you have not seen before, and use the mock interview sessions to assess how well you follow the process described in the Brainteaser Questions chapter (page 129).

Prepare a Mock Interview Script

A good mock interview script is short and to the point, because the goal of a mock interview isn't to replicate a full interview, but rather to break down the interview into segments so you can practice them independently.

A mock interview script should contain a list of questions that the mock interviewer can select from, so the mock interviewer can select the questions randomly in order to simulate pressure.

The following is a high-level mock interview script you can use to adopt. You can download a template from the companion website.

Table 21.1 - Sample Mock Interview Script

Category	Description
First Impression (page 45)	Pay attention to the immediate impression made by the candidate. Part of first impression - such as dress code - can only be tested once during a session, while others (such as handshake) can be repeatedly simulated. • Is the candidate neat in appearance? • Does the candidate dress appropriately? • Does the candidate dress to impress? • Does the candidate have a solid handshake?

Category	Description
	• Does the candidate hold your eye contact during the handshake and have a warm smile?
Meet and Greet (page 55)	Look for whether the candidate succeeds in making a quick connection with you. • Does the candidate use your name? • Does the candidate feel at ease? • Does the candidate carry out a conversation with you? • Does the candidate talk too much? • Does the candidate talk too little?
Interview Opening (page 65)	Ask the candidate to provide you with a hypothetical interview opening so this part can be tested. • Does the candidate ask questions during the opening? • Is the candidate paying attention to your words? • Does the candidate get ready to take notes of what you say?
Interview Body (page 71)	Ask the candidate questions (provided by the candidate) and pay attention to the following: • Does the candidate provide information relevant to the position at hand or just meander everywhere? • Does the candidate tie his answer back to how they can be used to help you? • Does the candidate use the STAR model for answering behavioral questions? • Does the candidate ask clarifying questions? • Does the candidate use a whiteboard/paper without being prompted? • Does the candidate get flushed with tough questions? • Does the candidate think silently?
Interview Closing (page 91)	Tell the candidate you have asked all your questions. Ask the candidate if he has any questions.

Category	Description
	• Does the candidate ask you any questions? • Does the candidate review the action items with you? • Does the candidate ask for your contact information if it hasn't been given?

Delivery is Key

During the reviews, you want the mock interviewers to talk to you about the following:

- Did you answer the question asked - believe it or not, interviewees sometimes answer the wrong question?
- Is your answer correct for the questions that have correct answers?
- Did you answer the question effectively, i.e., is your answer weak or strong? Do you cover the main points? Did you sell yourself?
- How is your nonverbal communication? Do you have the right posture, maintain eye contact, and have appropriate voice pacing, utterance, and tone? Do you appear calm and relaxed, or nervous and fidgety?

Your mock interviewer should be able to identify if you have any issues with regards to the above, point out how you can correct them, and then work with you multiple times to rehearse the issues in order to correct them.

If you work with friends and family for mock interviews, it can take them a while to understand what they need to watch for, so make sure you work closely with your mock interviewer to figure out the issues, and then jointly work to determine the appropriate resolution based on the guidance from this book.

Conclusion

Practice is the only way we get better at something, but practice alone isn't enough, you need to practice the right things.

You have many choices when it comes to finding a mock interviewer, but make sure to understand what it takes to run a proper mock interview, so you can help your mock interviewer to help you.

Chapter 22
The Night Before

How did you go about studying for an exam back in school? If you were like me, chances are you crammed for the exams, studied until the wee hours, relied on coffee or something even stronger to keep you awake, and powered through the exams on adrenaline.

This approach works for exams where your objective is to write down answers, but needless to say it won't work for interviews!

The main difference between exams and interviews is that in interviews, your "score" mainly comes from your interaction and communication with another person. When you struggle to stay awake without the stimulation of caffeine or feel jitters from overdosing, you won't project yourself optimally.

To beat out the competition, you must be in your most optimal state of performance. If the above doesn't describe your approach to taking exams, great, you are doing something right, and hopefully the tips in this chapter will propel your performance even higher. But if it describes you, definitely implement what is described in this chapter to help you get back on the right track.

> While we call this chapter the night before, you should really do this **every night before**, as it takes time for you to get proficient at the techniques with just about everything, and things listed in this chapter is no exception.

Sleep Time

Make sure you get ample of sleep. As stated before, if you are not at your most optimal state, your final result will be less than your best. After you have put in all of the hard work to get to this point, you will want to make sure that you do not shortchange yourself.

The amount of sleep time everyone needs varies – some need as many as 9 or 10 hours to properly function while others can get away with as few as 4 to 5 hours of sleep. If you usually need caffeine to feel alert in the morning, you are probably functioning on too little sleep, and should increase the amount of time you need.

The actual quality of the sleep itself matters as well. If you are constantly tossing and turning at night, chances are you will still wake up feeling under-rested. If you find your sleep interrupted at night multiple times, you might need to address your sleep environment – is your bed comfortable, is the room temperature conducive to sleep, and are you sleeping in an environment with appropriate level of darkness?

If you are stressed about the interview, you are likely to get poor sleep as well – we will talk about how to relax yourself in a bit.

Shutdown Time

Since it can take a while to transition from preparation mode into sleep mode, you will need to allocate time for you to unwind prior to your sleep time.

Interviews usually start early; that means you also need to go to bed early. If your interview starts at 8 a.m. in the morning, and it takes you 30 minutes of commute time to get there, it means that you should plan to leave your place at 7 a.m. in the morning, to account for 15 minutes of potential extra traffic, as well as arriving at least 15 minutes early.

And if it takes you one hour to get ready, and if you need seven hours of sleep, it means you need to wake up by 6 a.m., and go to bed by at the latest 11 p.m. at night. If it generally takes you 30 minutes to actually fall asleep, you need to hit the sack by 10:30 p.m. at night.

Backtracking this way tells you exactly when you need to fully shut down so you can fall asleep. In order for you to perform the rest of the exercises, you should give yourself at least another 30 minutes to relax as well. So prepare to stop all your preparation activity by 10 p.m. if the above describes your situation.

Deal With Your Nerves and Fear

Although it seems like relaxation is easy, the chances are that when you have an interview tomorrow, you can feel a case of nerves. Nerves are caused by one reason - you are focusing on yourself, instead of focusing on others.

It's perfectly normal, of course, to focus on ourselves. However, during the performance time, focusing on oneself achieves the opposite effect of what we actually want. It causes us to freeze in action and perform worse; this potentially creates a self-fulfilling prophecy.

Such focus is due to fear of failure. When we were young, stage fright is an unknown experience. Look at how little kids are able to perform in front of an audience without much concern, and even though they might not be great performers, their joy and lack of stage fright is something that all adult performers work hard to reclaim.

Can we do what little kids do? Yes we can - by stopping being concerned about our performances.

Allow Yourself The Room To Suck

> *Perfect is the enemy of good.*
> *-- Voltaire.*

In interview situations, it's actually worse than that. In wanting to put the best foot forward, we often end up shooting ourselves in the foot when we are so focused on being perfect.

Little kids do not know what being perfect is - kids **are** perfect, period. Anything they do is fine, and their enthusiasm and optimism carries the day.

Adults have more standards to live by, of course. But by not being concerned about how well you perform, you automatically become more relaxed, and actually end up performing better.

How You Can Help Others

It's actually a bit trickier than "stop worrying about how well you perform" though. Because whenever we tell ourselves not to think of something, that something is exactly what we think about.

What we need instead is to have "something else" replacing the "original something." The best "something else" in an interview situation is to think about how you can help others (page 34), by focusing on answering the following questions:

- How can you help the company?
- What problems are they trying to solve?
- How will you help solve their problems?
- What skills do you bring to the table?
- What intangibles will benefit your new employer?
- Are you the right person to help them?

The more you think in this fashion, the less you are concerned about your own performance, and the more value your interviewer will actually find you bring to the table.

The goal in the interview is to **immediately add value.** Why else would they be hiring you?

Always focus on the other party. You will reduce your own fear, and actually make others like you more.

Be Willing to Walk Away

The by-product of focusing on helping others is this - **if you are not the right person, you are willing to walk away** (page 34).

Think of it this way - if you are the wrong person, you might actually end up causing more problems.

You don't want to be the person who causes others more problems if you really are trying to help.

Hence - willingness to walk away signifies true desire to help others.

> And if you are willing to walk away - what is the reason to fear?

Practice, Practice, Practice

The more confident you are about your ability, the more confident you will be about your performance. Practice (page 175) increases your confidence.

If you have been following the plan laid out in this book, you will improve your interview skills and gain confidence, and hence reduce your fear of failure.

Happy Thoughts and Guided Imagery

When we don't know what will happen, it's easy for our minds to run wild and think of all sorts of crazy things, many of which are not conducive to our confidence and state of mind.

A simple method to counter your mind running rampant is to fill your minds with positive thoughts instead, so you are thinking about the happy thoughts rather than the negatives.

Instead of thinking:

- I'm going to suck at the interviews tomorrow.
- Interviewers are going to be hard on me.
- What do I do if I freeze up?

Think of:

- I'm going to perform splendidly.
- Interviewers are going to love me. If they want to challenge me, it's up to me to overcome the challenge, and I am up to the task.
- I used to freeze up before, but now I know what to do when I freeze up, and I can get myself out of the jam if it happens again.

When you think about positive thoughts, be as specific as possible, so you can form a visual imagery in your head and "picture" what happens as if it actually happens.

Imagine that you are in the room with the interviewer, with both of you sharing thoughts about how you can help the company. Imagine how his eyes lit up, his head nodding, and his smile widening as he listens to your answers. Imagine that he shakes your hand enthusiastically, and can't wait to hear back from you again.

Imagine the above, and notice how good it feels when you imagine it.

Positive imagery, when done correctly, can help you overcome fear.

You can even do contrast imageries. This works especially well when you have a specific issue that you know likely to occur again. What you do is as follows:

- Recall a past incidence where you have the particular issue.
- Fix your memory by overlaying what you would do instead of, on top of the memory.
- Vividly imagine the newly superimposed memory.

For example, let's say that you had problems in the past with freezing up in interviews.

Recall a past incidence where you froze up in an interview. Replay it in your head, and see yourself being asked a question, and then unable to answer it.

Pause right at the moment when you froze up, instead of recalling further.

At this moment, imagine yourself doing the things needed to unfreeze:

- Paraphrasing the question and asking confirmation for your understanding of the question.
- Asking additional clarification questions as necessary for you to fully gain the understanding to the question.
- Laying out a plan of actions of how you would go about tackling the problem.
- Walking through the steps of your plan to tackle the problem.

- Repeating as necessary with another approach.

As you imagine yourself going through the steps above, notice that with each step you take, you have moved yourself forward in answering the question instead of being frozen, and notice how good you feel by no longer being frozen.

Positive Visual Imagery can be applied to many human performance situations, and it is a technique widely used by athletes and performers. Spending your time learning the technique is well worth the benefit.

Occupy Your Mind with Other Things

Another approach to reducing your fear is to occupy your minds with other things, so it keeps your mind away from twisting itself into a knot. The easiest way to do so is to do something completely different, for example:

- Physical exercises.
- Play recreation sports with others.
- Hang out with friends.
- Watch a movie or listening to music.
- Any hobby that you can engage in easily.

When we spend too much time in one activity, we not only get our mind racing, it also has a diminishing effect, and oftentimes the best approach to relax is to do other things instead.

With you executing against a plan for preparation, you can safely spend time on other activities as long as your schedule permits.

Breathing Techniques

If you are already well practiced in activities like meditation or yoga, they will aid you tremendously in relaxation.

But if you have never done those before, an easy-to-learn skill to quickly relax is the breathing technique.

Not only are breathing techniques useful for interview situations, it has been taught and shown to be effective in even more stressful situations such as military combat. Retired Lieutenant Colonel of the Army Rangers, David Grossman, calls it "combat breathing" in his book "On Combat."

The key to using breathing to relax is as follows:

- Breathe slowly – no need to slow it down tremendously, but you must breathe slower than you usually breathe for it to be relaxing.
- Breathe deeply – breathe with your abdomen rather than your chest. You should see your stomach rise and fall, instead of your chest.
- Focus on your breathing – think only of your breathing when focusing. You can listen to the breathing, watching your nose or abdomen, or any other parts where you can focus.
- Repeat as many times as you note your anxiety fleeting.

The combat breathing technique mentioned earlier is as follows:

- Breathing in - count one, two, three, and four.
- Stop and hold breath - count one, two, three, and four.
- Exhale - count one, two, three, and four.
- Rinse and repeat.

Not only is the above breathing technique easy to learn, the best thing about this breathing technique is that you can use it anytime, anywhere. You don't have to do it as part of meditation or yoga, and you can do it while you are in front of another person, i.e., you can use it during interviews! Learn it to your great benefit.

Check List

Ensure you have the following items prepared for your interview the night before:

- Clothing.
- Paper resumes – as many copies as the numbers of the expected interviewers plus two.
- Business card – this is optional since your contact information is in your resume. If you do decide to have a business card, attach them to the resumes.
- Notebook and pen - if you want to use laptop or tablet to take notes, make sure you clear it with the interviewer.
- Laptops and other presentation aid, if you are giving a presentation.
- For people with perspiration issues:
    - Antiperspirant and liquid chalk.
    - Two of the most absorbent handkerchiefs you have.

You want to make sure that everything is ready to go by the night before the interview, so you would not be stressed about them in the morning. Luck always favors the prepared.

Conclusion

Making sure that you are in the optimal state takes more than you just "willing it to happen." It takes deliberate effort and planning to make sure that you can be in the optimal state when the day comes.

Take advantage of the relaxation techniques described in this chapter, make sure you have ample rest, as well as building up a routine to support that ample rest at the time you need it, will be the key toward putting you into the optimal state.

Imagine yourself walking into the interviewer's office fully rested, relaxed, and energetic! Keep that visual imagery in mind, and start putting the techniques described in this chapter to work for you.

Part V
Alternative Interview Types and After Interview

We have finished the deep-dive on the process and techniques for one-on-one in-person interviews. But we are not quite done yet!

We haven't talked about what happens in the After Interview stage, and we also have not talked about two other common interview scenarios - remote and panel interviews.

In this last part of the book, we will cover the following:

- How to handle remote interviews (page 195).
- How to handle panel interviews (page 203).
- How to follow-up after interviews (page 209).
- How to get the offer you want (page 225).
- How to keep improving yourself (page 255).

Without further ado, let's continue onto the last part of our interview mastery journey.

Chapter 23

Remote Interviews

As previously mentioned, a remote interview contrasts with an in-person interview (page 15) in the communication channel - you are at a different location from the interviewer, and this provides you with some advantages as well as some disadvantages.

The advantages for remote interviews, from the interviewers' perspective, are reach and cost. Remote interviews allow interviewers to cast a wide net to interview candidates from around the globe without incurring large expenses. Another advantage is that it can make the interview scheduling easier (this is not applicable in all scenarios).

On the other hand, the major disadvantage is the lack of in-person non-verbal communication, which makes a remote interview a poor tool to really get to know the candidate. This issue is improved if videoconferencing is used instead of phones, but videoconferencing still isn't prevalent enough to replace phones, nor is it good enough to fully eliminate this disadvantage.

From your perspective, the advantages are flexibility of location and scheduling - as long as it's not videoconferencing, you can even interview in your bathrobes! You can also have all the materials with you that you wouldn't have in an in-person setting, so you can be much more prepared.

The disadvantage is the same as the interviewer. You want to be able to get to know the interviewer to make your best possible impression, and a remote interview limits what you can achieve.

Due to its nature, remote interviews are often employed as an initial screen before an in-person interview. From your perspective, it means that you should prepare for a subsequent interview if you are scheduled for a remote interview.

There are two main types of remote interviews - phones and videoconferencing. As phones are still the prevalent channel, we will talk about phones first, and then talk about how videoconferencing differs.

Phone Interviews

The nicest thing about phone interviews is that you don't have to pick out a wardrobe (page 47) for your interviews. You can interview in your bathrobe or even your birthday suit, and the interviewer would not know the difference.

You can also have all your interview aids with you so that you can quickly look up the answer to a question if you are stumped. This can be hard to in practice though, as its success depends on the setup of your environment, the pace of the interview, and whether or not you are capable of finding the answer quickly enough for the pace.

It's important to remember the disadvantage of phones as a communication channel. Not only do you lose the ability to communicate via body language, you also cannot pick up the body language of the interviewer. What it means is that you will need to compensate for the loss.

Landline vs. Cell Phone

If possible - try to interview through a landline.

I know, you might not even have a landline any more, and cell phones today basically sound as good as a landline. This advice will eventually be irrelevant when all the landlines disappear.

But for today, if you want the best control over the quality of your voice, a landline is still the way to go.

Interviewers generally understand that if you are on a cell phone there will be a chance for poor signals, and they will give you the appropriate slack. You just don't want to leave things up to chances if you can help it.

Location, Location, Location

Make sure that you are in a quiet location for the interview. Your home is still likely the best choice. And if you have a landline at home, see above.

Cell phones enable you to be anywhere these days to take calls. It's extremely convenient, but environment can make the conversation unpleasant, which is not what you want the interviewer feeling.

Some interviewers will catch you by surprise because they want to interview you immediately with the first call - see the initiation process (page 38) on how to deal with them.

In all other situations, make sure when the call comes you are already in a quiet location for the duration of the call. Unless the interviewer calls you ten minutes earlier than expected, it's a faux pas to tell them to wait for you to get to a quiet location.

Make sure you aren't doing anything else either, and no one or things will bother you. If you are at home, make sure that your family leaves you alone during the call. Close and lock your room door if possible, so you can cut out outside noise and no one - including your kids and pets if you have them - can accidentally wander in and distract you.

Focus, Focus, Focus

Old habit can die hard it seems, even for interviews.

Most of us multitask when there is a phone call. We can often carry a conversation and at the same time do something else, like watching TV, washing dishes, taking out trash, playing with pets or kids, etc.

They are all no-nos when it comes to interviews.

When you are handling an interview at home, you will need to have the discipline to keep yourself focused because that is what you need in order to do better than other candidates.

It's extremely hard to multitask without the other party noticing. When the interviewer realizes that you are multitasking, he will question your dedication to the job.

If you really have something to do at this particular moment, like dealing with an emergency situation, apologize profusely and **reschedule**. No exceptions.

Speaking on the Phone

Have you heard your own voice on the phone?

Phones can distort your voice as they transmit a narrower range of frequency than your natural voice. A poor signal for your cell phone won't help either. And if you have a different accent from the interviewer, it can make the phone conversation even harder.

Adding on top of that, if you are a fast talker, you will have a difficult time communicate through the phone.

You might or might not have these problems, and if you have them, you might not be aware of them either.

You cannot rely on whether others tell you about the problem as the indicator though. Most people don't make it their life's mission going around correcting other people's problems - they are more likely to put up with you than tell to your face without you asking.

It is of course quite possible that you don't have a problem, but wouldn't be nice to be certain?

- Record your voice and play it back to yourself. At the very least, you get to hear what you sound like to the other party. You might also be able to tell whether you talk too fast.
- Find people you interact with on a daily basis and ask them if they have difficulty understanding you through the phone. Ask sincerely, and if you do have a problem they would respond to the sincerity.

Regardless of whether you have a problem, the following are good approaches when it comes to phone interviews:

- Speak louder without raising your voice. You want to make sure your voice carries and resonates. Raising your voice will come across as a lack of confidence, and even worse anger. So train yourself to project your voice without raising the pitch.
- Speak slower. Just about all the speaking problems can be overcome with a slower pace, as it gives the listener a chance to process what you are saying. Unless you have gotten feedback from others asking you to speak faster, you can always speak slower.

Find someone who is willing to work with you on your voice. It can be friends and family, or it can be a professional voice coach. You don't need to have the best voice in the world, but you want to make sure your communication is as good as it can be.

Preparing for Aid

As previously mentioned, one of the advantages of the remote interview format is that you can use interview aids, so you should take advantage of this. As long as you have control over your environment, you will have a much easier time to do so.

You probably won't be able to make use of the Internet to look up and find answers to the questions, unless it's an extremely simple question, so you should not count on being able to utilize the Internet.

What you can do though is to have all information about you ready to go, such as your resume. If you have gone through the preparations recommended in the book, you should also have quite a bit of additional aid created. They can come in quite handy for a phone interview.

Have all your aids laid out so they are readily accessible with a glance. Flipping through them will make you slower to respond, as well as making sounds that can be misconstrued.

Make sure that you have a pen and paper around - it can be just as hard for you to understand your interviewer, so you want to make sure that you take notes. They also come in handy as a substitute for a whiteboard if you are asked a scenario (page 120) and brainteaser (page 129) questions.

Make sure you use a headset, so you can have both of your hands free.

Video Interviews

Although the technology of videoconferencing has been around for a while, it's still far from replacing phones as the primary channel for remote interviews.

The reason is that both parties need to have them, and today's video-conference capabilities are still tied up in computers, so you will be more restricted in terms of locations comparing to phone interviews, although this is not necessarily a bad thing, since even with phone interviews, home is still likely the best location.

> Yes, you can use smartphone or tablet today for videoconferences. You are better off not to when it comes to interviews. You want to make sure that 1) both of your hands are free, and 2) the setup is solid enough that you don't accidentally tip them over.

Videoconferences are subjected to similar issues as cell phones since both rely on connections without a guaranteed quality of service. Your voice might sound even worse than on cell phones.

The primary advantage of a videoconference is the ability to see the other party so you can catch some of the body languages missing from phones. Combining with the advantage of being remote, videoconferencing will be more heavily utilized going forward, but it won't be replacing in-person interviews any time soon.

You also lose the advantage that you have with phones - you will now be seen and must prepare everything as you would in a regular in-person interview. In other words, videoconferencing retains the disadvantages of both in-person and remote interviews.

Let's take a look at what we need to pay attention to when it comes to video interviews.

Impressions

You need to treat a video interview the same as you would an in-person interview - i.e., you need to take care of your appearance and wear the appropriate attire. You will also need to make sure you have the right posture - you would most likely be sitting, so follow the rules described in the Impression chapter (page 45).

Make sure you use software that will let you see yourself the way the other party will see you, so you can verify how you appear through the camera. Adjust yourself so the camera captures you front and center, a bit like a mug shot, but with a bit more torso in view, i.e., including down to your upper chest region. If the camera is capturing your whole upper body, you are sitting too far back.

Eye Contact

Eye contact is where you need to pay special attention when it comes to video interviews. Since the focus of the video is likely to be on your face, it makes your facial expressions, especially your eyes easy to see.

This is where videoconferencing doesn't work well. When you are looking at the interviewer on screen, it appears to the interviewer that you are not looking at him, due to the location difference of the screen and the camera. This is more pronounced when the camera is located to either the left or the right of the screen. If the camera is right on top of the screen, it works a bit better since the height of the screen is less than the width of the screen, but it still looks a bit off.

The way to overcome that is to look primarily at the camera instead of the interviewer. You should definitely look at the camera when you are talking. It can be harder to pick up non-verbal cues this way, but it will work better for you if the interviewer thinks you are maintaining eye contact.

It might be hard not to steal glances at the screen this way. Do it as little as you need and rely on peripheral vision as much as you can.

Location, Location, Location

The same rule for phone interviews basically applies to video interviews. Given that the interviewer can actually see your location, you actually have to put more effort into making sure that what they see is what you want them to see, i.e., having things organized cleanly and neatly will be important to make an impression and show that you are organized.

The same goes for having others wandering into your camera's view. With the ability for your interviewer to see your place, you need to make sure you are in a secured area for videoconferencing so that doesn't happen.

Preparing for Aid

Although an interviewer can now see you through video, as long as you layout the aid well, you can still take advantage of them.

What you need to ensure is that they are viewable without you lowering your head though - that makes it too obvious.

Instead, get a stand so they can stand straight up so all you need to do is to drift your eyes over to steal a glance.

From the interviewer's perspective, it will appear as if you are thinking. Placing them on the left can take advantage of the fact that people think of you as recalling information when your eyes drift toward left.

Tell them ahead of time that you will be taking notes, so when you lower your head toward your note they know what you are doing.

Conclusion

Although interviewing remotely has its own sets of challenges, the majority of what you have learned for in-person interviews are just as applicable, so all you need to do is to adopt the additional changes tailored for remote interviews, and you will be just fine.

Chapter 24

Panel Interviews

As previously mentioned, when there are multiple interviewers involved in a single session, it's called a Panel Interview. In this chapter, we will take a look what it takes to be successful in panel interviews.

Interviewing with one interviewer is a stressful enough endeavor, having to interview with multiple interviewers at once can be downright scary. Luckily all of the techniques we discussed to this point apply just as well to panel interviews. We just need to look at the differences to see how we need to adapt accordingly.

Keep in mind that a panel interview can be either in-person or remote, so if it's remote, you will need to account for the issues described in the Remote Interview chapter (page 195).

Meet and Greet

When you meet and greet a panel of interviewers, start with the one closest to you.

That might seem obvious, but what you want to avoid is to spend too much time scanning the room to determine whom you want to greet first. It's a common urge for people to want to look through the surroundings first before greeting. That can create an interesting pause when it comes to greeting a group of people. Try minimizing that pause.

It is likely that one of the interviewers will come to lead you to the larger group, and in such case it's often that interviewer's job to introduce you to others. Sometimes that introduction will not happen; maybe they want to test you, or maybe the person isn't good at introductions. Do not wait too long, go ahead and immediately introduce yourself to the person closest to you.

Try not to rush through the introduction phase either. This is the time when you get to put a name to the face, and you are disadvantaged in having to remember many names. Unless it's a very formal place, you probably won't receive business cards at the beginning to help you remember everyone. Make sure to repeat the name of the person back during the introduction.

Seating Arrangements

Depending on the room configuration, you might or might not end up with a good seating arrangement.

What is a good seating arrangement? It is one where you can see all of the interviewers at once without having to turn your head like a Japanese pellet drum in action.

The worst type of seating arrangement is where you are sitting in the middle of a long conference table, with one interviewer sitting at each end from you. Although it's probably done unintentionally, it can feel like an interrogation if such a seating arrangement is used.

Luckily, as long as they aren't trying to test you on your reaction to a seating arrangement, you should be able to adjust your way to a favorable position.

What you try to look for is to have minimal head traveling distance for you to look at everyone, as well as finding the shortest distance from all the interviewers given the constraint of your viewing angle.

The following are some ways to arrange your seat from the panel interviewers:

If the room is narrow, you pretty much only have the option to sit close to the interviewers, and this means you will have a large head turning radius.

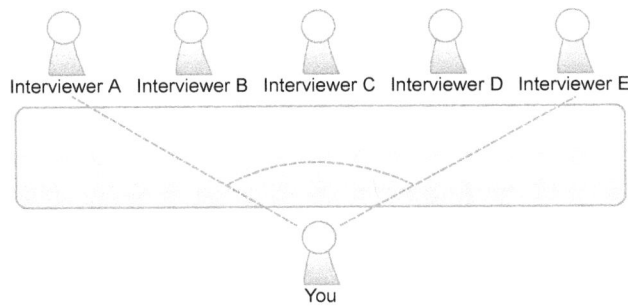

Figure 24.1 - Sitting very close to interviewers

If the room is very large, you can accommodate sitting far from the interviewers. This is usually a very formal type of interview, with the position of the seat already decided for you. This gives you a small head turning radius, but the interview will not be very personable.

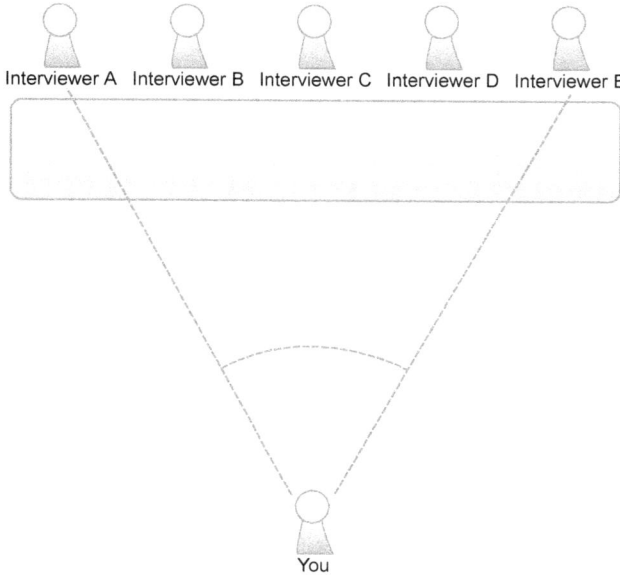

Figure 24.2 - Sitting very far to interviewers

In between is usually a good compromise. This still requires a room with an appropriate size, and can still feel a bit weird to sit far from the table.

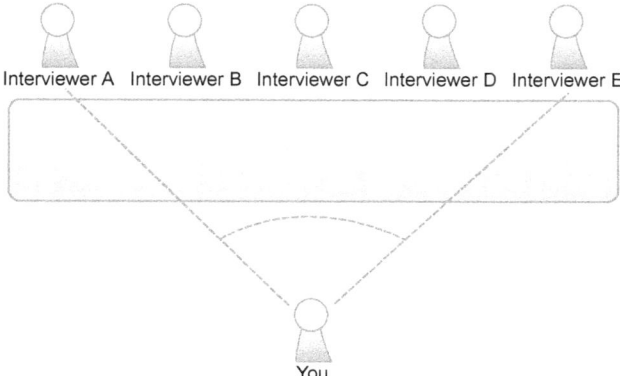

Figure 24.3 - Sitting in between the other two

What actually works best from the head angle perspective in such situation is to sit at one end of the table.

That's a power seat, of course, and it creates an imbalance of the interviewers' seating arrangement from you, which might or might not work in your favor. Choose this one if you are very, very sure of yourself.

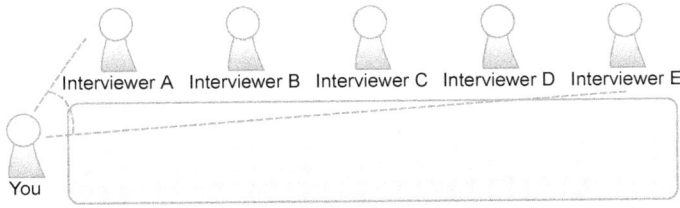

Figure 24.4 - Sitting at one end

Ideally, at a long table, the seat would have been decided for you, and interviewers will arrange themselves to make everyone more comfortable.

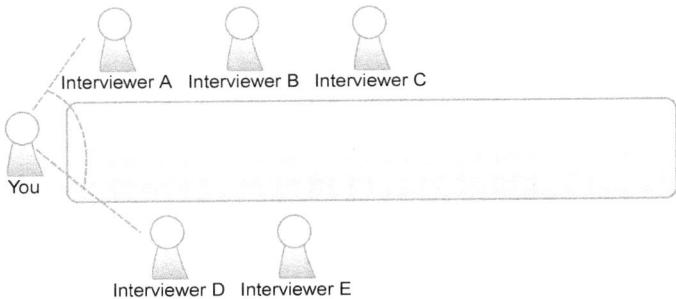

Figure 24.5 - Sitting at one end, balanced

But you can never count on it. When people point out a seat for you, you should take it, and adapt as well as you can.

Interview Opening

When it comes to a panel interview, you definitely want to make sure that there is an interview opening (page 65), even more so than a regular one-on-one interview.

The reason is because you need to remember everyone and what they do, and chances are you didn't really catch everyone's names during the initial meet and greet.

Since there are more people involved in panel interviews, they tend to have more structures and you are very likely to get an opening without you having to prompt for it. But just like in regular one-on-one interviews, pay attention to whether there is an opening, and ask for one if the interviewers automatically start asking questions.

Say something like this to help steer the interview toward an opening.

You   I'm sorry, but can we go through the room for a quick introduction again? I want to make sure I capture everyone's names and roles.

Given that everyone will have sat down by this time, you now can actually match the name to the person much more easily (you can draw out the seating on your notebook). Furthermore, make sure you ask for the roles of the interviewers, because you want to know whom the decision maker is.

Assess the Roles

If you ask for the roles during the opening, this part of your job becomes much easier.

For example, you want to quickly tell who the boss is, who the recruiter is, and who your peers are. Their titles alone should give you enough information.

But you probably won't know who the main decision maker is until the interview starts. Even though the boss might have the final decision, he likely relies on others to make that decision for him. That means that you still need to figure out who has the heaviest input to the decision.

This should be quickly determined once the interview starts. Often the person providing the heaviest input also takes a lead role during the discussion. He might not necessarily ask the most questions, but you will be able to see others besides the boss deferring to him. Make sure that you pay specific attention toward him and the boss.

Answering Questions

This is the part where it will be most similar to one-on-one interviews.

You still only answer one question at a time, no matter the number of people on the panel.

The main difference is that others will be observing your behavior while you are discussing with one of them. So you will need to make one additional change:

> **Look at everyone in turn.**

This is the reason why you want to find as favorable of a seating arrangement as possible. If you have to turn your head 180° in order to see everyone, it can be quite a jarring experience that reduces your effectiveness.

What you want to do is to talk primarily to the person asking the question, but as you speak, look at others as well. You want to make sure to pause longer for the boss as well as the lead besides the questioner.

If the answer is not long enough for you to sweep through everyone, make sure you cover those you missed in the next answer.

Make sure your voice projects through the room since you are likely to be in a larger room than you would be in a one-on-one interview. You want to make sure the farthest person from you can hear your voice, and you want to maintain that level of volume throughout the interview session.

If you have taken public speech classes before, the lessons come in handy for panel-style interviews. If you haven't done so before, it's never too late to get started now.

Leverage Ace as Appropriate

As we have stated in the Presentation chapter (page 139), the panel format lends itself well to presentations, and it might actually even have been decided for you to prepare for such a presentation. If not, consider whether it will be effective for your particular situation, and adapt it as appropriate.

Conclusion

Panel interviews can be scary, but they don't have to be, once we understand how they differ from regular interviews so we can adapt accordingly. Everything we learned for one-on-one interviews is still applicable; we just need to make sure we take care of talking to everyone as if they are having separate one-on-one interviews with you at the same time.

When you achieve that, you will have one heck of a panel interview performance.

Chapter 25
After Interview - Follow-Up

Although most candidates know that they should follow up with the interviewers after interviews, for many, once the interviews are done, it's an "out of sight, out of mind" deal.

That means if you really follow up during the After Interview phase, you can really separate yourself from the pack. Take advantage of it, and know that others' loss is once again, your gain.

The After Interview Phase

The duration of the After Interview Phase depends on whether you are an early interviewee or a late interviewee. Early means the company still has quite a few other candidates to interview after you, and later means a decision for the position is imminent. So you can expect the after interview duration to be longer if you are an early interviewee, and shorter otherwise.

This information isn't automatically shared though, so you should definitely ask. Interviewers can get so busy and not remember everything they have to do, and often interviewees feel being left in the dark. The easiest solution to this problem is to take upon yourself to ask the question "When can I expect to hear back from you" as discussed at the Interview Closing chapter (page 91). This will help you with getting the information you need for your planning.

Once a while, the after interview phase is so short that you hear the decision practically immediately after your interview, meaning that you hear the decision before you have a chance to do any follow-ups. Obviously whether that's a good thing depends on the actual decision itself, but if there are action items from the interview, you should still continue to follow through on them - see the action item section (page 215) for more details.

Should You Do Follow-Ups?

What are the chances follow-ups will improve your prospects? Let's be straightforward on what follow-ups do for you:

- If you are not a good candidate for the job, follow-ups won't change that fact and land you the job.
- If you are clearly the best candidate for the job, the job will be yours even if you do not follow up.
- However, if you are in a tightly contested race with a couple other candidates, doing (great) follow-ups can just be the tiebreaker that puts you over the hump.

Unless you know for sure that you are either the best possible candidate or not a good enough candidate, doing follow-ups does have the potential to tip the scale in your favor. Keep in mind that while follow-ups are strictly optional, this is actually a very well known interview advice that most people know and plenty follow to a degree, so not doing follow-ups might actually put you in a disadvantage.

But let's just say that you know for sure that you do not need to rely on follow-ups to aid your prospects, should you do follow-ups in such case?

While that's certainly up to your decision, here are some good reasons why you should still do follow-ups in such cases:

- Following through with words is the hallmark of professionalism. Follow-ups signal your commitment to being a professional, and such commitment will pay off in the long run, even if it does not pay off currently.
- People remember what you say, and whether you follow through. Even if you end up with the job, not following through on words can affect you in subtle ways.
- Relationships are longer than a single employment opportunity. A great follow-up makes good impressions, and companies are more likely to call back those they like more.

Obviously, the key to follow-ups, as in all previous parts of the interviews, is that you need to make sure that you are looking at it from the employer's perspective rather than just solely from your own perspective, and remember that you have an intense desire to help and are here to help them. Holding such thoughts allows you to put in a greater effort toward your follow-ups to actually make them stand out.

You can distinguish yourself with the effort you put into follow-ups, which we will cover next.

Follow-Up Planning

Many people equate follow-ups with just thank you notes, but there are actually multiple types of follow-ups:

- Thank you notes (page 211) – this is something that you send to the individual interviewers. You should send one to every single interviewer on the loop.
- Action item follow-ups (page 215) – this is also something that you send to the individual interviewers. Not all interviews create action items so you only need to send these to some of the interviewers.
- Official follow-ups (page 218) – these are follow-ups asking for the status of the hiring decision. This only goes to the official channel, usually the HR personnel.
- References (page 219) - a company might reach out to ask for references, so make sure you are prepared.
- Decision (page 221) - this is where you have made a decision on the position or a response to a decision made by the company. For example, you might have decided to take another job, or you might have decided to thank the company for the opportunity when you are notified that they hired another candidate.

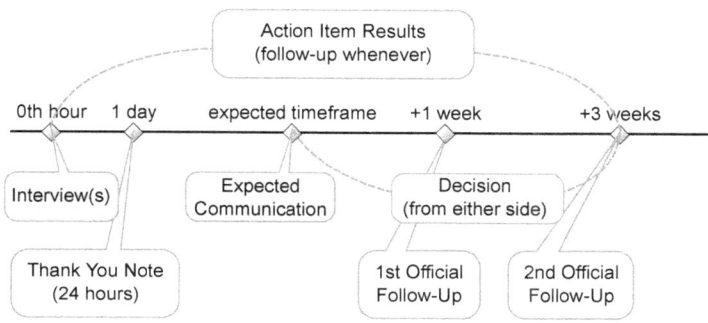

Figure 25.1 - Follow-Up Timeline

The whole process might sound complicated, but it really isn't - keeping this level of correspondence planning in one's head is expected of professionals.

Thank You Notes

When it comes to thank you notes, some of the usual questions are:

- When should it be sent?
- Should it be handwritten?
- Should we deliver it personally?

The way to think about it is that due to the advent of technology, people no longer look down on emails as thank you notes, so you now have options to use either email or physical notes.

> Keep in mind that for some industries there are still specific guidelines - in those cases follow the industry's norm.

Physical notes obviously still give a better personal touch - you can impress HR and interviewers with your excellent handwriting and great paper selections with any additional adornments that you have, you can even show strong initiatives by delivering them yourself. But physical notes, including physical delivery, isn't without drawbacks:

- It can actually be more inconvenient to the recipient. A big reason why email is now accepted is because that's the communication mode of everyone these days. Using a different communication channel makes it harder for the recipient to correspond with you.
- It is much slower in comparison to email. Since most people are used to almost-instant communications now, their expectation on the response turn-around has also increased. Choosing a slower communication mode might be misconstrued if they are waiting for your response.

So you should weigh the advantage of physical note vs. electronic note, and choose them appropriately depending on the situations.

> Keep in mind that options like texting or instant messaging are considered very informal and should not be used for thank you notes.

What to Include in a Thank You Note

One thing to keep in mind about a thank you note is that you should have one per interviewer on your loop.

This is why you should get all of the contact information from your interviewers. Your job here is to send a note to each one of them, addressing what has been discussed.

Sometimes it cannot be helped that you do not have all of the contact information. In such a case, make sure you ask for them with your thank you note to HR.

The formality of the note depends on the culture of the company you are applying to. The more formal the place is, the more likely that you have to maintain that formality. That being said, you should also strive to add a degree of collegiality into your note, since you have now actually met them in person, and going back to maintain full formalness can be seen as taking a step backward in relation building.

So, take the following into account to establish the appropriate tone:

- The formalness of the company.
- Whether you met the person (for example, HR might not necessarily be in your interview loop so you should maintain formalness).
- How much rapport was established during the interview, i.e. did you have a very casual or a formal conversation.
- Writing in general is more formal than conversation - make sure to account for that.

A Sample Thank You Note to HR

The key points to include in the thank you note to HR should include the following:

- Setting the context - whether you have met HR in person.
- Talk about the outcome - how did your interviews go with others.
- Reiterate your interests.
- Confirm next steps - figure out where you are in the process and when can you expect a decision.
- Additional requests - asking for contact information, etc.

Dear <name>,

Thank you so much for setting up the interview yesterday, and it was great to finally meet face to face with you. I thoroughly enjoyed our conversation, learning about you and the company in depth. I must say I am very impressed by what I have seen and learned. I just want to send you a quick note stating my appreciation for your time and effort for my consideration.

I also have great conversations with all the interviewers. Everyone was very kind and shared great information with me. I am very appreciative of their time as well. I feel like I am that much smarter about the company, and I can't wait to contribute as much as I can.

My understanding is that the hiring timeframe for the position is expected to be two weeks. Please let me know if my understanding is correct, and if there are any additional information you need from me, please do not hesitate to let me know.

I look forward to hearing from you soon.

P.S. I did not have <so and so>'s contact information - I'd love to drop him a thank you note as well. Please let me know what his contact information is, or if I should send it through you.

Sincerely,

<Your name>

A Sample Thank You Note

The key points to cover in a thank you note with the interviewer should include the following:

- Setting the context for the meeting.
- Talk about the outcomes - what is your take away from the interview.
- Discuss your action items.
- Next steps.

Dear <name>,

Thank you so much for interviewing me yesterday. I thoroughly enjoyed our conversation, learning more about you and your company in the process. I must say I am very impressed by what I saw and learned. Everyone I met with was friendly and top-notch. Working with great people excites and energizes me. I just want to take a bit of time to tell you my appreciation for your consideration.

Your description of the problem helped me understand the challenge very well - I am now much more knowledgeable about your needs. This is something dear to my heart - I have been tackling and addressing this exact need my whole career, and I believe my experience will enable me to contribute to your goals, and I can't wait to contribute as much as I can.

The following are action items I took away from our conversation:

- <Action item 1>
- <Action item 2>
- <Action item 3>
- ...

I will start on them as soon as I can and will keep you informed.

In the meantime, I have come across this article that discusses one of the challenges you mentioned. Please take a look.

<Insert the article link>

Again, just want to let you know I appreciate the opportunity and consideration. My understanding is that a decision will be reached within the next week; please let me know if that is correct. If there is anything else you need from me, please do not hesitate to let me know.

I look forward to hearing from you.

Sincerely,

<Your name>

Action Item Follow-Ups

If you have been taking notes diligently (page 67) during the interview, you are likely to capture some tasks for you to perform after the interview. They are your action items.

Although not enough people send thank you notes, plenty do. In contrast, very few people follow up on their action items from interviews.

Usually, there aren't any action items coming from the interviewer, so most people think there are no action items coming out of an interview.

That doesn't mean there are no action items.

For example, every question you did not get correctly should automatically become an action item.

Think of the message you send by following up with your interviewer on researching the question and finding the answer afterward.

Many people claim they are go getters, problem solvers, self-motivators, and **perfectionists**, but yet they miss the chance to demonstrate all those attributes as soon as they walk out of the interview.

You can demonstrate **all the above attributes** by simply follow through with your action items. The action items can be as simple as all the questions that you are not one hundred percent confident on.

Even if you answer everything correctly, it doesn't mean you cannot improve upon the answers, either. You can always do more research to form more knowledge and deeper insight. You can openly discuss with the interviewer how to tailor the knowledge toward their problems. You can **demonstrate initiative**.

This is again one of the reasons why you should take diligent notes. You won't remember a thing when you get home if you don't take notes.

But if you do, you have just **created a huge advantage for yourself**, as most people don't do this.

You will be **working** with the interviewer while other candidates wait.

> One thing to keep in mind with the action item follow-ups is that you should not use it as a request for your hiring status. See the next section for that.
>
> Some places have stigmas about allowing contacts with interviewers after interviews. It won't be advertised, so you should ask during your interviews if you can follow-up on the action items.

Action Item Follow-Up Frequency

The way to follow-up on action items is to treat it like work. You can discuss the issue whenever, but you should periodically provide status.

At work, one week is often a good duration to discuss status, but that's a bit long for interview purposes unless you are very early in the cycle. Every 2 or 3-day period usually works well for interviews.

But you can also immediately provide the status when you have resolved one of the action items. No need to wait until the end of the period.

But if you have not resolved the problem at the end of a period, make sure to take it upon yourself to send a status update, so your interviewer knows that you are working on the issue.

The interviewer might or might not respond, but your effort will be noticed.

Action Item Status Update Template

Since action items are work you are doing with the interviewer, you should make your conversation as collegial as possible. Some level of formality should still be maintained, but your goal here is to make it appears as if you are already part of the team.

Dear <name>,

Hi, I just want to give you a report of where I am with my action items.

- <Action item 1>

I was able to do research on this issue, and so far this is what I found. ...(Describe what you found)...

My next steps from here will be ...(describe what you will do next)..., and I will keep you updated.

- <Action item 2>

...(Repeat the above)...

...(Repeat for each action items)...

Please do let me know if you have any questions or thoughts. I look forward to hearing from you.

Sincerely,

<Your name>

Official Follow-Ups

An interview is a bit like a "hurry-up and wait" game from a candidate's perspective. Oftentimes, we are rushed through a whirlwind of interviews, and afterward it becomes a black hole where no information can escape.

Companies are supposed to follow up with you. Unfortunately, they do not always do so because they are quite busy. It isn't a proper excuse, but it's the reality of the game. In order for you to gain information, you must be proactive yourself. In a way - think of this as a test of your resourcefulness. We are masochistic that way.

You can consider the thank you note as the first follow-up. In the thank you note, you ask for a confirmation for the time frame. If you get a response back telling you that you should hear back in say, two weeks, you should wait for an additional amount - such as a couple of days up to a week - beyond the two weeks to follow-up to allow them a chance to catch up with their daily work. If you did not hear a response to your thank you note, use one week as a guide to do your first follow-up.

Beyond that, you can do one or two more follow-ups. If there are still no responses at that time, you should go ahead and move on from the opportunity.

No matter how you are treated - make sure that you do not consider things personal, as getting mad at companies is not only a waste of time, if you act on your anger, it will be remembered long after you regret your actions.

You should consider the official follow-up a separate process from the action item follow-ups. They will go to different people - the official follow-up goes to HR (or directly to hiring manager if there isn't an HR), and action follow-ups go to the other interviewers. Do not mix the two.

Official Follow-Up Template

If you have been working on your action items, the official follow-up letter will be a lot easier to write for you, because you will now have things that you can include to show that you are adding value rather than just checking in for status.

If you did not take care of action items - try to do additional research to show your initiative and include it with the follow-up letter.

Dear <name>,

I am checking in to see how you are doing. I want to thank you again for considering me for the position. I am very excited for the opportunity, and since the interview I have been doing research and collaborated with <name of the interviewer> on the following topics, and we have made good progress.

- <Action item 1>
- <Action item 2>
- ...

I am definitely looking forward to having the pleasure to formally contribute to your company. Please do let me know if there are any additional questions I can answer for you.

Thanks for your time and consideration - I look forward to hearing from you soon.

Sincerely,

<Your name>

References

If you still are listing your references on your resume. Don't. Take them out. Provide references only when requested.

Having references listed on resume is rife with issues:

- It removes your ability to change to a different set of references as needed. You never know when you need that since it's possible that you might come up with a better reference down the line, and someone might no longer be available to be your reference.
- You remove your ability to control when the employers reach out to your references. They might even call them before they decide to interview you.
- Your references will no longer get the heads up from you on when interviewers will call. They will be under-prepared, and might even get annoyed with you and stop being your references.

Interviewers are very used to requesting references as needed. Take them out, and provide them when requested.

You can definitely assume that your interview went well if the employer asks for your references because it's an unnecessary and wasteful step if you are no longer in the running. Just be sure not to assume that you have won the job. They might uncover things that they don't like during checking references, or they might like another candidate's references better. In other words - be excited, but do not assume everything is set in stone.

Asking for Reference

The most important thing to do when the employer ask for references is for you to reach out to your references and **ask them for reference.** You should not assume that you automatically have references:

- The person might not be reachable or available, in which case you have to find another reference.
- Your reference will be unprepared and end up giving a poor reference.
- Your reference might not be happy to be blind-sided, in which case you might get a bad reference, and possibly also lose a future reference.

Prepare Your Reference

Make sure that you also prepare your reference so he knows what's coming. You are not "coaching" your reference what to say, but you should certainly let your reference know what to expect:

- What the position you are applying for is, as well as its background context.
- What the employer likely look for, such as verification of your past experiences.
- Remind him the experiences you guys have had in the past.

The last point is especially important - **do not assume that your reference recalls everything you did together five years ago**. This is very important for references that have worked with you in a distant past. You want to keep your references updated and refreshed with newer knowledge of you.

> **Provide your most recent resume to your reference, and provide additional explanations and highlights from the time you work together**

> until now, so he recalls what you've worked on, as well as gaining new knowledge of your more recent experiences.

The more you can prepare your reference and help him refresh his memory of your experiences together, the more he can provide you with a stellar reference with clarity and authority that can wow your prospective employer. Do yourself a favor - do not skimp through this step to just rely on your reference's memory.

Decision

As you go through the follow-up process, eventually you will reach the decision point - the company will either offer you the position or reject you; and you might choose another offer before this company makes a decision. The following are the potential outcomes:

- The company rejects you.
- You receive an offer from another company. You are still waiting to hear back.
- The company offers you a position.

We will examine the negotiation process in the next chapter (page 225). For now, we will just have a few quick words about the process.

What Happens if You Did Not Get the Job

As noted earlier, you might not receive this notice at all. Some companies are really poor at following up, and it's an open question mark whether you really want to work there. In such a case, you should go ahead and move on.

In the case where you receive a rejection, it can be through letters. Not many people like to deliver bad news in person so they can avoid being shot as a messenger.

What it means is that you might also choose to respond via either email or letters. The choice is up to you, of course.

Do not worry about arguing for your case. It won't matter, as the position has already been given to **another person who has accepted** (companies do not reject candidates before the top candidate accepts - if they do that, they might end up with no one). What you need at this moment is to graciously accept the decision and show your professionalism and commitment to growth.

Also, ask for feedback again at this time. Make sure to ask sincerely so the company knows it's for your personal improvement and can feel comfortable enough to give you feedback - if you don't ask, you will never get it.

If you are not yet done with your action items - commit yourself to finish them, as it builds long-term relationships.

Dear <name>,

Thank you very much for informing me of the decision. I am very happy for you that you have found a great candidate who can contribute to your cause at this time. I believe in your cause and am excited about the future of your company.

I would like to ask for a very special favor - if you don't mind sharing with me what I can improve on so I can become a better candidate next time, I will make sure to take suggestions to heart and work on them. This is for my personal use only and will never be shared with anyone for any purpose. I grow through feedback, and I would greatly appreciate if you have any for me.

Also, I am about 80% done with the action items, and I am committed to finishing them with <the name of interviewer>. If you think it's better I stop, please let me know.

If there were other opportunities opening up, I would love to be considered for them. Please do keep me in mind.

I look forward to any future opportunity to work with you again.

Sincerely,

<Your name>

What Happens if You Receive an Offer from Another Company

Congratulations! You now officially have an offer in your hand. This is a big leverage, and luckily the timing worked out for you that the two opportunities can line up around the same time.

Chapter 25 After Interview - Follow-Up

Obviously, you know which one you like more - maybe the one that is giving you the offer, or the one you are still waiting on.

In either case, there is nothing wrong at all with seeing what options you have, and when you have an offer in hand, it means options for you. It means you can finally achieve what we the job candidates all want from our interviews (page 9).

This is the time that you are permitted to go on the offensive. Employers - at least the good ones - will want to know that they have other competitors. They will appreciate you giving them a chance to bid on your service if they do in fact want your service.

So, leverage your offer to gain a decision from the slower company. Write them an email immediately, followed up by a call at the same time.

Dear <name>,

I am checking in to see how you are doing.

I just want to inform you that I have received an offer from a different company. This offer is very competitive and I need to consider and respond. I realize things are very busy and you are in the middle of the hiring cycle, but as I will need to make a decision quickly, I would need to know if I am still in the running for your position.

As previously stated, I am very excited about your opportunity, and I would love to contribute to your cause if I'm still indeed in the consideration.

I will also leave you a voicemail to make sure this reaches you in time. I look forward to hearing from you soon.

Sincerely,

<Your name>

Afterward, **call!**

If the company is very interested in your service, they will ask for a bit of time to put together an offer - in which case, you can now leverage them against each other. If the company is not interested in your service, you will know and can move on with closure. Although no one can guarantee that this won't offend the company, they should have enough experience to know it's just business, and you have the better leverage.

What Happens if You Did Get the Job

Again, congratulations! If you are waiting on another opportunity, just do the same above steps (page 222)!

Getting multiple offers at the same time requires work and a little of luck on your part, so make sure you take advantage of them.

Whether you have multiple opportunities or just one, once you receive an offer, it is time to move into negotiation mode, which we will discuss next (page 225).

Conclusion

As you can see, there is actually quite a bit of work after interviews, and by doing them correctly, you can put a big distance between you and the other candidates, which will especially benefit you if the competition is close.

Following through with the effort will pay off beyond just the short-term job as well. Your interviewer will really get a chance to see how you work in action, even if you are not the one that ends up with the job. This builds relationships, as well as building your character.

Let's look at the final step in the interview process, the negotiation.

Chapter 26

Getting the Deal You Want

It's not personal. It's strictly business.
-- Michael Corleone, The Godfather

When the dust has settled, the company will choose one winner among the candidates who have interviewed for the position. If you have put in the necessary preparation, practice, and potential mastery, with your skills and experiences, chances are good for you.

Obviously the actual outcome depends on the quality of the competition versus how well you interview. If you did not succeed this time – just know that the experiences and the feedback you have gained - you did **ask for feedback** (page 92), right? - are invaluable toward your interview skill mastery and can only benefit you in your subsequent interviews! Remember, **you do not need this job** (page 32) – you are glad that someone better matched can help them, as well as having learned valuable skills toward finding your dream job.

If on the other, they called you and offered you the job, congratulations. You have now entered into the "end game" – to negotiate the offer to ensure that you are compensated equitably.

The Loss Art of Haggling

When it comes to negotiations, we usually conjure up images of Hollywood movies in which actors portraying lawyers or executives jockeying for positions to beat each other down. We think of how to maximize our positions.

This is only natural because we do this all the time ourselves as well. In the past, before the practice of listing prices became widespread, if you wanted to buy something, you haggled with the seller to get the best price you could. The seller would in turn ask for as much money as possible. Eventually, the two might arrive at a mutually acceptable price point – if so, the sale took place; if not, no deal.

Although the widespread of listing prices has removed most of the opportunities for us to haggle, it still exists at various places like flea markets or car dealerships. Although the elimination of haggling reduces the cost of sales for both the buyers and the sellers, from a negotiation skill perspective, it is unfortunate that for many of us, haggling is no longer something that we get to experience on a daily basis, as it means that most of us are simply unpracticed when it comes to the art of haggling.

A good haggling is a sight to behold for those who haven't seen it. The buyer, who is very interested in buying the item in question (otherwise he will not be there in the first place), continues to raise objections about the quality of the item (such as how broken, how stale, how expired, how out of fashion the item is), wanting to show why the item is not worth the asking price. The seller in turn counters each of the objections raised, either by defending the objection successfully, and thereby justifying the asking price, or agrees to knock off some of the price in concession to the buyer. This process repeats until there are no more objections and results in a deal, or until the price has reached the seller's bottom line without the buyer being satisfied, and hence no deal.

If we analyze the process a bit, we can see that it is a particular form of sale process – one in which that the buyer already wants to buy something, but need to be sold on the item's monetary value by being reminded why it is worth the asking price.

And if you want to negotiate, you need to be able to justify your asking price as well. Because **you are the seller when it comes to job hunting.**

Thick Skin Required

We might not think of "finding a job" as "selling ourselves," since that has a negative connotation. But if we remove ourselves from the equation and look at the process at a distance, we can readily see it for what it is - we are exchanging our time, services, etc. for money from the customer, in this case, the employer.

When it is up close and personal, our perspective often changes, and emotions enter into the picture. Although emotions make us human and make the world worth living, they are big time liabilities when it comes to making a sale as a seller.

To understand why, you just need to put yourself in the buyer's position, one that we are quite familiar with.

Let's say that you walk into an antique shop and see a coffee table that looks like it belongs in your living room collection. You inquire for the price and the seller gives you a price that's about twice as much as you are willing to pay for, so you want to haggle it down.

You	2,000 dollars? I can build a table myself that's twice as nice and costs less than 500 dollars!

At this particular point in time, you expect the seller to counter with the reason why it costs so much, or seller will have to give you a price concession.

Seller	Of course, looking at you I can tell you are a master carpenter, and a fabulous coffee table is obviously easy for your skill level. But this is a coffee table from the first settlement in Oklahoma, already over 100 years old. The craftsman is also top notch – look at how sturdy it is, and how beautiful the carvings are – you won't find many from this time period at all. Your own table will obviously be a great one, but you can't find another one like this.

The above seller has successfully defended the value of the table without giving a price concession. If you want a better price you have to find other objections.

What you don't expect is the seller getting emotional.

Seller	I can't believe you don't see this little gem's value! Are you an antique owner at all? Where under the sun are you going to find another coffee table made during the Oklahoma settlement period? Go ahead, make your little coffee table yourself – buy one from IKEA for all I care! This table deserves an owner who understands its value!

Would you buy from such a seller? While the buyer in this case can start with a less aggravating counter, if the seller gets emotional at all, the chance of him making a sale is very slim indeed.

While it's unlikely that the employer will utilize such a blunt tactic to drive the price for your services down, as a buyer they want to pay as little as they can for your services, so you need to be able to **defend your value without getting emotional** like the seller above.

Buyer's Rights

Does the fact that the employer wants to pay as little as possible for your services offend you? If so, remember that your job as a seller is to leave emotion out of the equation, no matter what your philosophical and political stances are.

The dichotomy of buying vs. selling is an interesting one – when we are the buyer we want to pay as little as possible, but when we are the seller we want to sell for as much as possible. The existence of both stances in the same person might seem contradictory, but it is fact of life that all buyers, no matter in which market – including the labor market – want to pay as little as they can get away with.

As consumers, even when we are shopping for items with listed prices, we compare shop at multiple places – the Internet makes it very convenient to do so – in order to find the place with the best price. We spend time asking questions and take up the salesperson's time at a store, only to buy later at another place that has the best price. We take our right to do so as a natural right.

And that is the correct stance. That is the only right that buyers, or consumers if you prefer, have – the right to decide whether they will actually buy. This applies to all buyers, in any market. Sellers who want to sell must find a way to get buyers to agree to the price, without alienating the buyer. Remember, you are the seller, and the employer is the buyer. The one buying gets to decide what, when, where, and whether to buy.

Seller's Rights

Sellers are not without recourse, of course. We seldom think of stores as "poor little things" that require protection. In fact, we often think of stores as taking advantages of us (food for thought - could this be a rationalization of our desire to pay as little as we can?). Any store that has lasted a few years is obviously making a profit, or else it would have gone out of business already.

Nonetheless, the recourse of sellers doesn't come from the fact that some of the stores survived business competition and prospered beyond what we think they have a right to. It comes from the fact that sellers do not have to sell at all. Their goals are to transform their goods and services into money, but only at a price point they can agree to.

Hence, buyers and sellers are like Yin and Yang, diametrically opposed to each other, and utterly dependent on the other for existence and mutual benefit. Buyers only part with their money when they believe the goods are worth the money spent, and sellers only part with their goods when they believe that the money earned from the goods is profitable so their selling effort is worth it. Both mutually benefit in such transactions.

Needless to say, as a seller of your services, you do not have to sell unless you can agree to the price. Remember that you don't need this job?

General Negotiation Approach

At a high level, your approach to negotiation can basically be broken down into the following:

- No negotiation (page 229) – i.e. take the offer immediately.
- Light negotiation (page 229) – try to negotiate a little bit and win a few concessions.
- Heavy negotiation (page 230) – try to maximize whatever you can get immediately.
- Representation negotiation (page 231) – have someone represent you in the negotiation.

Let's look at each in turn.

No Negotiation

Depending on your particular circumstance and the offer, it can be completely valid to take the offer without negotiation.

You don't have to negotiate for the sake of negotiation if the offer is good enough from your perspective.

One might argue that if you do not negotiate, you are sending the signal that the other party has overpaid. If you are concerned about this potential perception, feel free to lightly negotiate, and then agree to the offer even if they do not give any concession. There is little harm in practicing a bit of negotiation.

But if you simply want to get on with your job as soon as possible, do not worry about sending the signal that the others have overpaid. They wouldn't remember it for long – everyone involved has real jobs to focus on other than dwelling on whether they have overpaid for you. Your performance and contribution on the job, as well as continuous career improvement (page 260), are the most important factors for determining your earning power going forward, not the immediate starting point.

Light Negotiation

The difference between a light negotiation and a heavy negotiation is a matter of position – what you expect to get out at the end of the process.

The goal of a light negotiation is to win a bit of concession from the other party quickly, but "leaves some money at the table." This approach obviously has the downside of not maximizing your earning immediately, but has the following advantages:

- It allows you to practice your negotiation skills without getting yourself in trouble.

    Unless your specialty is in negotiation (in which case you wouldn't be reading this anyway), chances are the longer you negotiate, the more likely you will make mistakes, especially on the emotional front. Keep in mind that the other party has emotions too, and keeping track of your words and actions' influences on them can be difficult for novices.

- It allows you to win some quick concessions.

    You are likely to get quick concessions from the company since they expect the initial offer to be countered, so they are prepared to sweeten the deal without giving away the farm.

- It allows you to get onto your job quickly.

    A heavy negotiation requires a prolonged timeframe, which you might or might not be able to afford. Starting a job quickly might be a higher priority for you at this moment than winning another small amount of base increase after months of delay.

Remember – it's not about where you start, but where you finish.

Heavy Negotiation

The goal of a heavy negotiation is to exact as many concessions as possible from a single transaction – i.e., you are trying to maximize your earning power immediately.

The key to heavy negotiations is leverage – the larger of a leverage you have, the more likely the other party wants to stay in the negotiation and give concessions to you.

Obviously, leverage is created whenever you simultaneously hold multiple offers. But another way to create leverage is for you to have unique skills and capability difficult to find on the market. For example, in professional sports, you can regularly see top draft picks take a longer time to negotiate their contracts than the lower round draft picks. This is because the top draft picks are evaluated to have more talent and hence can afford to take a longer time to negotiate.

Although there is a potential for you to "win the farm," heavy negotiations come with higher risks:

- You need a longer runway to hold out for an extended timeframe.

    Depending on your situation, this might or might not be desirable.

- The negotiation might fail.

    It is difficult to keep a tight balance when you are trying to win the farm at the same time without pissing off the other party. The goal to win everything now might backfire if you do not have strong enough negotiation skills.
- It might put you in a more adverse position to start.

    A higher salary generally comes with higher expectations, and it's possible the increase in expectations can actually put you in a more difficult position when it comes to evaluation time.

    You only need to look at the examples of professional athlete holdouts. Many holdouts struggle to learn the new playbook in a shortened timeframe and end up struggling on the field.

It can take a long time and dedicated practice to acquire enough skills to pull off a heavy negotiation. This is the reason why that people with the most to gain or lose (like professional athletes who have relatively short careers) employ agents to represent them in contract negotiations.

Unless you have been haggling all your life and negotiate professionally, I would advise you to either do a light negotiation or hire a representation for the heavy negotiations.

"Win the farm" negotiation is out of scope for this book.

Representation Negotiation

Besides negotiating yourself, you can also hire representation, like hiring a lawyer in a court case.

Since HR departments deal with candidates all the time, and you hopefully only have to interview and negotiate offers occasionally, the chances are that the HR department are better at negotiations than you, even with the decline of the haggling culture.

Scratch that – you should expect the HR to be **much better at negotiation than you** unless you grow up with haggling blood.

For certain jobs, such as high-end senior executives and professional athletes, hiring representation for negotiation is an option. Representation will give you professional negotiation capability that will be hard to train in a short time for yourself.

However, this option isn't broadly available to all positions since the cost involved will not be worth it for either you or the agent. So for most of the jobs, we will need to learn how to negotiate ourselves if we do choose to negotiate.

Light Negotiation vs. Heavy Negotiation

It can be difficult to know the line between a light and a heavy negotiation if your goal is to maximize as much as possible without turning it into a heavy negotiation.

The difficulty exists due to a lack of practice coming from an aversion to haggling, and unless you gain a lot of practices it simply is difficult to figure out. But here are some ways to tell when you have veered into a heavy negotiation:

- You want to visit every single issue during the negotiation.
- You expect lots of concessions from the employer and expect to give few in return. You don't really care if the employer "loses."
- You aren't satisfied with a single round of negotiation; you want to visit the conversation multiple times to get as much of a concession as possible.

If you are able to accomplish the above without the employer rescinding the offer, you don't need the help of this book - or most negotiation books, actually. That's why we aren't covering that in this book - a chapter certainly won't be enough. You probably can write such a book yourself, and should do so to share your wisdom.

If you don't have the above mentality, chances are your negotiation won't come across as heavy and you will be fine. I'd certainly encourage you to do some negotiation - even though "no negotiation" is completely valid - because that is the only way you get better at the skill. But if you are really concerned and want to stay completely within the light negotiation boundary, try the following:

- Pick three to five issues to negotiate, and be okay with not winning all of them.
- Understand the rule of quid pro quo (discussed later).
- Negotiate in a single round if the situation allows.

As long as you negotiate well, the above will ensure that you stay on the light negotiation side. With experiences and gain in skills, you can push the boundary further.

Goal of Negotiation

The goal of negotiation is very straightforward - it is to produce a situation where **both sides perceive that they got what they wanted**. This is

Chapter 26 Getting the Deal You Want

usually called "win-win scenario," but whatever you want to call it, the key is that **both sides** must feel like they are **better off after negotiation** than before.

In order to accomplish that, you need to understand the motivations on both sides.

The motivations for the employer:

1. Finding a great addition to the organization.
2. At as good of a price as possible given the market condition.

The fact that an offer has been made to you confirmed the first point from the employer's perspective - they'd rather have you over the other candidates at this particular point. They now hope to land you at as good of a price as possible.

The motivations for you, on the other hand:

1. Finding a great place to work and provide your services.
2. Earn as much as possible given the market condition.

Now, if we are honest with ourselves, point one and point two might actually be reversed for many people, as many are willing to put up with a lot of crap if the pay is good enough.

> The desirability of a job is often priced into the market averages. Jobs that are generally considered undesirable, such as garbage truck drivers, pay more in order to compensate for the undesirability. Jobs that are very desirable, like singers or actors, pays next to nothing until you become famous.

But we still derive satisfaction from a great place to work. Gaining the name of a high profile employer on your resume is worth something (and HR knows that), having to work in nice conditions is worth something, and not having assholes for bosses is worth something, as there are only so much crap we are willing to put up with for a particular price. So it's important to think through what that single line item entails, as it might point to things that you can negotiate:

- Flexible work hours
- Longer vacation packages
- Payable vacations (rather than just losing the unused time outright)
- Telecommunication
- Training benefits
- Professional events to attend

- Healthcare benefits
- Shortened review and promotion cycles
- Ability to bring pets or children to work
- Signing bonus
- Probation period
- Dedicated parking spot
- Window office
- Office closer to a particular location (bathroom, kitchen, door) for special accommodations
- Anything else that's important to you

Even if your mind is dead set on increasing your base pay, you should still think through these issues to see which ones are important to you in case of a fall-through in negotiating the base pay that you have something else you can trade concessions for.

So - identify the most important issues to you when it comes to work besides the base pay, and making sure you have them ranked in order of priority so you can give them the attention they deserve during the negotiation.

Game of Negotiation

The game of negotiation can be summed up as **quid pro quo**, i.e., something for something. If you are asking for something of value, you are expected to give up something in return.

Note that what you give up isn't always necessarily of equal value! As a matter of fact, most of the trades occur because people perceive values differently.

When you decide to pay ten thousand dollars for a car, it is because you value having the car more than having those ten thousand dollars. Likewise from the seller's perspective, the seller values the ten thousand dollars you have more than wanting to keep the car.

Although this point is simple, it can be difficult to grasp, because most of the time we think of value in monetary terms, i.e., a car sold for ten thousand dollars is worth exactly ten thousand dollars. But it isn't - it's worth more than ten thousand dollars for the buyer, but less than ten thousand dollars for the seller, or the trade will not take place, because no trade is frictionless and costs time and effort, and a trade alone is only worth going through if the exchange brings value to both parties.

> If the information contained in this book were worth exactly the cost of the book, you wouldn't buy it. You buy it because its information is worth much more to you than the money. The effort took to organize and compile the information alone will make purchasing the book worth it comparing to research and compile the information yourself.

One thing to keep in mind is that quid pro quo is more than just a phrase that coins the phenomenon of exchange; apparently this is built into human psychology and is known as The Law of Reciprocity. The social nature of humans seems to encourage if not outright dictate, whether innately or culturally, a reciprocal return of favor when a favor is made.

This can be as trivial as the other party making a concession - you'll find yourself feeling urged to make a concession as well in order to return the psychological debt. The sales technique - down selling - relies strongly on you feeling more obliged after the salesperson conceding to your decline of the higher priced items.

In offer negotiations, companies usually have quick concessions that they can make on the spot, all with the goal of extracting a concession from you (in this case - agreeing to the offer) as soon as possible.

So, be mindful of the concessions asked and made - you want to make sure you get the concession you are looking for, not simply returning the favor of a concession with a concession of your own.

Know Thyself

When you negotiate, you need to know where you stand, or else your ask will not be defensible. Yes, you can certainly think of a negotiation as a form of debate, though one that you would want to handle with as much tact as you can muster. You don't want to be like the first seller who gets emotional. For that, you will need objective answers to the following question:

- What is your market value (page 235)?
- How much leverage do you have (page 236)?
- What is your bottom line (page 237)?

Market Value

We all like to think ourselves as uniquely capable in this world, but what we offer to the world has a market value. Yes, this often gets abbreviated to just "your market value" so it can offend some people's sensibilities, but I'll keep it that way here so we can practice having thick skins.

Depending on your skills, specialties, and experiences, your services have a market value – this value is determined as an aggregated average of the prices paid by various customers who purchased services from people who offer similar services as you. Understanding your market value will give you a position for negotiation, since you know (and the employer knows too) that if their offer is much lower than the market average, you can find better deals elsewhere, and you will be motivated to do so (they also want to know the market average so they don't overpay).

Market value comes as a range rather than a single number – this is because a range provides more information. With a single number, you cannot know whether and where you fall within the distribution – your offer might be only 10,000 dollars off, but the lowest end of the distribution might be only 2,000 off. With a range, better yet, a bell curve showing to actual distribution, will inform you how far of an outlier your offer is. If you see you are on the 10th percentile, you can reasonably infer that you can find better deals elsewhere. If you see that your offer is lower than the range, you can further infer that the employer has low-balled you.

But if you find your offer is around 45th to 65th percentile, while you can continue to find better offers, you will need to weigh it against the effort you'll exert in finding better offers, and you might not necessarily find the additional effort worth it.

Given how easy one can find salary information today, you have no excuses not to have this information before you start the negotiation process.

> One thing about getting the salary information is that depending on the freshness of the data, you might need to adjust the range up and down depending on the market condition, and especially when there are sudden swings. This way you can be sure you are negotiating from the latest condition of the market.

Leverage

If your market value is your base, leverage is the rocket that can launch you into the sky.

The most important advantage you can have in a negotiation is **your ability to walk away** - remember the seller's right not to sell. If you cannot walk away for whatever reason, such as needing to meet a late payment immediately, you have seriously curtailed your ability to negotiate.

This is another major reason why in this book I have preached about having the mentality that you don't need this job. Besides enabling you to be more relaxed and perform better in interviews, it gives you a strong leverage when it comes to negotiations.

However, some people might find that the mentality alone is not enough. The easiest and surest way to fully buy into the mentality that you don't need this job is when you have **alternative real offers**. Unless you botch the negotiation with all of them, you can secure at least one offer out of the bunch (a simple way to ensure you don't botch all offers is to not negotiate the fail-safe option).

Another benefit of having multiple offers to choose from is that you can gain a true sense of what your market value is, since the multiple offers are likely to form a range of its own. This gives you confidence in your negotiations with the lower offers since you know for sure that your market value is higher.

Without having multiple offers, your leverage is limited unless you are willing to walk away - so if you want to have the leverage, instill in yourself the willingness to walk away from an offer you dislike.

Bottom Line

Leverage is your ability to walk away from an offer; the bottom line is where you will absolutely walk away.

Everyone has a different bottom line and different reasons for arriving at a bottom line. Only you can know for sure what that is.

The following are often used as the criteria to determine the bottom line:

- Salaries of previous employments. For people who are still employed, it makes no sense to leave the current job if the new offer is lower than the current one.
- Monthly expenditure plus some discretionary funds. For people who are out of jobs for a while, their expectations are lowered to meeting their expenditure needs (which might also have been curtailed).

But even the monthly expenditure isn't the lowest possible bottom line - bottom lines below monthly expenditure (including zero) exist for the following:

- People who have infinite runway can consider working for free. This includes young adults (i.e. unpaid internships) as well as volunteer work.
- People who have little savings but lots of expenditures need to plug a leaky hole as quickly as possible. They will of course be motivated to look for another job as soon as they can.

In all situations, it is important that you are realistic about where you stand, so you can decide the appropriate bottom line – the higher the bottom line (i.e., more inflexible), the less room there is to negotiate; and the lower the bottom – being more flexible – the more room there is to negotiate.

Know Thy Enemy

The amount of leverage you have, as well as your actual bottom line, form the basis of your negotiation range.

Knowing the above alone though doesn't form a complete picture. As usual, we need to look at and understand the other side.

Generally speaking, if you are dealing with large companies with a dedicated HR department, you are dealing with companies that have formal compensation procedures and guidelines that they follow. The uniform approach, similar to listing sticker prices, enables them to efficiently process "transactions" without getting into too many lengthy and sticky compensation discussions. Large companies, when making offers, will also likely give you a shorter timeframe to respond than smaller companies.

Many large companies also are better at refraining themselves from entering into a bidding war in order to avoid driving up salaries. They know that auctions benefit sellers, not buyers, and their goal, like all customers, is to pay as little as possible.

So it is possible that you might not be able to string together multiple offers at the same time to form the leverage you want, and you need to make a decision for each offer separately.

But luckily, even when offers are driven from guidelines, there are still ranges that leave you room for some negotiation.

Steps to Negotiate

The following offers a blueprint for you to negotiate your salaries yourself.

1. Determine Your Value (page 239)
2. Name the price (page 240)
3. Thank the offer (page 242)
4. Review the offer (page 242)
5. Discuss the offer (page 243)
6. Discuss other compensations (page 248)

Determine Your Expected Market Value

As soon as you start looking for a job, you should start to determine what your expected market value is. This informs your negotiation position.

Imagine a hypothetical haggling situation where you have to defend your market value like the antique furniture seller, you would want to be able to explain and defend your asking price:

- The market value for the position
- Your unique value that you bring to the table

Research the Market Value

As previously stated, in the information age, you have no reason not to figure out what the market value is for the position you are applying for. Salary sites can easily provide you with such information.

You want to be able to dissect the information as much as possible, in the following dimensions:

- Geography - as specific as possible, as the cost of living differs between various places.
- Job position - this is the key to finding the actual salary data. Some of the sites will provide salary information on related job titles for you as well.
- Skills and qualifications - keyword-based skills, certifications, and education degrees all apply here.
- Years of experience - use your career number rather than years of experience in a particular job title.
- Industry - some sites will allow you to filter down to a particular company.

You should adjust the parameters and see how the salary range changes. Run through with as many different combinations of parameters as you are allowed so you can get multiple sets of salary ranges for you to really get a sense of where your market value is.

If the salary calculator you use has data on the specific employer you are discussing with, make sure to contrast the salary range from the company against its peers and the industry to get a sense of how the company pays, so you can have a clue of how you should prepare for negotiation.

Determine Your Unique Values

What are your unique values? They are your skills, experiences, attributes, or flexibilities you have that are desirable for the job but not required.

For example, the United States Army pays additionally for the following:

- If you know another foreign language fluently.
- If you are a medical or dental officer.
- If you are a parachuting instructor.
- If you are assigned to locations where the living condition is substantially lower than conditions in The United States.
- If you are a pilot.

For hourly-wage jobs, overtime pay is a way to compensate for workers putting in extra efforts.

You need to consider the job, and what particular skills, experiences, attributes or flexibilities you have that can be desirable for the job that results in you getting compensated:

- At the hourly-wage level, willingness to work overtime or night shift will bump you into a higher paying table.
- At the high-end jobs, your Rolodex - the contacts you can open for the company - can be used for negotiation as well.
- Foreign language skills will come in handy in an increasingly more global world.
- Certifications - depending on the particulars, of course - can also be valuable to the employer, especially if employers rely on providing services to generate revenue (like consulting, for example).
- Are you willing to travel for extended period of time? Unless the job requires you to travel, if the position generally doesn't require traveling but might have such potential, this can also be discussed.
- Are you somewhat "overqualified"? Your over-qualification can come in handy providing backups in case it's needed.

Name the Price

As part of receiving a formal offer, it should also have come with a dollar value associated with it. When you have it, you can start negotiating in earnest.

Sometimes, however, the employer will continue to insist on you naming your price first before revealing their numbers. Such is life.

The prevailing thinking on naming the price is that "The person naming the price first loses." This is especially true during the interview stage - from your perspective, it makes zero sense to talk about a salary range and have that as a filter. Not only are you at risk of being filtered, but also the employer is at risk for focusing on the bottom-line to the point of filtering out great candidates that might be flexible.

However, as we have stated earlier - the goal of negotiation is to ensure that both sides walk away from the table feeling like they've gained something, so while the sentiment of "first to speak **loses**" makes intuitive sense, that's not how we want to set our perspective.

Instead, the way to think about it is that "the first to name the price sets the negotiation parameter."

In general, having the employer name the price first makes sense, and this is usually accomplished as long as you can ward off salary discussion during interviews.

What we are talking about here though, is that you are free to name your price first, as long as the following conditions have been met:

- No salary discussion during the interview.
- You have done your homework to arrive at your determined market value.

Once you have done that, the next point is the key to naming your price:

> **Name the price at a defendable point higher than the amount you are looking to earn!**

For example, let's say that after diligent market research, you have determined that the market range for an equivalent position ranges in the low-end of $60,000 to the high-end of $110,000.

You love to get the top number, of course, but you are happy as long as you are getting north of $85,000. What you will do then is to pick a number higher than $85,000 as the starting point, because you should expect to get negotiated down.

That means that if you want to end up in the high-end, which is $110,000 in this example, you'll have to start with a number higher than that!

If you pick a number that is within the expectations of the employer, you are less likely to be challenged on how you come up with the number. So if you desire to obtain the high end of the range (or even go beyond), make sure that you practice defending the number.

If you end up naming the offer first, the chance is that they will take the number into consideration into presenting you an offer before they will try to negotiate with you. But if they try to immediately talk about your price being too high, just tell them "In that case, please do provide me with a concrete offer so we can start the discussion" to put the ball back into their court.

Thank the Offer

Once you have a concrete number in hand, the first thing to do is to **thank the employer for the offer**.

You   Thank you very, very much for the offer.

Then the next thing you do is - **tell them you will review the offer**.

You   I will need a bit of time looking through the offer, when do you need me to get back to you?

Many companies already know that you will take some time to review the offer and have set a timeframe with the offer for you to get back to them, in that case, say

You   I will get back to you as soon as I have reviewed the offer, at the very latest by the timeframe stated in the letter.

You can always come back to ask for an extension if the timeframe is not enough - just make sure you do so as soon as you know that, and before the due date!

Review the Offer

Go through the offer in detail - you want to know as much information as possible - base salary, signing bonus, stock options, commission structures, performance bonus structures, benefits and perks, etc. If anything is not clear in the offer, call and ask for clarifications!

Create a chart with a list of things you expect, and what is offered, and whether the offer matches your expectation. It looks like the following:

Table 26.1 - Offer Comparison Worksheet

Criteria	Expectation	Actual	Result	Action
Base Salary	$90,000	$85,000	Too Low	$88,000 bottom line
Signing Bonus	$0	$5,000	Good	N/A

Criteria	Expectation	Actual	Result	Action
Year-End Bonus	$0	$0	OK	N/A
Relocation Expense	N/A	N/A	OK	N/A
Vacation	3 weeks per year	2 weeks per year	Low	Ask for 3 weeks. 2 weeks acceptable.

Go through this exercise - this table will give you the plan for you to discuss and negotiate the offer.

Make sure you sort the rows in the order of discussion priority. This way, you will be in control of the order of the discussion, and make sure that you can be satisfied with the discussion.

Discuss the Offer

When you get back to the table to discuss the offer with the employer, start with thanking for the offer again:

You I want to thank you so much for the offer again. I have a chance to review the offer, and I have **a few points** that I would like to talk to you about.

Make sure to stress the "a few points" part - it informs the employer that you have multiple things to discuss, but doesn't bind you into the specific numbers of things that you have in mind. You don't need to wait for a response before you get onto the first item of the discussion, which, for most people, will be the base salary.

For base salary, if you did not previously mention a number, you want to discuss it in the following fashion:

You For base salary, the offer is $85,000. That's lower than I expected, can you tell me what flexibility you have?

The employer might come back with:

Employer What number do you have in mind?

And that is when you present your figure that's higher than the number you hope to arrive at. Make sure you provide a solid number at this time instead of a range, because a range is redundant - the employer will take the lower number anyway - and it makes you look uncertain in negotiations, which is not a trait you want to demonstrate.

You I am looking for a base salary of $95,000.

It can feel scary to throw out a number just like that without some justifications for the number, especially if you are more into relationship building and collaboration. Justifications are strictly optional though, because as long as you are prepared, you can defend when you are asked to back up the number. But you can certainly pre-empt the question if you are concerned, with:

You Based on my research of the job market and what I bring to the table, I'm looking for a base salary of $95,000.

The differences between the two approaches are:

- The first is a more "assured" approach. There is a good chance that the employer won't ask you to defend the number at all as long as the number is reasonable. But for people who are less "assured," there is a concern that it can come across as aggressive.
- The second method appears more solid and less demanding because you are stating your reasoning at the same time. There is still a good chance that you won't have to further defend, but calling them to the attention of your reason can draw them toward that direction.

The second approach is easier initially but might not be easier in the long haul, so I'll suggest practicing the first approach, unless you find it unpalatable, in which case pick the method you are most confident and comfortable in (but remember - uncomfortableness is par for the course in negotiations - if you want to get good at it, you need to get used to it).

As long as your number did not scare off the employer, you will likely get a bit of concession from them because they start from a low point:

Employer We can't do $95,000, that's too high for us, but we can do $88,000 - this is as much as we can do.

You will obviously have to decide if you want to accept that offer or make them come up further.

Further Haggling

If you do decide to further haggle beyond the above, you have to remember - you are **the seller**, not the buyer!

That means your job is to defend your value, but not to challenge the buyer, i.e., you want to be the second antique seller, not the first.

What that means is that you want to bring highlight to your value, just like the second antique seller highlighting the value of the furniture:

You As you know, I not only possess the skills of an excellent customer service rep, in addition, I can also back you up in the leadership position given my experiences serving in the capacity. My Spanish skills also come in handy these days as well.

By your diligent research of your skills and what the company needs, your highlighting of your unique skill set will be the value defense for you to employ.

The employer has a few different options to respond to your value defense:

1. Challenge you on your value defense (page 245).
2. Agree with you but argue that's priced in (page 246).
3. Come up further on the offer (page 247).
4. Plead to lack of additional budget (page 247).
5. Ask you to consider other forms of compensations (page 248).

Challenge Your Value

If the employer picks option one, he risks alienating you, so this will be the last resort, but the first one you have to prepare for since it's the hardest.

The key when being challenged is to stay as detached as possible, and focus on discussing your value.

If you are challenged for not possessing a skill:

Employer We did not assess you having the necessary leadership skills to act as a backup supervisor. (Tear down, ouch!)

You Well, as we (or with another interviewer) discussed in the interview, we spent quite a bit of time talking about my taking over for my supervisor when he was on leave without any hiccups. I'm fully confident - during the interview as well as now - you will not regret having my ability to act as a backup supervisor when required. **It will alleviate you the problem of having to find or train another person to take that role.**

Remember - you are here to add value, point out the value to them!
If you are challenged for possessing an unneeded skill:

Employer We weren't able to assess your Spanish skill, and we don't really know if we need it.

You I'm happy to speak in Spanish with anyone you want to assess my fluency, but let me assure you that it will come in handy - in my previous gig, the numbers of Spanish customers calling in increased three-fold during my tenure there. This reflects the growth of the Hispanics population, and they very much appreciate hearing their native tongue - **it reflects very well on the company**.

Again - add value, and address the point without getting emotional is the key to success in such negotiations.

> You might be wondering whether you want to work for someone who challenges you on your value. No matter your decision, do not let it cloud your emotion and affect the negotiation.

Priced-In Argument

The employer can also take the tact to argue that the additional increase reflects your additional value.

This one can be difficult to defend against if you haven't done your homework, but you will still have to proceed focusing solely on defending your value rather than attacking the employer's position.

Employer The increase has already reflected the additional skills you bring to the table.

You Thank you very much for taking my additional skills into account. My research on the average market value for people without my additional skills is that they only earn $500 less than this offer on average, which I promise you will be made back if the supervisor is out for two days.

Defending against priced-in arguments is why you also research for market average with parameters different from yours. You need to know how you relay to your peers, and why you are worth more.

If you cannot do such a defense, you will concede the point and agree with the current price.

Additional Increase

This is the outcome you are looking for! Although the increase might yet again is less than you sought.

Employer   All right, I can add another $2,000 and that's my final offer.

You again have to decide whether you should proceed further. You need to determine whether the employer has signaled reaching his bottom line, if so, you risk pushing beyond the line the employer is willing to go and might end up not having a deal.

If you determine it's safe to proceed, the idea remains the same - continue to demonstrate where you bring value and why that's worth raising your base salary to the employer. As you get closer to the employer's bottom line, make sure to proceed with caution so you do not veer into a heavy negotiation.

If you choose to not proceed further with this topic, go ahead and move onto other topics of discussion as appropriate.

Lack of Budget

Another approach that can be taken by the employer is to plead the lack of budget. Your value is not challenged in this approach.

Employer   We'd love to pay you more, but we don't have the budget to do so.

This is also an effective stopper because you don't actually have the picture to the budget, and the plea makes it that if you want more, you will have to give up something instead.

Your choices?

1. You can **accept the plea** - you would in effect agree to the current price.
2. But it doesn't mean you **have to** accept the plea. You can **continue to negotiate**, just realize that in this case, the quid pro quo is on the side of the interviewer.

   You   Well, that's a bummer. Is there any potential for increasing the budget? (Explicit)

   You   I really love to work with you here, is there a way for us to meet in the middle? (Less explicit)

In either case - the idea here is the same as the before - proceed cautiously to ensure you are not going beyond a point where the employer can go.
3. Last but not least - you can do the employer a favor by turning it into other negotiation leverage. Remember, your value is not challenged and you are within your rights to extract values.

You   I see, well, can we look at other ways to make this up?

This is exactly the same as the next case, only that you are the one bringing it up rather than the employer.

Other Forms of Compensation

In this case, the employer also concedes your value, and would like to ask you to consider other ways of making it up.

Employer   We'd love to pay you more, but we don't have the budget to do so. What we can do is give you a $2,000 signing bonus.

You are getting a further concession, just not the particular one you asked. Keep that in mind - the quid pro quo says that the employer did something for you just now. In the previous case, the employer's plead gives you the chance to do a favor. In this case, the employer directly does you a different favor.

You are of course free to reject this alternative offer, but keep in mind that this offer comes about because the employer is drawing a line on the base pay, so you would need to overcome the objections raised (in this case, a lack of budget) and make sure you proceed cautiously toward the line.

You can, of course, move on to negotiating the signing bonus if that's a topic you want to discuss as well. The idea is the same; continue to emphasize your value.

Finally, you can also choose to ask for a different favor instead, i.e., maybe you would like the bonus to be at year-end instead:

You   Thank you very much for the offer - can we consider switching it for a $3,000 year-end bonus instead?

Discuss Other Compensations

Although we negotiate the base salary first in this book, you can negotiate from other things first if that's more suited to your style. This particular approach - if you are able to structure correctly - can take advantage of the phenomenon that once a person has said yes to you - he is more likely to continue to say yes than no.

This phenomenon is not absolute, though. The opposite is the tracking of concession/favors - the more the other side gives up, the more urge you will feel to agree to things once asked. The danger of this approach is that you have so many small favors piled up and you end up agreeing to the offer before you get to the base salary. So weigh the approaches accordingly. There isn't a right or wrong answer; there is only what works for you.

Negotiating other compensation topics does not differ from negotiating the base salary. They follow exactly the same approach - you want to make sure that:

1. Ask what you want - without asking, you won't ever get it.
2. Defend your value when negotiating rather than attacking the employer's position.
3. Keep track of favors done for each other.

Keeping track of favors is important - remember, the goal of negotiation is for both parties to win, and if you cannot remember any favor you did for the other side, you probably haven't done any.

Anything you have written down as a priority during the offer review phase (page 242) is negotiable:

- Signing bonus – either money or stock options
- Dedicated parking spot
- Window office
- Office to be closer to a particular location (bathroom, kitchen, door, etc.) for special accommodations
- Amount of training
- Numbers of professional events to attend
- Review period
- Ability to work remotely
- Ability to bring pets to work
- Starting date
- Healthcare payout (if you do not use their healthcare provider)
- And anything else you feel that's important to you

The key to understanding about negotiation is that the less important it is to the other party, the more likely you will win a concession.

Things like base salary are likely the one of the most important criteria for the employer, so you might need to put in some effort to bump it up. Getting and increasing the hiring bonus in comparison is likely easier for you to win, since it's only a one-time payout compared to the base salary.

Likewise, a window office might be an asset hotly contested by those within the company, and it'll be harder for them to concede one to you unless you are hired into a senior position. But if it's important for your office to be closer to the bathroom to accommodate specific health needs, it's probably something much easier for the company to oblige.

Also, if a company has an extensive training program set up, increasing your training allotment is probably easy and cost little to them (after all, many people don't end up taking advantage of the available trainings). Training is valuable to both the employer and the employees in the long run.

You can also potentially negotiate for a healthcare payout if you have the ability to opt out using their healthcare provider, such as when your spouse's employer already provides healthcare for your family. Depending on their arrangement with their healthcare provider, you might just find yourself with additional payout added to your check.

The more creative you are, the more likely you can come up with scenarios that benefit you but don't cost them. You are more likely to have success with these types of concessions compared to the base salary. Do not overlook these easily; they can add up to something substantial.

Last Review

After you are done with the negotiation, in principle all issues are resolved and you can arguably take the offer on the spot. Resist that temptation unless you are fully ready to get started.

A well-run company will automatically tell you that they have to recreate the offer package for you, which will give you an additional opportunity to review the offer again. But if not, all you have to do is to ask:

You — Thank you very much for discussing the offer and working through the issues with me. I would ask for one more favor - could you put the offers in writing again so I could do a final review and get back to you as soon as possible?

The employer might want to know whether there is a verbal agreement barring additional findings, you can say so if you are ready, but if you are still reviewing other offers, make sure they understand you are not agreeing to the offer yet.

Chapter 26 Getting the Deal You Want

The idea of the last review is to give you enough time to make sure that you are completely okay with what you are signing up. You would be expected to make decisions with same rigor once on the job, so do not cave into the pressure to make a decision on the spot.

You — One more review will allow me to make sure there aren't issues we missed - this is the same diligence I will bring with me to work everyday.

So - take your time to review, and if everything looks good - congratulations on a long and rewarding effort!

Multiple Offers

As previously mentioned, having other offers (or being still currently employed) is the most concrete way to know your market value, as well as giving you the best leverage for your negotiation, because the winner of your derby will be the one that offers the highest compensation for your service, and if they want you, they need to bid high.

In such a situation, it can present an interesting dilemma for you - do you pit them against each other?

As soon as you have an offer in hand, as discussed in the follow-up section (page 222), you are fully within your rights to notify every other company in your pipeline that you might be off the market soon, and thus help them hurry up if they are still interested in your services. This can lead you to having multiple offers in hand if you play everything right. And at this point, they should be aware that they are in a competition with other employers, and the highest bidder wins.

Given the above, all of your offers should come in with the understanding that another offer is in play, i.e. there is no reason for you to be explicit and in their face about it.

Obviously, having another offer firmly in hand helps make negotiation discussions easier, because when you say it's low, it means there is another better concrete offer:

You — For base salary, the offer is $85,000. That's lower than I expected, can you tell me what flexibility you have?

The employer will interpret it with the understanding that you are asking him to outbid the competition - no need for you to mention it unless they inquire it:

Employer   Sounds like I'm outbid. Do you mind telling me what my competition offers?

You are free to reveal the number, or not. I personally stay away from revealing the number just because I don't want to create too explicit of a bidding war, but it's completely your choice. You will come out winning anyway, so just make sure you keep the uncontrollable urge to laugh out loud down.

Obviously, for this to play well, what you do is to negotiate the lower offers first, before you negotiate the higher offers. Sort all the offers you have accordingly.

A few issues to keep in mind when juggling multiple offers:

- Make double sure that you are not leaving the impression that you agree to take the offer at the end of a negotiation.
- Do not agree to one offer first and then negotiate against another offer in the hope of getting a higher offer so you can rescind the first one. Many companies stop negotiating once they found out that you have accepted another offer.
- If an employer has not interviewed you yet, you probably won't be able to include them in the derby unless they can bring you in for an interview immediately.

Think of having multiple offers as having multiple dates that all expressed the desire to go exclusive. It's great, but handling things with tact and care is important for everyone involved, you most of all. This will feel like the best time of your life - utilize it, but handle it well and tactfully allows you to keep bridges open.

Conclusion

This chapter covers a lot of points, so let's do a quick review.

- The goal of negotiation is to have both sides coming out feeling like they have won.
- Negotiation can be summed up as quid pro quo - keeping track of the favors you made and owed will be crucial to your success.
- Never get defensive and emotional when you are a seller.
- Determine your market value via research and understanding of your unique skills, above and beyond other candidates.

- Researched market value is your base, and leverage is your weapon in negotiations - the best leverage is when you can literally walk away from the job because you have other offers or are still employed.
- Remember - you don't need this job!
- It's okay to name your price first, as long as you did not do so during the interview, and you have researched your market value.
- Review the offer before negotiation, and review again after negotiation. Call and verify (but do not negotiate) if you have questions.
- When reviewing, make sure that you sort the priority of issues for discussions.
- When negotiating the base salary, just ask it.
- Understand when you have veered into a heavy negotiation, because that unbalances the quid pro quo.
- When challenged with reasons, always make sure to emphasize the value you bring to the table, instead of challenging the employer's positions.
- Look out for opportunities where you can make a favor - that can be leveraged for additional concessions.
- Multiple offers are like multiple dates looking to go exclusive - leverage as much as you can, but handle with care.

The pitch never stops. You should always be closing.

And the mastery will be yours if you keep at it. Good luck with your job-hunting endeavors!

Chapter 27

It is Just the Beginning

We have covered everything from the beginning of the interview initiation to the end of the negotiation. Hopefully, the knowledge contained in the book is able to help you succeed in acing your interview and land your dream job.

The thing about interviews, as we said in the beginning, is that it's one of those things that we hopefully only have to do once a while, so most of us are perpetually beginners or intermediates. That's actually okay, as it makes no sense to go through a rough lifestyle just so we are good at a particular skill, unless you are masochistic that way.

A job interview you just had, whether successful or not, is a step in your career journey, and is a beginning to the rest of your career. In this final chapter, we will take a look of where to go from here:

- If you did not succeed this time, how do you make sure you can improve from this point (page 255)?
- If you did succeed this time, what do you do from this point on to put yourself in the right position to supercharge your career (page 260)?
- How do you benefit both yourself and others at the same time with your new earned knowledge (page 263)?

Let's take a look at each in turn.

Self-Evaluation of Failure

Nobody likes it when things didn't work out, but a consummate professional knows the seeds of success are planted in the lessons of failures, as long as we are willing to face them to extract the seeds. Self-evaluation will require you to face yourself honestly, critically, and positively.

First, remember that you have **an internal locus of control** (page 29). You are **making things happen**, instead of having things happen to you. That means that even when things don't go well, you know **you can fix them, and do better next time**.

The following steps form the approach for self-evaluation:

- Determine what happened (page 256).
- Based on the determination, identify the cause(s) (page 257).
- Come up with a plan to tackle the cause(s) (page 259).

Determine What Happened

During the interview cycle, the following are situations that constitute failures:

- An offer was made, but withdrawn or rescinded.
- An offer was not made, although references were asked and checked.
- An offer was not made, and references not checked, although you feel you succeeded in the interview.
- An offer was not made, and references not checked, and you know you tanked the interview.

Given that an interview is a linear process where the next step is only taken if the previous step is passed, it's not hard for you to pinpoint exactly what happened, even without explicit communication from the employer's side.

However, it's important to realize the value of feedback from the employer's side. We talk about getting feedback both during the interview closing phase (page 92) and the follow-up phase (page 221). Getting honest feedback from the employer will beat your second-guessing of the exact issue. The feedback might be much more precise than your own diagnosis as well, so make sure to ask for feedback as sincerely as you can to make the interviewers comfortable enough to provide you feedback.

The identified situation will allow us to narrow down a host of reasons:

- If an offer was made but withdrawn, it means you were considered the best candidate, but issues happened during the negotiation phase.
- If no offer was made, but your references were checked, it means that you were considered one of the finalists, but others beat you out at the end, and this can be due to the strength of the other finalists, or the weakness of your references.
- If you feel quite good about your interview but no references were asked, it means that you were not one of the finalists. This can be due to you having a false impression of the interview, or other candidates were simply stronger.
- If you know for sure that you tanked the interview and no references were asked, you know you will have to focus on improving your interview skills.

Once we have the reasons, we can then work on identifying the actual causes.

Identify Cause(s)

The reasons we determined during the previous phase will inform us the area to determine our problems.

Failed Negotiation

If it's an issue during negotiation, pretty much the only reason is that the two of you cannot come to a mutual agreement.

That's usually the symptom that you are asking more than they perceive you are worth, and that can happen due to:

- You are asking for more than they are willing to pay.
- You are negotiating in a way that makes people angry.

It obviously can also be both.

Note in the first case, it isn't necessarily you asking above the market price - it could have been that they are paying below the market price. Go back and determine your market value (page 239) again to ensure that you are within normal expectations. As long as you are, you are within your right to ask for market price.

In the second case, it can be due to either your stance (i.e. heavy negotiation) or what you say (i.e. not paying attention to etiquettes). Remember both are not recommended. Learn to keep track of favors, give as many as you ask, so you do not come across as a heavy negotiator. Also, remember to always defend your value rather than attacking the other's positions - you are the seller!

Others Are Better

Sometimes we just happen to go up against people who are better than us. When that happens, the outcome is not surprising.

Keep in mind that you don't need this job (page 32), and you are here to help (page 34) so you are happy to walk away if you are not the best person (page 34). You know they are in good hands, and you are happy that they can be successful.

You know you can get better, and you want to find people and places that want you the most, so congratulate them, and congratulate yourself for a job well done, and go on to the next bigger and better things.

Weakness of Reference

References can make or break your prospect at landing the job. Make sure they are as solid as possible.

Go through your references again, and verify the following:

- Are they your actual fan? Some people ask references from people who don't know them well, or worse, from people who actually dislike them.
- Are they updated on what you are up to? References that are too old will be much weaker than references that are recent, since unless they know what's going on recently with you, they cannot really speak gushingly about your current performance.
- Do they know a reference check is coming? If they don't know and get caught by surprise, don't be surprised that their impromptu responses won't be their best work.
- Are they as prepared for the reference check as they can be? After all the preparations you go through for your interview, are you going to leave things up to chance on how well the reference feels that day?

It will be hard for you to reverse-engineer to know where exactly references go wrong. So the best way is to make sure to prepare your reference as much as possible (page 219) going forward, so they can make you successful.

False Impression of Interview

Sometimes we think we did better than we actually did. A false impression hurts because it sets the wrong expectations.

False impressions can come from many places. When we come across friendly interviewers, we generally think things are going well, but friendly interviewers might also be tough graders, and their friendliness can cause us to misjudge our performance.

Depending on the content of the interview, you might also have a harder time knowing whether you did well. Interviews focusing on soft skills and experiences generally have more of such issues, since it's more of a subjective call. Interviews focusing on hard skills usually abuse the notion pretty quickly since it's much easier to know whether an answer is good or bad.

A false impression of an interview can be easily corrected by simply asking for feedback before leaving the interview (page 92). Make sure you practice asking that question at every interview going forward!

Poor Interview Performance

Obviously, a bad interview will not beat the competition - it might not even cross the bar of the interviewer.

Bad interviews happen due to one of these reasons:

- You are outmatched for the position.

    Sometimes this happens. Not all jobs with the same title are created the same, and that means you can come across a job that demands more than you currently have. Due to the inexact nature of resume filtering, it unfortunately means we can walk into a mine trap that leaves us feeling a bitter taste.

    When this happens, the right thing to focus on is to continue to build up your skills and experiences, and treat it as an aspiration that such level of demand exists, and it means you can overcome it.

- You are qualified for the position, but your interview skills leave much to be desired.

    You might not have enough time to become an expert in interviews even with this book's help, but remember that this experience is now part of you and can only add to your future success, so continue to focus on interview skills - it is definitely learnable and improvable.

    Go through your interviews with fine-tooth combs to identify your issues. Create plans to improve those particular issues, go through the book again and again to absorb the lesson. Practice, practice, practice!

- You are qualified for the position, your interview skills are up to par, but you tanked the interview due to inexplicable reasons.

    In other words, you freeze up for your performances. Your nerves got the best of you. Stage fright is a very common phenomenon, unfortunately.

    There is no other way to conquer stage phenomenon except to practice. You want to be like Michael Jordan, who practices so hard that the actual games are easy by comparison. That might not necessarily eliminate your stage fright, but it will make your stage fright irrelevant.

    Practices do reduce nerves and increase confidence, so the more you practice, the more you will be confident, and the less you will experience issues on stage. Coupled with the relaxation drills (page 185), you will be able to overcome your nerves in no time.

Tackle the Causes

This whole book serves as your blueprint to tackle the causes of your job interview outcome.

Once you know the cause(s), follow the steps outlined in the Planning chapter (page 149) to incorporate them into the goal of your next interview preparations.

Make sure that the goals are followed throughout the plan execution. Make sure that your mock interviewers are clued in and focused on helping you improve these specific weaknesses. Your goal is to see visible improvement with your issues for your next interview. If the improvement is great enough so you succeed at the next interview, great, but if not, rinse and repeat the process again to feed into the next one. When this process is repeated multiple times, you will be surprised at how much improvement you can make.

Continuous Learning

We love to do things "just in time," and usually this is a sound approach, but when it comes to managing your career, just in time - like cramming for schools exams - might not be the optimal approach.

Depending on how long you stay at your current job, you might be quite rusty the next time you hit the job market again. You will have this book to help you, but wouldn't it be nice for you start off from a higher point the next time around, instead of looking to cram for success again?

To do so, you need to have a continuous learning mindset, and become proactive about your career and your training.

Remember the concept of leverage (page 236). The more leverage you have, the easier it is for the negotiation to favor you.

When do you have the best leverage? When you have an infinite runway, i.e. when you have a job in your hand.

The best time to job hunt is when you are actively working!

There is no ethical quandary about looking for jobs while you are employed today. While employers will always try to demand your loyalty, you won't get reciprocal loyalty when they change direction. Enlightened employers know this and will not frown upon you looking around, but you owe it to your career, your family, and yourself to do so. You are worth it.

The above concepts are pretty easy to understand, but chances are many people won't carry it out, and still end up in the same spot the next time they look for jobs? Why? Because it's much, much easier to be comfortable, than to do the right thing. People might say that life gets in the way, and things become busy. All true, but also all excuses, and no one cares about these excuses except you, no one is impacted by the consequences of these excuses except you. So why not try to overcome them by being proactive?

Your Continuous Career Plan

If you don't know what you are trying to accomplish, you are unlikely to accomplish it. So in order for us to keep the rudder of our career, we will first need to figure out a plan for it.

Now, since a full-on career planning is another book in the making, in this section we will just restrict to talking about how to keep ourselves fresh so we continue to build up our job interview and job seeking expertise.

The plan is simple, on a recurring basis, do the following:

- Update your resume (page 261).
- Networking (page 262).
- Go on job-hunting (page 263).

Update Your Resume

How often do you update your resume? Only when you are looking for a new job?

Just like refreshing your interview skills right before interviews is an ineffective approach, updating your resume as you seek new job is a sure way to make sure you have a sub-optimal resume, because obviously you will not remember everything you did in the last job if it's of any significant duration, like more than three months.

Writing a great resume is out of scope for this book, but the quick tip here is that you should update your resume with the following approach:

- At a minimum - review and update your resume **once a quarter**. Even if there isn't anything to update, at the very least, reviewing it every quarter will let you have a chance to verify that is the case.
- Optimally - track what you do on a weekly basis, and update your resume once a quarter. In order for you to know for sure what you have accomplished, you should have a way to refer back through all the details of your work log, and then utilize that to summarize and update your resume. When you do not have that, you are operating blind.
- When you update your resume, go through the process discussed in the Refresh and Synthesize chapter (page 165) to test your resume, to make sure what you track works for your purpose.

Remember to sign up on the companion website for the upcoming resume writing book, you will not be disappointed.

Networking

I'm sure you have heard about networking being the key to job-hunting a hundred times already. The question is - have you done it?

You probably have gone onto a few networking events here and there, and the chances are that even if you have made some contacts during the networking event, they are never followed up and cultivated. Yours truly is as guilty of this as anyone.

A full-on networking technique is also outside the scope of this book, but the following are techniques you can leverage for your networking:

- At a minimum, force yourself to go to a networking event **once a month**. Once a month ought to be a frequency that you can plan your work around.
- When I say force, I mean exactly that - you should treat your networking event as serious as your work because they are an important routine for your career. Make sure that you really plan your work around and do not deprioritize network events just because you might feel delivery pressure.
- Understand the goal of networking - it is for people to **mutually benefit from each other**. What it means is that you should be prepared to benefit others in order for others to benefit you.
- Make sure you select networking events where you can mutually benefit each other.
- Make it a goal to meet one new person during a networking event.
- When making contact during the networking event, make sure you not only grab the contact, but also understand the following
    - What the person does.
    - What would help the person to do more.
- Always cultivate contacts. That means to follow-up after the initial meeting during the event. Make sure that the follow-up occurs within a few days.
- Remember the rule of three - it takes at least three contacts for people to remember you. Add value in these three contacts.
- Even when there are no responses, keep providing value by regularly sending contents you find that the person can use.

Networking is a **long-term investment** - any returns on the investment only occurs if you **invest your effort** in it, so make sure you are actually adding value in your networking effort rather than just making the trips.

Job-hunting

As we said earlier, the best time to find a job is when you already have a job because you have an infinite runway and a great leverage!

Most people, however, do not take advantage of their situation, and instead operate in a feast or famine mode - i.e., they only look for a job when they need to.

Remember the fable of the grasshopper and the ants? The best way to prepare for the rainy days is to start when it isn't raining yet.

Your goal when it comes to job-hunting is to try to do the following:

- Go job-hunting at a minimum once every six months. This rule is for you to **proactively** look for positions.
- You should also entertain as many qualifying offers as you can if they find their way to your footstep. Of course, if you are very popular, you might not be able to entertain all such offers, so as long as you entertain an offer once a quarter, that should be plenty.

Putting yourself regularly on the job market gives you the following advantage:

- You will have a pulse on the job market and the conditions.
- You will have a good idea of what your market value is - and guess what, this can be fed back to your current employment to make sure that you are being compensated fairly and equitably.
- The more you go through the process, the easier it will be for you to go through the process.

No matter how much you love your current work and have no plan to leave, you will benefit from the above activities.

Spread the Knowledge

The best way to learn something is to teach it to another person

I really believe this is the case. I always find my own learning jumping through the roof every time I have to teach it to another person. Not only do you have to synthesize what you already know, you will also have to research for more information, which adds to your knowledge. And you cannot teach it to another person without trying to crystallize the knowledge yourself first. The more I try to teach, the more I learn. And this book is the result of the effort of my teaching and hence learning.

You have the chance to pick up that mantle now. You have a book in your hand that can be leveraged as the starting point for you to teach to another person, so you can enhance your learning at the same time.

Not only does teaching enhance your learning, it also allows you to impact other people's lives, and at the same time networking with others. It is one heck of a value you are gaining for yourself and people you teach!

Join local meet-ups on job interviews. Create one if you are good at starting and organizing meet-ups. Offer mock interview practices. Create job-hunting support groups. Participate in local speaker networks. All these are good deeds that will pay you back multiple folds in the long term, even just for the sheer joy that you get from seeing people getting jobs. I know I will be happy beyond words when people use this book to find jobs, and so will you.

Conclusion

No matter what the outcomes are, your experience this time will lay the foundation for you next time, and experiences are the only things in this world that stay with you - no one else can ever take them away from you.

Remember to take advantage of the resources on the companion website, as well as the resources in the appendix to help you improve your interview skills. The companion website is a simple registration away and will be updated and improved, so you owe it to yourself to check it out.

Life is a never-ending journey, and we are always learning. Hope you have learned what you are looking for from this book, and good luck job-hunting!

Appendix 1
Bibliography

- Schreiner, Michael. "Magical Thinking." Evolution Counseling, 23 July 2012. Print.
- "Illusion of Control." Wikipedia.org Print.
- Wiseman, Richard. "Self Help: Forget Positive Thinking, Try Positive Action." The Guardian, 30 June 2012. Print.
- Wargo, Eric. "How Many Seconds to a First Impression?" *Observer*. Assoiciation for Psychological Science, 1 July 2006. Print.
- Goman, Carol. "Seven Seconds to Make a First Impression." Forbes, 12 Feb. 2011. Print.
- *Interview Handbook*. Management Recruiters of Lynden. Print.
- "Clothing for Interviews - Women." University of Illinois Extension Print.
- Runyan, Anna et al. "What Should I Wear To An Interview-Skirt or Pant Suit?" Classy Career Girl, 27 Dec. 2012. Print.
- Raphael, Rina, and By TODAY.com. "TODAY.com." TODAY.com, 20 Sept. 2011. Print.
- Pine, Karen, Ben Fletcher, and Neil Howlett. "The Effect of Appearance on First Impressions." 1 Sept. 2011 : n. pag. Print.
- Pine, Karen. "Fashion Psychology." Karen J. Pine Print.
- Martinez, Astrid. "Job Interview – Skirt or Pants?" Resume Advantage Pro, 2 Jan. 2012. Print.
- Hansen, Katharine. "The Great Pantsuit vs. Skirtsuit Debate: What Should Women Wear to a Job Interview?" Quintesessential Careers Print.
- Howlett, Neil et al. "The Influence of Clothing on First Impressions: Rapid and Positive Responses to Minor Changes in Male Attire" *Journal of Fashion Marketing and Management* 31 Dec. 2012 : n. pag. Print.
- Bay, Jason. "What to Wear (and Not Wear) to a Game Job Interview." Game Industry Career Guide, 15 Oct. 2014. Print.
- "Selecting Interview Attire for a Technical Job Interview." Stackexchange.com Print.
- "How to Dress for an Interview as a Man." WikiHow Print.
- Doyle, Alison. "Dressing for Success." About Print.

- Fenton, Lois. "Men's Interview Fashion Tips." Monster.com Print.
- Smith, Jacquelyn. "How To Dress For Your Next Job Interview." Forbes, 19 June 2013. Print.
- Lubarsky, Michael. "How To: Dress For a Job Interview." askmen.com Print.
- "Knowing What To Wear To An Interview." fashionsunrise.com, 22 Jan. 2014. Print.
- McKay, Brett, and Kate McKay. "The Art of Manliness." The Art of Manliness, 21 June 2009. Print.
- "Tips to Maintain Good Posture." American Chiropractic Association Print.
- Breene, Sophia, and Kate Morin. "The Ultimate Guide to Good Posture." The Greatist Team, 28 Nov. 2011. Print.
- Connolly, Reg. "NLP, Eye Contact & Rapport." *The Pegasus NLP Newsletter*. Pegasus NLP Print.
- Carey, Benedict. "You Remind Me of Me." New York Times, 12 Feb. 2008. Print.
- Thompson, Jeff. "Mimicry and Mirroring Can Be Good... or Bad." Psychology Today, 9 Sept. 2012. Print.
- Kain, Debra. "'Mirroring' Might Reflect Badly on You." Science Daily, 28 July 2011. Print.
- Hedges, Kristi. "Five Easy Tricks To Make Your Presentation Interactive." Forbes, 27 Jan. 2014. Print.
- "Presentation Tips." *Do-It*. University of Washington. Print.
- Poundstone, William. *How Would You Move Mount Fuji?: Microsoft's Cult of the Puzzle -- How the World's Smartest Companies Select the Most Creative Thinkers*. Little, Brown and Company, 2004. Print.
- "Fermi Problem." Wikipedia.org Print.
- Levitin, Daniel. "How to Solve Google's Crazy Open-Ended Interview Questions." Wired Magazine, 22 Aug. 2014. Print.
- Williams, Kawana, Jasmine Plummer, and Myrna Hoover. *Preparing for a Telephone Interview*. The Career Center of The Florida State University, 2009. Print.
- Stock, Judith. "6 Steps To Nailing A Job Interview ... Over The Phone." Forbes, 22 Oct. 2013. Print.
- Fertig, Arnie. "7 Tips to Ace a Phone Interview." US News & World Report, 17 Feb. 2014. Print.
- Doyle, Alison. "Phone Interview Tips." About.com Print.
- Vogt, Peter. "Mastering the Phone Interview." Monster.com Print.

Appendix 1 Bibliography

- Patkar, Mihir. "How to Ace a Job Interview Over Email or Skype." Lifehacker Print.
- Wilson, Patti. "Are You Prepared for a Remote Executive Interview?" *Executive Career Insider*. Blue Steps, 9 Dec. 2013. Print.
- Corcodilos, Nick. "Are Skype Interviews Good for You?" Ask The Headhunter, 6 Feb. 2012. Print.
- Locatis, Craig et al. "Comparing In-Person, Video, and Telephonic Medical Interpretation." Nih.gov, 1 Apr. 2010. Print.
- Lester, Margot. "Should You Send a Thank-You Letter After an Interview?" Monster.com Print.
- Quast, Lisa. "Job Seekers: No, The Interview Thank You Note Is Not Dead." Forbes, 25 Aug. 2013. Print.
- Doyle, Alison. "When Should You Send a Thank You Letter After an Interview?" About Print.
- Green, Alison. "How Much Do Thank-You Notes Really Matter after a Job Interview?" Ask a Manager, 24 Aug. 2011. Print.
- Doyle, Alison, and By Expert. "Do Companies Have to Notify Job Applicants?" About Print.
- Triffin, Molly. "The Handwritten Thank-You Note After an Interview: Necessary or Passé?" Learn Ve$t, 6 June 2014. Print.
- Hairston, Shirell. "Why You Should Send a Thank You Letter After the Interview." Employmentguide.com, 12 Aug. 2013. Print.
- "Do You Send Rejection Letters to Applicants?" Citehr.com Print.
- Besson, Taunee. "How to Deal With Waiting to Hear Back After a Job Interview." Careercast.com Print.
- "Post-Interview Call Back Do's And Don'ts." Hcareers.com Print.
- Muse, The. "4 Non-Annoying Ways to Follow Up After an Interview." Forbes, 29 May 2012. Print.
- Fisher, Anne. "The Job Interview Is Over. Now, How Do You Follow Up?" Fortune, 27 Feb. 2014. Print.
- Lauby, Sharlyn. "5 Expert Tips for Following Up After a Job Interview." Mashable, 22 Feb. 2014. Print.
- Ann, Ronnie. "Template for a Follow-up Note (Letter or Email) After a Job Interview." CAREER NOOK by Ronnie Ann, 21 Mar. 2014. Print.
- Smith, Jacquelyn. "What To Do When You Don't Hear Back After A Job Interview." Forbes, 19 Feb. 2013. Print.
- Podesta, Sandra, and Andrea Paxton. "201 Killer Cover Letters." McGraw-Hill Print.

- Doyle, Alison, and By Expert. "How to Ask for a Reference." About Print.
- By Anne Pushkal, January. "The Right (and Wrong) Way to Ask Someone to Be a Reference." Themuse.com Print.
- "How to Ask for a Reference from an Employer." wikiHow Print.
- Costa, Kim. "How to Ask for a Reference." Snagajob.com, 29 Aug. 2012. Print.
- Lauby, Sharlyn. "Does Providing References Mean You've Got the Job – Ask HR Bartender." hr bartender, 13 Jan. 2014. Print.
- Sheridan, Jerry. "Tactical Breathing Can Stop Stress on the Spot." Onresilience.com, 2 June 2011. Print.
- Wood, Christina. "Negotiating? Keep the Upper Hand." Hrworld.com Print.
- Rossheim, John. "Salary Negotiation: What to Expect from Top Talent." Monster.com Print.
- Hopkinson, Jim. "Getting Your Moneys' Worth: Salary Negotiation Tips for Employers." Monster.com Print.
- Heathfield, Susan. "Tips for a Successful Salary Negotiation." About Print.
- *Salary Administration Rules for Managers, Confidential and Unclassified Employees.* Commonwealth of Massachusetts Human Resources Division, 2014. Print.
- "What HR People Won't Tell You About Salaries and Raises." Reader's Digest, 4 Mar. 2011. Print.
- *State of North Carolina Salary Plan.* State of North Carolina, 2013. Print.
- Green, Alison. "What to Say When You Negotiate Salary." Ask a Manager, 19 July 2012. Print.
- Green, Alison. "What's Wrong with 'do What You Love,' How Employers Can Get Your Salary History, and More." Ask a Manager, 13 Feb. 2014. Print.
- Ryan, Liz. "How To Negotiate A Job Offer." Forbes, 26 Jan. 2014. Print.
- Sugars, Brad. "Up Sell, Cross Sell or Down Sell." Actioncoach.com, 12 Mar. 2008. Print.
- Scocco, Daniel. "Up-Sell, Down-Sell and Cross-Sell: Do You Know What They Mean?" Make Money Online With The Kidblogger, 15 Sept. 2010. Print.
- "SPECIAL PAY: FOR SPECIAL DUTIES & SKILLS." goarmy.com Print.

- Green, Alison. "How to Juggle Multiple Job Offers." US News & World Report, 20 May 2012. Print.
- Fisher, Anne. "Can You Negotiate Higher Starting Pay at a New Job?" Fortune, 16 May 2013. Print.
- "Evaluating and Negotiating a Job Offer." n. pag. Print.
- "Trachtenberg School Career Development Services Career Guide." n. pag. Print.
- Hoover, Myrna. "Negotiating Job Offers." n. pag. Print.

About the Author

Yin-So Chen is a software professional in the high tech industry. During his time at a multinational consulting company, he has helped interviewed and staffed hundreds of IT professionals, as well as having to frequently interview for positions himself. This book is a crystallization of the lessons learned from both sides of the interview desk.

www.ingramcontent.com/pod-product-compliance
Lightning Source LLC
LaVergne TN
LVHW051824080426
835512LV00018B/2719